PARTNERS OR PRISONERS?

Partners or Prisoners?

Christians thinking about women and Islam

Ida Glaser and Napoleon John

solway

Copyright © Ida Glaser and Napoleon John, 1998

First published 1998 by Solway

04 03 02 01 00 99 98   7 6 5 4 3 2 1

Solway is an imprint of Paternoster Publishing,
P.O. Box 300, Carlisle, Cumbria CA3 OQS UK

British Library Cataloguing in Publication Data

A catalogue record for this book is available from the British Library.

ISBN 1–900507–35–8

Typeset by Photoprint, Torquay
Printed in the UK by Mackays of Chatham

Take this book in Thy wounded hand,
Jesus, Lord of Calvary;
Let it go forth at Thy command,
Use it as it pleaseth Thee.

Amy Carmichael

Acknowledgements
and frequent references

Bible: Scripture quotations taken from the HOLY BIBLE, NEW INTERNATIONAL VERSION, copyright © 1973, 1978, 1984 by International Bible Society. Used by permission of Hodder & Stoughton Limited. All rights reserved. "NIV" is a registered trademark of International Bible Society. UK trademark number 1448790.

Qur'an: Unless otherwise indicated, quotations are from A. **Yusuf Ali**, *The Holy Qur'an: Text, Translation and Commentary*, Jeddah: Islamic Education Centre, 1946.

Other translations and commentaries referred to are:
Al-Galaleen, *The Commentary of Al-Galaleen*, Egypt: Al-Azhar, 1983.
Ali, F., *Al Qur'an Al-Hakim* (Urdu translation), Lahore: Chand Company, 1969.
Al-Zamakhshari, *The Commentary of Al-Zamakshari*, Dar: Al Kasshaf, undated.
Azad, A.K., *The Tarjuman al-Qur'an*, translated and edited by S. Abdul Latif, Lahore: Sind Sagar Academy, 1968.
Ibn Kashir, *Commentary* (Urdu), Karachi: Noor Muhammad, undated.
Pickthall, M., *The Meaning of the Glorious Koran*, New York: Mentor Books, undated.

Maududi, S.A.A., *Towards Understanding the Qur'an*, English translation by Zafar Ansari, Leicester: Islamic Foundation, Vols. I-IV, 1988–93.

Usmani, S.A., *Tafsir-e-Usmani*, translated as *The Noble Qur'an* by M.A. Ahmad, Lahore: Aalameen Publications, 1991.

All the above translations and commentaries will be referred to by author, as indicated in **bold**. Since most of them are available in various languages and editions, references will be to the Qur'anic verses at which comments occur rather than to page numbers.

Hadith Collections

Sahih Muslim, tr. A.S. Hamid, Vol. 1–4, New Delhi: Kitab Bhavan, 1986.

Sunan Abu Dawud, tr. A. Hasan, Vol. 1–3, Lahore: Sh. Muhammad Ashraf, 1988.

Sahih Al-Bukhari (Arabic, with English translation by M.M. Khan), Vol. 1–9, Lahore: Kazi Publications, 6th edition, 1986.

Mishkat Al Masabih (tr. J. Robson), Vol. 1–2, Lahore: Sh. Muhammad Ashraf, 1981.

Passages of over 100 words from *Sunan Abu Daud* and *Mishtat Al Masabih* are used by permission of Sh. Muhammed Ashraf.

These will be referred to by title, as indicated in *italics*.

The passage from F. Mernissi, *The Harem Within*, London and New York: Bantam Books, 1994, is quoted on p. 70 by permission of the author.

Some stories of individuals are composite or have had details altered in order to preserve confidentiality.

Special thanks to Elaine Frame and Pat Moreland, who discussed how they have observed that the patterns of the world-gone-wrong for women can be seen in Elswick, and shared their findings with Ida.

Contents

x

Prologue
Ida Glaser
Napoleon John

Muslim women. For many westerners, the images that immediately spring to mind are of silent, submissive creatures covered with black tents. Yet there are many different Muslim women, from many countries, with different cultures, different dress styles, different levels of education, different personalities, and different experiences of life.

From our experience in different countries, we think of

- Teenage girls having the lengths of their school uniform skirts checked, to ensure they are no more than two inches above the knee.
- Girl Guides shinning up coconut trees and learning how to fish.
- An overseas student completing a doctorate in mechanical engineering in London.
- A highly educated woman restricted to domestic activities because her husband does not permit her to go out to work.

- A village woman coming to weep with her Christian friend who has experienced a family tragedy.
- Women organising a countrywide health campaign.

Teachers, doctors, government officials, writers, lecturers, high-powered administrators: we have met Muslim women in different places who carry out all these roles as well as Muslim women who spend most of their lives in their homes. But there are two particular encounters that have motivated our writing of this book.

Ida:

One morning, when I was considering writing this book, a Muslim friend came to visit me in great distress. Her husband was on holiday in their home country. She had been caring for their home and their six children, managing on social security since he had been out of work for several years. She had just heard from her sister in Pakistan that he had married a second wife.

The first wife was not consulted. The new wife is but fourteen years old — younger than his oldest daughter. Doubtless her impoverished parents felt that they were doing well for her by finding her a rich husband. Little can they realise that the apparent riches are only what he has been able to glean from his social security allowances, and that his family in the UK will have to continue to live without whatever he siphons off to support the new wife.

I was angry, and helpless. My friend was hurt, but also angry and helpless. There is nothing she can do but fight to care for her children with the little that she has.

There is little I can do but support her. But I am convinced that God sees and God cares, and God is more upset and angry than both of us put together.

And that left me with the question: *Whose fault is it?* How did life get to be so unfair for my friend, and for so many other women who seem to be at the mercy of their husbands, their fathers or their brothers?

Some would say that it is the fault of Islam — that Islamic law systematically discriminates against women and reduces them to the status of chattels.

Many current Muslim writers would say that it is not the fault of Islam at all. On the contrary, they would claim that Islam liberates women as does no other system. Problems arise because of particular cultural practices that have nothing to do with Islam, or because people misuse the Islamic system.

Moreover, they would say, other systems have misused women. In particular, the Christian faith, especially in the West, has given women little status until recently. Christianity, they say, degrades women in many ways, while Islam protects and honours them.

Who is right? Or is it that the predicament of women is universal? Christians believe that all people are sinful: that, although God created us good, we have 'fallen' so that every culture has gone wrong. Perhaps my friend's problems are just a particular case of the problems that we all share because we are part of a world gone wrong.

Napoleon:

I met Suzanna in a sixth form college in Walthamstow. I was invited there by the Christian union. The theme of the evening was 'grill a Christian', so I was not given any special subject to speak on. I was just to respond to the questions people would ask me.

The meeting began and even with all my experience in dealing with people I was nervous. The small room was packed with people, the vast majority of whom (perhaps 90 percent) were Muslims. In whichever direction I looked I saw young but hostile Muslim eyes gazing at me. Even behind my chair there were some tables, and these were also occupied by the young Muslim students. I think I understood how Daniel felt in the lions' den.

But in the middle of frantic chanting of '*Allahu Akbar*', 'Allah is Great', I found some comfort when I noticed that there were a few white faces which I thought were Christians. But soon a white girl wrapped in her Iranian-style *chador* reminded me that in today's Britain it is wrong to judge people's religion by the colour of their skin. She had converted to Islam.

The questions were mainly asked by the Muslim girls and boys. Most of their questions were about the authority of the Bible. But Suzanna, the white girl, changed the course of the discussion by asking, 'I know what Islam has given me as a woman, but what has Christianity to offer?' Before I could answer her question I was bombarded by Muslim girls and boys with all sorts of quotations from their literature to tell the people present how wonderful the religion of Islam was and how good it was towards the women. Again and again they would attack the Bible and say that there was nothing for women in Christian faith or the Bible. I promised Suzanna that I would write to her about the question she had asked me.

How many other western women, I wondered, do not know what Jesus Christ has to offer them? How many Muslims have only read the books which say that the Bible oppresses women? Some of my letter to Suzanna is in this book — and much more.

1
Introduction

> You have stolen my heart, my sister, my bride, with one
> glance of your eyes, with one jewel of your necklace.
>
> How delightful is your love, my sister, my bride! How
> much more pleasing is your love than wine, and the
> fragrance of your perfume than any spice![1]

So speaks the Holy Bible of the wonder of a woman. A
good wife, it tells us, is more precious than rubies (Proverbs 31:10ff.), and the very first male greeted the very first
female with great joy. He had found no suitable companion amongst all the creatures God made, and it was not
good, God judged, for him to be alone. The woman was
'bone of his bones and flesh of his flesh' (Genesis 2:23).
She was like him but not the same as him. Together they
would rule the world.

But it has seldom been like that.

> Down the ages a system has been built up which aims at
> destroying the ability of women to see the exploitation to
> which they are subjected, and to understand its causes. A
> system which portrays the situation of women as a destiny
> prescribed by the Creator who made them as they are,
> females, and therefore a lesser species of the human
> race.[2]

So argues the Egyptian doctor, Nawal El Saadawi in her introduction to *The Hidden Face of Eve: Women in the Arab World*. The stories she recounts of her observations of the lives of Muslim women are sobering and sometimes shocking, yet she does not blame the problems on Islam in itself. In its essence, she believes, it is no worse than other faiths. Her historical study of the plight of women at different times and in different places leads her to conclude that:

> Islamic, Arab or eastern cultures are not exceptional in having transformed women into a commodity or a slave. Western culture and Christianity have subjected women to exactly the same fate . . . the oppression of women exercised by the Christian Church and those who upheld its teachings has been even more ferocious.

> The oppression of women is not essentially due to relig-ious ideologies, or to whether she is born in a Western or Eastern society, but derives its roots from the class and patriarchal system that has ruled over human beings ever since slavery started to hold sway.[3]

The thesis of this book is that she is largely right. Islam as it has been practised has often encouraged the dominance of men over women, but it is not alone in that. Every analysis of the oppression of women through Islam could be matched with an analysis of the oppression of women in the West or in the name of Christianity. Which system has had the worst record is debatable: that all have much to be ashamed of is undoubtedly true.

The question is, why is this so? Why has oppressive patriarchy emerged so widely that it affects almost every culture and place? It is all very well to say that the problems arise from class and patriarchal systems, but where do these come from, and why are they so tenacious? And why have two religions which have both inherited the beautiful story of Adam and Eve so distorted their partnership that, far from men and women justly ruling the world together, men have unjustly ruled women?

From a Christian point of view, the root of the problem can be seen in the second half of the Adam and Eve story — that of their disobedience to God and its consequences. Following their sin, the world went wrong. Their relationship with God was spoilt, and one of the results of this was that their relationships with each other were also spoilt. Ever since, there has been a basic tendency towards gender inequality in human nature. This is but one manifestation of what Christians call 'the fall', which the Lord Jesus Christ came to deal with.

Another manifestation of the fall is a tendency for human beings to blame other people, and not to acknowledge their own weaknesses and wrongdoings.[4] Nawal El Saadawi is bold in her criticism of both her own religion and others, but not everyone is like her. It is possible to find books by Christians that criticise Islam, but show little appreciation of either the positive aspects of Islam or of the negative ways in which their own faith has been used. And there are increasing numbers of books by Muslims which, like the students met by Napoleon in Walthamstow, criticise Christianity without acknowledging either the positives of the Christian faith or the negatives which can be found in Islam. Sometimes, even the scriptures can be misused.[5]

The following quotation is taken from S.M. Khan's preface to *The Status of Woman in Islam* by Jamal A Badawi:

> Judaism and Christianity, beginning with the concept of original sin regarded women not only as inferior but as evil. Even today the Bible does not recognise women's right to voice their opinion in the Church. In the Bible, concerning the subject of women, we read:-
>
> . . . She gave me of the tree and I did eat (Gen. 3:12);
>
> . . . It is good for a man not to touch a woman (1 Cor. 7:1); . . . But if they cannot contain let them marry for it is better to marry than to burn (1 Cor. 7:7–9) (p. 5).

What might this communicate to someone who is not familiar with the Bible and the context of the verses quoted? Napoleon showed it to a couple who came to him for marriage preparation, and asked the woman what she understood from it. She replied, 'According to this it seems that the women are witches and they should be burnt, but for marriage purposes one can spare them'. He then read the whole passage from the Bible:

> I wish that all men were as I am. But each man has his own gift from God; one has this gift, another has that. Now to the unmarried and the widows I say: It is good for them to stay unmarried, as I am. But if they cannot control themselves, they should marry, for it is better to marry than to burn with passion.

She was astonished to see the difference.

Christians may feel that the Muslim writer quoted above has misunderstood western Christian culture. But there are also many Muslims who think that Christians have understood nothing about Islam and its culture. As

Christians, both writers of this book recognise a duty to seek understanding of all people, because Jesus commanded that we love all people as we love ourselves (Matthew 22:35–40). We very much want Muslim people to understand us, and to hear clearly the message of the Bible. We have different reasons for writing, and that will be evident from what follows; but we both want to understand what is going on in Islamic societies, and to listen to all aspects of Islamic teaching on women.

5

As a Pakistani Anglican priest working in an area of London which has a large proportion of Pakistani Muslims, **Napoleon** has had many encounters with Muslims who have attacked his faith in their attempts to convince him of the truth of theirs. He has often felt that they have made little effort to understand what Christianity really teaches, and that some are ignorant of parts of their own faith. They seem to know only the positive aspects of Islam, and to study Christianity only to find fault with it.

He wants to set the record straight on what Islam and Christianity teach about women: to understand and to be understood. He wants people to recognise that Islam has negative as well as positive sides. He also wants to challenge the accusations that Muslims level against Christianity in its treatment of women, and to help people to understand what the Bible teaches.

As a white woman living and working in a deprived inner city area, **Ida** has met many Muslim women who face great difficulties in life. They are mostly from rural backgrounds in Pakistan and Bangladesh, have little education, and have come to Britain to join their husbands' families. Many are struggling valiantly to cope with diffi-cult situations, that are made more difficult by the attempt to transplant traditional gender relationships from rural Asia to urban UK.

6 She wants to see all women treated as fully human, of infinite value in God's sight. She wants to know why her Muslim friends get into such predicaments as described in the prologue, and what it is in their particular cultures that make it so difficult for them to do anything but acquiesce. She wants to set the record straight on what women actually experience, and to find ways forward.

Yet our different reasons are two sides of one coin. Napoleon is familiar with problems experienced by women in Pakistan, his home country, and he and his wife know many Muslim families in Britain. Ida has responded to her concern for her friends by studying what Islam and Christianity have to say on the subject. We cannot separate what happens in practice from what our faiths teach in theory.

Both of us are also convinced that true liberation for all peoples is only to be found in the Lord Jesus Christ. That liberation has not only to do with how we treat each other, what we think about gender relationships and how we divide roles within families. In the end. true liberation is, we believe, a new relationship with God, which changes the whole direction of our lives and so enables us to live in relationship with each other as God originally intended. That is, we need to be set free from personal rebellion against God and slavery to self-interest more than we need liberation from any oppression by fellow human beings.

We will try to avoid the all too common debating method which compares the best theory of one system with the worst practice of another. We are both aware that, whether we look at Christianity or Islam, women have good and bad experiences, and that both religions have taught both positive and negative things about women. We pray that God will help us to balance these, and to write only what is true.

We start by listening to Muslim people: both men and women who defend the Islamic system and women who have found themselves oppressed within Islamic cultures. In Ch. 2, Napoleon reviews the writings of apologists who claim that Islam is the only system that offers true freedom to women, and Ida explores some sociological analyses and Muslim women's own stories which suggest quite the opposite. We find totally conflicting accounts of Islam's treatment of women.

The next step is therefore to look at the sources of Islam, to try to see why Islam has produced so much suffering for women despite the positive picture painted by the apologists. In Ch. 3, Napoleon explores material that has given rise to misogynist attitudes, and Ida looks at how Muslim feminists have sought to re-interpret it. We find that, while traditional interpretations of the Qur'an and the *Hadith* have often denigrated women, these interpretations can be challenged.

The situation is closely parallel with that obtaining in Christianity. There are those who argue that Christianity offers the one way of true liberation for women, but there are also those who have documented how societies influenced by Christianity have exploited and oppressed women. Turning to the Bible, there is material that has been used as the basis of misogynist attitudes, but there are also those who challenge such uses of the Scriptures.

Rather than arguing which Book has been most used against women, Chs. 4 and 5 consider biblical teaching about women. In Ch. 4, Ida considers Genesis, the first book of the Bible, and its teaching about how life has gone wrong for all women. She then explores how this works out in the very different cultures of South Asian Muslims and white British people in the inner city area in which she lives.

To see what is wrong is not sufficient: we want to find ways forward. In Ch. 5, we turn to the life of Jesus Christ, the centre of our Christian faith, and consider his dealings with women. Ida reflects on how he reversed the pattern of spoilt gender relationships described in Genesis. Napoleon considers how this works out in the teaching of the New Testament on several controversial issues that have been raised in the discussion about women in Islam — marriage, divorce, and male authority.

Having done all this, we ask what Islam and Christianity share in their attitudes to women, and where they differ. Ch. 6 leads us into some fundamental differences between the faiths. We see that Christians and Muslims have different attitudes to law which imply different problems of interpretation, and find that the key underlying question has to do with what has gone wrong with the human race. It is then that we can answer Suzanna's question, 'What has Christianity to offer women?'

We have prayed for God's guidance as we have written: we pray that he will guide you as you read and reflect on what we have to say. May our work bring glory to him, and contribute to the welfare of the whole human race; for God himself loves every person, and he will come to the aid of all who are oppressed:

> Blessed is he whose help is the God of Jacob,
>> whose hope is in the Lord his God,
> the Maker of heaven and earth, the sea and all that is in
>> them —
>> the Lord, who remains faithful for ever.
> He upholds the cause of the oppressed and gives food to
>> the hungry.
>
> The Lord sets prisoners free, the Lord gives sight to the
>> blind,
>> the Lord lifts up those who are bowed down,
>>> the Lord loves the righteous.
> The Lord watches over the alien
>> and sustains the fatherless and the widow,
>>> but he frustrates the ways of the wicked.
>
> Psalm 146:5–9

Notes

1. Song of Solomon 4:9–10.
2. N. El Saadawi, 1980, p. 5.
3. Ibid., p. 211.
4. See Ch. 4.
5. See, for example, Afzal Qutb, *A Treatise on Competing Faith Oriented Family Norms: Hindu, Christian and Islamic Principles*, which, in our judgement, both overstates the Islamic case and misrepresents Hinduism and Christianity

2
Listening to Muslims

Sharif Muhammad, in a Friday sermon published by the Institute of Islamic Studies of the United Kingdom, concludes:

> . . . there is no doubt that Islam has immensely improved the status of women compared to the Judaeo-Christian tradition. The Qur'an has offered women dignity, justice, and protection which, for long, have remained out of their reach. That's why it is no surprise to find that most converts to Islam, today, in a country like Britain are women. In the US women converts to Islam outnumber men converts 4 to 1.
>
> The problem is that the majority of the population in the West do not know these facts. They easily believe the media's distorted image of Islam.[1]

There are some serious accusations here:

- The Judaeo-Christian position denies women such dignity, justice and protection as is found in Islam.
- Most westerners are ignorant of Islamic teaching about women, and are also ignorant of the oppression promoted by Judaism and Christianity.
- The western media distort Islam, and the images of Muslim women common in the West are false.

Christian people, especially those living in the West, need to listen to these accusations, and to give due consideration to those Muslim writers who explain what Islam has to offer. In this chapter, we are seeking to do just that. We will start by exploring recent Muslim apologetics, so that we can listen to Muslims who tell us that Islam liberates women.

But we will also listen to the other side of the story: that of Muslim women themselves. Sharif Muhammad may well be right in saying that the western media give a distorted image of Islam, for media are necessarily selective. It is not news if a hundred Muslim women are living happily, but it is news if one is beaten to death by her relatives. Similarly, the media often give distorted pictures of Christianity and even of western society itself. We will therefore not go to the media for our study of the condition of Muslim women.

Neither will we rely on our own experiences. Both of us have had extensive contact with families in several different Islamic communities, and have met many women who have experienced oppression; but we would not wish to break their confidence, or to claim that we know better than Muslim people. We will therefore explore the actual experience of Muslim women through published writings by Muslim women from several different countries.

We want to set the record straight: to listen to those who are telling us that Islam, at least in theory, liberates women, but also to listen to the experience of Muslim women themselves. What we hear is contradictory; and it is the tension between the two different views of Muslim women that underlies the rest of the book.

Sharif Muhammad is not addressing Christians in his sermon: he is speaking to Muslims, and the challenges he brings out are for them:

12

> Therefore, it is a must that we change our defensive attitude towards the whole issue of women in Islam. We must stop being apologetic. We have nothing to be ashamed of. What the Qur'an has given to women is unparallelled in the history of religion.
>
> Instead of always reacting to the consistent barrage of articles defaming Muslim women, we have to take the initiative . . . We should boldly initiate discussions with our friends and colleagues regarding the true status of women. Tell them how the Qur'an has ended so many injustices against women found in other scriptures.[2]

His sermon is evidence that he has followed his own advice. He puts Qur'anic teaching about the dignity of women alongside quotations from Christian and Jewish sources that have denigrated them. We take two examples:

First, the Qur'an's silence about any separate part for Eve in the temptation and disobedience in the Garden of Eden is put alongside such comments as those of the influential early Christians Tertullian and St Augustine:

> Do you not know that you are each an Eve? The sentence of God on this sex of yours lives in this age: the guilt must of necessity live too. You are the devil's gateway: you are the unsealer of the forbidden tree: you are the first deserter of the divine law: you are she who persuaded him whom the devil wasn't valiant enough to attack. You destroyed so easily God's image, man.[3]

What is the difference whether it is a wife or a mother, it is still Eve the temptress that we must beware of in any woman.[4]

He also quotes from the New Testament:

I don't permit a woman to teach or to have authority over a man; she must be silent. For Adam was formed first, then Eve. And Adam wasn't the one deceived; it was the woman who was deceived and became a sinner.[5]

Secondly, the Qur'anic condemnation of the female infanticide practised by pre-Islamic Arabs (Surah 16:59) and affirmation that daughters as well as sons are gifts from God (Surah 42:49) are put alongside quotations from the ancient Jewish book, Ecclesiasticus:[6]

The birth of a daughter is a loss . . .

A man who educates his son will be the envy of his enemy . . .

Your daughter is headstrong. Keep a sharp look-out that she doesn't make you the laughing-stock of your enemies, the talk of the town, the object of common gossip, and put you to public shame.

He also refers to the instruction on the Biblical book of Leviticus (12:2–5) that the period of a woman's post-natal ritual impurity is twice as long for a girl as for a boy.

In neither case does he admit that Islam has parallels with the Jewish and Christian teachings that he condemns; nor does he ask where these teachings fit into the overall picture of the religions. He seems unaware of either how present day Jews and Christians handle Levitical ordinances or the centuries of debate about the interpretation of texts. He certainly does not quote any of the Bible's positive statements about women.

We want to set the record straight here too. We will not try to deny the fact that Christian history contains much that Christians should be ashamed of, as well as much that brings glory to God. We will not pretend that the Bible itself does not contain material that has been used to oppress and insult women. We will make every effort to resist the temptation to compare what is best in Christianity with what is worst in Islam. But we want to make it clear that Sharif Muhammad and others who follow similar methods of comparison of the faiths are not telling the whole story.

2.1 Listening to the apologists

Napoleon John

In recent years Islam has gained new strength and confidence. There is hardly a news bulletin in which some Muslim nation or its affairs are not mentioned. New confidence has given a new boldness to Muslim writers and apologists. They claim that, whatever the issue — related to world peace, economy, the social order or the welfare of women — the Qur'an and the *Hadith* have the answer. They also claim that there is no other religion or philosophy under heaven which can outweigh Islamic teachings on all aspects of human life. Hammudah Abda-lati, an eloquent spokesman for Islam, writes:

> The outward function of the Qur'an embraces all walks of life and covers the principles of the entire field of human affairs from the most personal matters to the complex

international relations. The Qur'an reaches areas un-
known to any secular system of law or code of ethics and
inaccessible to any popular doctrine of religion. . . . It is
man's spiritual guide, his system of law, his code of ethics,
and, above all, his way of life.[7]

Such a tone is common amongst today's Muslim writers,
whether they come from Arab lands, the Indian sub-
continent or Africa.

15

Often, confidence in Islam goes alongside criticism
of other religions and systems of thought. For example,
the Indian writer, Afzal Qutb, compares the family norms
of Hindus, Christians and Muslims in his book, *A treatise
on competing faith oriented family norms*. He concludes with a
quotation from the Qur'an (Surah 13:17):

> He sends down water from the skies, and the channels
> flow, each according to its measure: But the torrent bears
> away the foam that mounts up to the surface. Even so,
> from that (Ore) which they heat in the fire, to make
> ornaments or utensils therewith. There is a scum likewise,
> thus doth Allah (by Parables) show forth Truth and Vanity.
> For the scum disappears like froth cast out; while that
> which is for the good of mankind remains on the earth.
> Thus doth Allah set forth Parables (p. 138).

It is clear from his work that, to Qutb, the 'scum' are the
other faiths and philosophies of the world and 'that which
is for the good of mankind' is the religion of Islam.[8]

Even teachings which, just a few decades ago, were
felt an embarrassment to Islam are now proclaimed with
zeal. One area which has been a particular target for the
opponents of Islam has been its treatment of women.
Several of the current generation of Muslims are claiming
that Islam is the only religion which liberates women and

gives them status and equality. They claim that in the past Islam's position on women has been misunderstood and misrepresented by the world in general and by the West in particular.

Westerners, they say, need to re-examine Islam's position:

16

> In order to understand what Islam has established for woman, there is no need to deplore her plight in the pre-Islamic era or in the modern world of today. Islam has given woman rights and privileges which she has never enjoyed under other religious or constitutional systems . . . The status of woman in Islam is something unique, something novel, something that has no similarity in any other system[9]

Whilst some Muslims, especially women, go back to see how Muhammad improved the position of women in his times, and thence argue for liberation today[10], Abdalati sees this as unnecessary. He and other apologists see the traditional Islamic position as itself good for women, giving them a status equal to that of men and roles appropriate to their nature.

At the forefront of this argument are some white western women who have embraced Islam. B. Aisha Lemu, for example, considers that her fellow Westerners have grossly misunderstood the status of women in her adopted religion:

> The popular view combines the fantasy of a Hollywood version of the Arabian Nights, with a picture of deprived and repressed victims of a man's world. Neither approaches the truth, but ignorance and prejudice have supplied facts to fit the case. Closer examination of the role assigned to women in the teaching of the Qur'an

reveals a quite different picture, in which women lead a life balanced between freedom and protection possibly more fitting to their needs than the competitive struggle the more 'liberated' women are embarking on in the West.[11]

Westerners, she urges, could learn much from Islam's teachings about women.   17

It is true that non-Muslim writers can be very critical of Islam's treament of women. Here are some typical views:

> Marriage and family laws place women under the dominion of men, despite the protest of some Muslims. According to the Shariah a man can marry up to four wives. The man has the right to discipline, guide, and educate his wife and, if necessary, to strike her. In most Islamic countries the man can divorce his wife at any time. The children always belong to the father only. In court, the testimony of a man counts as much as the testimony of two women. In the case of inheritance, the female is always underprivileged.[12]

A former missionary to North Africa asserts that one of the controlling factors of Muslim women's life is fear:

> From early childhood a girl's brothers are encouraged to beat her and to dominate her life . . . When married, the fear of divorce hangs over her head like the sword of Damocles. She fears her autocratic mother-in-law who controls the household. When young, the mother-in-law had been made to suffer, so she will see to it that her daughter-in-law suffers as much, or more, than she did. When there is a co-wife, each is afraid that the other woman will plot against her so that her husband will turn her out.[13]

A Nigerian writer has this advice to give to young women who plan to get a Muslim husband:

> And if you are a young woman, engaged to marry a Muslim, take note. As a husband, your man has permission from Allah in Surah 4:34 to beat you up anytime you misbehave. As an alternative he may refuse to move close to you for a long time as a punishment, since he has others inside or outside.[14]

To Muslim apologists, such comments represent a total misunderstanding of the Muslim faith and culture. Ghulam Sarwar in his book *Islam: Beliefs and Teachings* (p. 166), says that Islam holds women in much higher esteem than do other religions. He cites as evidence three *hadith*:

> (Woman's) importance as a mother and a wife has been clearly stated by Prophet Muhammad. The Prophet said, 'Paradise lies at the feet of your mothers.' Once a person asked the Prophet, 'Who deserves the best care from me?' The Prophet replied, 'Your mother' (he repeated this three times), 'then your father and then your nearest relatives' . . .
>
> The Prophet also said, the best among you is the one who is the best towards his wife (p. 166).

Muhammad's final address to the Muslims also affirms women:

> In his farewell speech at 'Arafat' in the tenth year of the Hijrah, the Prophet said, O people, your wives have certain rights over you and you have certain rights over them. Treat them well and be kind to them, for they are your partners and committed helpers (idem).

These sayings of Muhammad are clearly positive about women, yet, observes Sarwar: '. . . there are still people, especially in the West, who have misgivings about the status of women in Islam. To these people, the Muslim woman is seen almost as a prisoner in the four walls of the house, a non-person, and someone who has no rights and is living always under the domination of a man' (idem).

Hammudah Abdalati, who has been quoted above, writes:

> The attitude of the Qur'an and the early Muslims bear witness to the fact that woman is, at least, as vital to life as man himself, and that she is not inferior to him nor is she one of the lower species. Had it not been for the impact of foreign cultures and alien influences, this question would have never arisen among the Muslims. The status of woman was taken for granted to be equal to that of man. It was a matter of course, a matter of fact, and no one, then, considered it as a problem at all.[15]

Such writers are clear that Islam assigns very different roles to men and to women. However, they insist that this does not suggest difference in worth:

> Equality and sameness are two quite different things . . . Equality is desirable, just and fair, but sameness is not . . . There is no ground to assume that (woman) is less important than (man) just because her rights are not identically the same as his. Had her status been identical with his, she would have been simply a duplicate of him, which she is not. The fact that Islam gives her equal rights — but not identical — shows that it takes her into due consideration, acknowledges her, and recognizes her independent personality.[16]

Differences in role, then, arise from the different natures of men and women, and can be considered entirely positive.

Answering objections

Having said that westerners misunderstand Islam, and explained the basis of the Islamic position, Muslim writers then go on to answer various standard objections. The issues which most frequently come under the Christian or western microscope and in return are defended by Muslim apologists are as follows:

- The status of women
- *Hijab* and segregation of sexes
- Polygamy and divorce

1. The status of women

Equality of nature Critics say that Islam makes women second–class citizens. Muslim apologists insist that the Qur'an makes women equal to men. Perhaps the most quoted verse is Surah 33:35.

> For Muslim men and women —
>   for believing men and women,
> for devout men and women,
>   for true men and women,
> for men and women who are patient and constant,
>   for men and women who humble themselves,
> for men and women who give in charity,
>   for men and women who fast (and deny themselves),
> for men and women who guard their chastity,
>   and for men and women who engage much in God's
>   praise —
> For them God has prepared forgiveness and great
>   reward.

According to tradition, this verse was given when some of Muhammad's wives asked why the Qur'an addressed itself to men and not to women, and some of the other believing women asked whether the verses about the wives were for them alone or applied to all women.[17] The answer came in this verse: women are equal to men in spiritual matters, for they are equally assured of God's reward if they live in the way of Islam, and the Qur'an applies just as much to women as it does to men.

21

Aisha Lemu quotes this verse[18] and adds that Islam gives men and women intellectual equality. Two *hadith*, one addressed to all Muslims and another specifically to both men and women, confirm this:

> 'The search for knowledge is a duty for every Muslim (male and female).'

and

> 'Seek knowledge from the cradle to the grave' (p. 15).

There is further evidence for this in the fact that 'A'isha, Muhammad's wife,

> is remembered primarily for her intelligence and out-standing memory. She is considered to be one of the most reliable sources of *hadith* by virtue of these qualities (p. 16).

Next, it is argued that the Qur'anic accounts of the creation of woman and the temptation of Adam and Eve allow no room for male superiority. In this, they are contrasted with the biblical accounts, and the use made of them by Jewish and Christian misogynists.

First, it is said that the creation of the woman is independent of that of the man and thus superior to the creation story of the woman in the Bible which says woman was created from man. Two verses are usually mentioned:

> And among his signs is this, that he created for you mates from among yourselves, that ye may dwell in tranquility with them, and he has put love and mercy between your (hearts) (Surah 30:21).

> O mankind! reverence your Guardian Lord, who created you from a single Person, created, of like nature, his mate, and from them twain scattered (like seeds) countless men and women — reverence God, through whom ye demand your mutual (rights), and (reverence) the wombs[19] (that bore you): for God ever watches over you (Surah 4:1).

In his comments on Surah 4:1 J. A. Badawi writes:

> From it here refers to the kind, i.e. from the same kind, or of like nature, God created its mate. There is no trace in the Qur'an to a parallel of the biblical concept that Eve was created from one of Adam's ribs.[20]

Next, it is pointed out that there is no idea of the woman being tempted separately from the man in the Qur'anic version of the garden of Eden story. It does not name Eve or describe her activities separately from those of Adam. Adam is told, 'dwell thou with thy wife in the Garden' (2:35), and Eve's presence thereafter is only indicated by dual word forms. Surah 20:120 even has Satan whispering to Adam, not to Eve.

Abdalati writes:

> The Qur'an makes it very clear that both Adam and Eve were tempted; that they both sinned; that God's pardon was granted to both after their repentance, and that God addressed them jointly (2:35–6, 7:19, 27; 20:117–123). In fact the Qur'an gives the impression that Adam was more

to blame for that first sin from which emerged prejudice against women and suspicion of her deeds.[21]

The Qur'an cannot be used, as the Bible has been used, to blame women for the 'fall' or to show that women as a whole are dangerous temptresses.

23

> It is not the tone of Islam that brands woman as the product of the devil or the seed of evil. Nor does the Qur'an place man as the dominant lord of woman who has no choice but to surrender to his dominance. Nor was it Islam that introduced the question of whether or not woman has any soul in her. Never in the history of Islam has any Muslim doubted the human status of woman or her possession of soul and other fine spiritual qualities.[22]

The implication is that the Qur'anic versions of the origins of human beings are far more fair to women than are the biblical versions. Some Muslim writers quote, like Sharif Muhammad (see p. 12), Jews and Christians who have used the stories of Eve to denigrate women. Others point out mistreatment of women in countries which have a Christian tradition.

> In France in 587 CE, a meeting was held to study the status of women and to determine whether a woman could be truly considered a human being or not! Henry VIII in England forbade the reading of the Bible by women, and throughout the middle ages, the Catholic church treated women as second class citizens. In the universities of Oxford and Cambridge, female students were not given the same rights until 1964. Before 1850, women were not counted as citizens in England, and English women had no personal rights until 1882.[23]

Abdalati further contends that, although women now have more rights in the West, this did not happen for the right reasons:

> The rights of woman of modern times were not granted voluntarily or out of kindness to the female. Modern woman reached her present position by force, and not through natural processes or mutual consent or Divine teachings. She had to force her way, and various circumstances came to her aid . . . (p. 186).

And perhaps the rights that have been gained are not in the interests of women anyway:

> Whether all women were pleased with these circumstances being on their side, and whether they are happy and satisfied with the results of this course is a different matter. But the fact remains that whatever rights modern woman enjoys fall short of those of her Muslim counterpart. What Islam has established for woman is that which suits her nature (idem).

Inheritance and witness There are two areas of Islamic law which, to the outsider, seem to indicate that women are less valuable than men: they are to have half the inheritance of males (Surah 4:11), and the testimony of two women is worth that of one man in a court of law (Surah 2:282). The argument is that these rulings do not diminish women, but that there are practical reasons for them.

It is said that the difference in inheritance is due to social circumstances. Women have different roles than men, and therefore need less inheritance. Abdalati argues that the fact that women are to have an inheritance at all is positive. In pre-Islamic times, he says, not only was she deprived of inheritance, she herself was considered as property to be inherited (*Islam in Focus*, p. 187). He points out that the male does not inherit double in all circumstances, and explains that there are good reasons why men are likely to need more wealth than women:

- The man is responsible for the maintenance of his wife, his family and any needy relations. It is also his role to contribute to charitable causes.
- The woman is provided for by a male relative — husband, father or brother. Even if she has no relations (in which case she would have no-one to inherit from!), it will be the state's duty to provide for her. She will never be responsible for the maintenance of anyone else, so anything she inherits will only be used for personal expenses and luxuries.
- Since inheritance is not earned, it should be considered an extra rather than a right — a sort of aid. 'And,' says Abdalati, 'any aid has to be distributed according to the urgent needs and responsibilities, especially when the distribution is regulated by the Law of God' (p. 188).

So, he concludes:

> If we deprive the female completely, it would be unjust to her because she is related to the deceased. Likewise, if we always give her a share equal to the man's, it would be unjust to him. So, instead of doing injustice to either side, Islam gives the man a larger portion of the inherited property to help him to meet his family needs and responsibilities. At the same time, Islam has not forgotten her altogether, but has given her a portion to satisfy her very personal needs (p. 188).

On the matter of the value of their testimony, Abdalati argues again that the very acknowledgement of the place of women as witnesses is positive. 'It gives woman a role to play in civil life and helps to establish justice' (ibid, p. 189).

Two women are needed for one man, he says, because they are not usually so experienced in public life as are men. If there are two women, they can support and correct each other: 'This is a precautionary measure to guarantee honest transactions and proper dealings between people . . . At any rate, lack of experience in civil life does not necessarily mean that woman is inferior to man in her status. Every human being lacks one thing or another, yet no one questions their human status' (idem).

Another writer, Professor Dr. Jamal-un-Nisa, suggests that there are not only practical but also scientific considerations behind the Qur'an's ruling. In his foreword to *Why Two Women Witnesses* by Shamshad M. Khan, he writes:

> The intellectual status of a Muslim woman is neither marred nor degraded by the commandment that if two Muslim male witnesses are not available then one Muslim man and two Muslim women should be invited as witnesses (Al-Qur'an: 2: 282). The writer has given in this book logical explanations supported by scientific evidences that make us realise the practical view Islam has taken about the witnesses (p. 1).

Khan explains that there are scientific and psychological reasons for women's apparently inferior position. These, he implies, make the Qur'anic wisdom the more remarkable because Muhammad was illiterate[24], and so could not have of himself come to such understanding — and, of course, he lived many centuries before modern scientific analysis.

> Allah (S.W.T.), the Creator, with his infinite wisdom gave the directives best suited to humankind . . . As for women we are aware of the cyclical psychological strains that she has to encounter. The symptoms during early pregnancy, the ante-natal and post-natal depressions, the phenomenon of menopause, the physiological and psychological problems due to infertility and last but not least the psychological problems faced after miscarriage. It is under these situations that women can experience extraordinary psychological strains giving rise to depression, lack of concentration, slow mindedness and short term memory loss (pp. 5–6).

Khan then goes on to give a number of references from different studies conducted in the West to prove that because of woman's physical make up she can sometimes be subject to slow mindedness and short term memory loss. The implication is that it is scientifically correct that her testimony in the court of law is worth half that of a man. For example:

> On the phenomenon of menopause in an article in Newsweek International May 25th 1992, Dr. Jennifer Al Knopf, Director of the Sex and Marital Therapy Programme of Northwestern University writes: . . . women never know what their body is doing to them . . . some reporting debilitating symptoms from hot flushes to night sweat, sleeplessness, irritability, mood swings, SHORT TERM MEMORY LOSS (pp. 10–11 (his emphasis)) . . .

He concludes: 'These are reasons enough for a genuine inquirer and as time progresses no doubt more will be unveiled. The aim of presenting these research findings on a number of aspects related with the theme is to indicate that a woman by her own biological constitution faces such problems' (p. 15).

28

Marriage Where Christians and Westerners have suggested that the Muslim wife is very much a second class citizen, the apologists tell us that, in truth, Muslim marriage is *kafa'*, which means that it is between the two equals.[25] Abdalati writes: 'It is noteworthy that the Islamic provisions of marriage apply to men and women equally. For example, if celibacy is not recommended for men, it is equally so for women. This is in recognition of the fact that women's needs are equally legitimate and are seriously taken into consideration' (*Islam in Focus*, p. 115).

The main points made by the apologists are:

- The Qur'an says that both man and woman are created from a single soul, so they must be equals. 'Oh mankind! Be careful of your duty to your Lord Who created you from a single soul and from it created its mate . . .' (4:1, Pickthall).
- God says that man and woman are to be each other's helpmeets, which implies equal partnership. 'And of his signs is this: He created for you helpmeets from yourselves that ye might find rest in them, and he ordained between you love and mercy . . .' (30:21, Pickthall).
- Islam gives a woman the right to refuse marriage to a person proposed for her. No one can force her into marriage.

- Critics say that, in Islam, woman is required to work like a slave at home and has few rights. But Muslim apologists say that if she is responsible for maintaining the house, her husband is responsible for looking after her. They are equal partners with different roles.
- If a man has the right to divorce a woman, she has an equal right to divorce her husband.

Equality is worked out in the marriage relationship. Suzanne Haneef, a western convert to Islam, explains:

> Islam assigns the leadership of the family to men, for in general they have been endowed with somewhat greater physical and emotional strength and endurance than women. For this reason, they have also been made responsible for supporting and maintaining women — not only their wives and daughters but also female relatives who may be in need of help and support. (Haneef, *What Everyone Should Know about Islam and Muslims*, p. 143)

She then quotes a verse from the Qur'an which we will be meeting again in Ch. 3:

> Men are responsible for women because God has given the one more than the other, and because they spend of their property (for the support of women). Virtuous women are therefore obedient, guarding in their (husbands') absence that which God has guarded (4:34) (idem).

As we will see, there has been much controversy over this verse, but Haneef sees it as entirely positive, and as defining a family order that meets the needs of both sexes. The wife's role she explains thus:

> The wife is her husband's companion and helpmate, who is, together with him, responsible for the affairs of the

household, the physical and emotional well-being of its members, and the training of the children . . . she is also responsible for the proper management of her husband's possessions and property, for the guarding of his honour, dignity and respectability, and for reserving her sexuality exclusively for the man she has married (idem).

30

She goes on to point out that, in Islam, a wife continues to own her own property, and retains her own family name.

The Western stereotype of the Muslim woman as a mere household drudge, preoccupied from morning to night with cooking, cleaning and looking after children, with no spirituality, interests, personality or life of her own, who is debarred from contributing in a constructive manner to society, has no basis in the Islamic teachings (pp. 143–4).

Further, although women usually do the housework without help from men, this is not a requirement of Islam: 'A husband should help his wife with the household work following the example of the Prophet (peace be on him), who used to assist his wives, mend his own clothes and participate in manual work' (p. 146).

She and other writers insist that the division of roles is liberating because it accords with the God-given natures of men and women, and that it does not in the least detract from the equality of status of all human beings. 'The rights and responsibilities of a woman are equal to those of a man but they are not necessarily identical with them. Equality and sameness are two quite different things' (Abdalati, *Islam in Focus*, p. 184).

Fatima Heeren, another western woman who has embraced Islam, quotes the verse

Women have the same (rights in relation to their husbands) as are expected in all decency from them; while
men stand a step above them. (Quoted in Heeren and
Lemu, *Women in Islam*, p. 43).

She comments: 'Those who want to find fault with
Islamic regulations, consider this detrimental to the dignity of women. But I am of the opinion that this one
sentence includes all that is necessary for my happiness as a
woman' (idem).

It gives her, she says, the right to be educated, own
property, manage her household and get a job; but it also
gives her the right to depend on her husband. The desire
to have a 'powerful, just, wise and considerate husband'
who takes full responsibility for caring for his family lies,
she believes, in the very nature of women.

This, I think, is the ideal family life as envisaged by Islam.
(idem)

2. *Hijab* and the segregation of the sexes

During the Spring of 1985, I came to visit Britain for the
first time with my wife. We stayed in East London with a
Finnish friend. Britain was very different from what I had
expected, and there were many things to surprise and even
shock me. One evening when I walked down the road
with my Finnish friend, I saw some very young girls of my
own background, covered from head to chest in white
cloth.

'What is the matter with these girls?', I asked. 'Why
are they covered like that?' My friend was surprised at my
question. 'How can a Pakistani man not understand what

the girls are wearing?' he wondered. I could not imagine what being Pakistani had to do with it. I had seen nothing like it in Pakistan. My friend explained that the girls were Muslims and were going for their Qur'anic lessons and wearing *hijab*.

Although brought up in a Christian village, I went to university in Lahore, where I lived amongst Muslims and had many Muslim friends. I never saw young girls wearing *hijab*. We thought such things were only for very old village ladies or a certain category of women who came from a particular area of the city and went to 'Data's Durbar' (a Muslim shrine in inner Lahore).

A few months ago I went to a college to address a group of students. Most of my listeners were Muslim girls and boys, and several of the girls wore *hijab*. At the end of the meeting, I stopped to talk to some Christian students in the college compound. As we were talking, three Muslim girls in *hijab* passed us by. One of the Christians standing beside me said, 'Goodness me! Until last week these girls were more westernised than Europeans; what on earth has happened to them'? The use of the Muslim *hijab* is increasing amongst Muslims in the UK, and elsewhere in the world.

In the West, *hijab* is understood as an Islamic way of dressing: an outer garment which covers a woman, usually from head to foot. It is seen as a symbol of oppression, of segregation of sexes and limitation to the freedom of women. This is yet another aspect of Islam that Muslims feel the West has misunderstood.

Yes! This is the same 'veil' which Europe loathes and detests, and the very vision of which weighs heavily on the western conscience, and which is regarded as a mark of oppression, narrow mindedness and barbarism. Yes, this is the same thing that is mentioned first of all in pointing out the ignorance and backwardness of an Eastern nation. So much so that when a person has to describe the cultural and social advancement of an Eastern nation, the first thing that he mentions with great satisfaction is that it has discarded the 'veil'.[26]

A leaflet distributed by Muslims in London explains:

> If we look at creation then we find that Allah has ordained for each and every valuable thing a type of preservative . . . the pearl is preserved in a shell . . . Also it is an instinct of the human being to want to place safely items of value, away from the sight and touch of others. We find that the jeweller puts his jewels in a safe. Is it not natural then to want to guard the beauty of the women from the gaze of other men and protect her body from those who may harm her?[27]

The writer believes that Allah himself ordained the *hijab* to give women freedom and dignity and to create a healthy society. The dress does not oppress women, but protects them. The wearing of *hijab* is therefore positive, and a duty for Muslim women. The same leaflet rejoices in its increasing use.

> Alhamdulillah (praise Allah), we see the wearing of hijab by more sisters as an indication of the growing awareness of Islam. However, we find that still a large proportion of sisters are ignorant of this Islamic duty, which Allah (SWT) has stressed in the Qur'an (Idem).

This western Muslim's view does not represent the breadth of Islamic understanding of *hijab*.

Veiling is much older than Islam, and was commonly practised by respectable women of the East. A Christian writer explains to her fellow Christians:

> From ancient times respectable dress for Eastern women was veiling and continues to be so in many countries until today. Respectable Greek and Roman women covered themselves in the street with a large (usually white) veil. This is evident in sculptures and paintings and it is often draped around their bodies as a shawl for the purpose of the artistic pose . . .
>
> However in Arabia, beyond the scope of the Graeco-Roman empire, women did not practise veiling until the prophet Muhammad's wives were obliged to veil, apparently as a sign of honour. Soon after, all Muslim women adopted veiling.[28]

This is probably the correct order of events, but I do not think many Muslim writers would be happy with her way of describing it. For Muslims, veiling was not adopted but entered Islam at Allah's command, for the verses on veiling are found in the Qur'an. Secondly, according to the Qur'an *hijab* is for all believing women and not just for Muhammad's wives. It is not only about manner of dress, but about the whole demeanour of women in home and society.

> O Consorts of the Prophet! Ye are not like any of the (other) women: If ye do fear (God), be not too complaisant of speech, lest one in whose heart is a disease should be moved with desire: but speak ye a speech that is just. And stay quietly in your houses, and make not a dazzling display, like that of the former Times of Ignorance; and establish regular Prayer . . . (Surah 33: 32–33).

Verse 53 of the same surah also refers to Muhammad's wives:

> And when ye ask (his ladies) for anything ye want, ask them from before a screen: that makes for greater purity for your hearts and for theirs.

But verse 59 includes all believing women:

> O Prophet! Tell thy wives and daughters, and the believing women, that they should cast their outer garments over their persons (when abroad): that is most convenient, that they should be known (as such) and not molested.

In the early years of Islam, there was no veiling. Tradition tells us that it was Umar's (Muhammad's close companion, father-in-law and the second Caliph) zealous concern for Muhammad's wives which provoked the 'descent' of the *hijab*. Suyuti in his *Al Itqan* quotes the *hadith*:

> Anas and Ibn Ummar told that Umar said: I agreed with my Lord regarding three matters. I said, Messenger of God, would that we could take Abraham's station as a place of prayer! and the revelation came, 'And take Abraham's station as a place of prayer. I said, Messenger of God, both pious and profligate come in where your women are. If only you would order them to seclude themselves! Then the verse about secluding came down.

Today, although *hijab* is advocated by all the different branches of Islam, it means different things to different Muslims. The four schools of Muslim interpretation of the Qur'an and the tradition differ on the matter:

> As for the views of the scholars of the four famous schools of jurisprudence regarding which part of the woman's body must be covered, they are basically divided into two camps. The Maaliki and Hanafi position is that the woman

may legally expose her face and hands to male strangers. As for the Hanbali and Shaafi'ee scholars, it has been mentioned that they adopted the view which states that the whole of the woman's body (including the face and hands) must be covered before male strangers.[29]

36 There is, though, another view, held by modern Muslims who seek to break away from traditional Islam but are nevertheless proud of their Muslim identity. An example is Pakistan's Prime Minister, Benazir Bhutto, a product of western universities but proud of her Asian and Muslim heritage. In her autobiography she makes it clear that her *hijab* is that of inner modesty. She describes when she wore her *burqa* veil for the first time. On reaching the home her mother proudly told her father about it:

> Pinkie (Benazir's nickname) wore her burqa for the first time today, my mother told my father when we reached Al-Murtaza. There was a long pause. She doesn't need to wear it, my father finally said. The Prophet himself said that the best veil is the veil behind the eyes. Let her be judged by her character and her mind, not by her clothing. And I became the first Bhutto woman to be released from a life spent in perpetual twilight (pp. 32–33).

The holders of this view cite a number of *hadith*, and the Quranic verse:

> Say to the believing men that they should lower their gaze and guard their modesty: that will make for greater purity for them . . . And say to the believing women that they should lower their gaze and guard their modesty; that they should not display their beauty and ornaments except what (must ordinarily) appear thereof; that they should draw their veils over their bosoms . . . (Surah 24:30).

To many Muslims, the *hijab* is not a sign of oppression but a sign of dignity and worth. It can also make a religious and political statement about the wearer's loyalties.[30] Christians and westerners in general see veiling as segregating the sexes and creating un-natural behaviour. But to very many Muslims it is a way of life prescribed by Allah himself. It is a way of creating a healthy society and avoiding the evils of the free societies of the West. 'What a contrast with western fashions which every year concentrate quite intentionally on exposing yet another erogenous zone to the public gaze!' (Lemu in Heerem and Lemu, *Women in Islam*, p. 25)

3. Polygamy and divorce

At the beginning of this century it was only the most orthodox Muslim writers who advocated polygamy. Modern and educated Muslims saw it as an old-fashioned and impractical custom. I can still hear the sound of a song from a famous Pakistani film in the late 1960s or early '70s. It goes: *Duusari Shadi naan karnan; ho jaiy ga khana khrab* (Do not have a second wife: you will be doomed).

With the current return to more traditional values, scholars from Muslim countries as well as European converts to Islam are re-assessing this judgement and saying that Islamic polygamy so far has been misunderstood. Had the West not been prejudiced towards Islam, they say, it could have helped to solve some of the problems of society. Aisha Lemu writes:

Islam does not impose polygamy as a universal practice. The Prophet himself was a monogamist for the greater part of his married life, from the age of 25 when he married Khadijah until she died. One should therefore regard monogamy as the norm, and polygamy as the exception. Although it has been abused in some times and some places, polygamy has under certain circumstances a valuable function. In some situations it may be considered as the lesser of two evils; in others as a positively beneficial arrangement.[31]

38

Circumstances often said to be best resolved by polygamy are those obtaining when, as the result of war, there are more men than women in a community.[32] Jamal A. Badawi, in his debate with the Arab Christian Anees Shorrosh, said: 'Polygamy is progressive in our day because if you go to Afghanistan with 1.5 million loss of life, it is much more humane that those who survived the battle would look after the widows and orphans of their colleagues who fell and gave their lives. Yes Dr Shorrosh it is much more humane.'[33]

Ghulam Sarwar of the Muslim Educational Trust sees polygamy as a possible way of ensuring that men do not have 'mistresses', but keep their sexual practices within the limits of legal marriage. It therefore protects both women and children:

> Islam has given dignity to women by marriage and has protected them from the exploitation of greedy and selfish men. Having more than one wife is better and more dignified than having a number of mistresses. Islam holds you responsible for your actions. You cannot just enjoy and have no responsibilities of fatherhood (*Islam: Beliefs and Teachings*, p. 171).

Anyway, he argues, a Muslim woman has the right to veto a second marriage for her husband, and a woman to refuse marriage on the grounds that she would be a second wife.

> But if a woman happily consents to her husband marrying again and the second wife agrees, why should anyone else object to it? . . . Islam is a practical way of life. It has responded to reality and necessity. It has also put a check on human tendencies and ensured balance. The system is full of wisdom and is perfectly scientific, completely logical (idem).

39

Abdalati (*Islam in Focus*, pp. 167–174) expands on these ideas:

- Imbalance of males and females in society. There are few women who can manage without 'the permanent and assured companionship of men' (p. 167). The overwhelming majority need to belong, to have their own home and family, and to have someone to care for them, or they are in danger of suffering mental instability. They also have sexual needs. To share a husband is better than having none.

- If there are not enough husbands to go round, a woman may enter into relationships with men who are already married. This can break the man's family, but is also very insecure for the woman. She has no rights, while the man can continue to use her as long as he likes. A polygamous marriage gives the woman rights and the man responsibilities.

- A man may not be happy with his wife, and it is a hard fact that he is then likely to look elsewhere. Islam 'does not try to evade the question or ignore the problem' (p. 169). If he is bound to be monogamous, this may lead to hypocrisy, adultery, illegitimacy, abortion and many other troubles. Islam avoids these by forbidding them. 'There is no other alternative except to allow legal polygamy' (p. 169).

- A wife may be unable to bear children, and full adoption is not permitted in Islam, because a child must be known by the natural father's name.[34] She may be incapable of carrying out her household duties because of illness, and bringing another female in to help may just complicate the emotional dynamics of the home. A second wife can solve such problems, without the first wife losing her security through divorce.

- Men have particularly strong sex-drives. If they have to spend long periods away from home, for example, on business, they may be tempted to immorality. A better alternative is to have a second home with a second legal wife. This also gives both women concerned more security and peace of mind.

Heeren, who admits to having been somewhat awe-struck when the registrar at her marriage warned her of the possibility of polygamy should she move to a Muslim country, agrees that the Islamic laws make sense. She considers that some men have a 'polygamous disposition' and that permission for polygamy will keep this in check.

> Hardly any man will merely for the sake of his greediness support more than one wife and the children of this liaison, justly dividing his attention between the wives and off-spring. He will think more than twice before he acts, while in societies without such sensible rules it is so terribly easy to jump into bed and walk away afterwards.[35]

Divorce The western Muslim writer Fatima Heeren commends Islamic divorce:

> In matters of divorce, I hold the Islamic system to be much superior to any others I know. If for any reason, seldom though this does happen in practice, husband and wife consider it impossible to live together any longer, there is no loathsome chain keeping them together by force.[36]

Western critics see Islamic divorce as very easy and liable to exploit women. A man can simply say three times, 'I divorce you', and a woman has lost her husband, her home and probably her children, with no possibility of objection or redress. Muslim writers see the possibility of divorce as a necessity for human welfare, and point out that Islam has, in fact, many regulations surrounding it. Doi, for example, considers the possibility of three 'divorces' being pronounced at once a heretical innovation (*bid'ah*).

> This form of divorce leaves no room for reconsideration and no chance for repentance. This is usually done by ignorant Muslims to satisfy their selfish motives. When these ignorant people pronounce divorce thrice at one and the same sitting, they commit a heinous sin against the precepts of the Shari'ah. The Holy Prophet has very severely denounced this practice and Sayyidna 'Umar used to whip the husband who pronounced divorce thrice at one and the same sitting.[37]

The Islamic way of marriage and divorce is presented as a more humane, fair and scientific way of social life than any other. People should live together only if the relationship works: it is better to depart in dignity than to suffer:

There must be a successful marriage or no marriage at all. Marriage is too solemn a contract to be stationary or non-effective. So if it does not serve its purpose or function properly, it may be terminated by divorce with conservation of all rights of the parties concerned. This is because there is no point in keeping a nominal and worthless contract, and to save human kind from being tied by vows which cannot be honoured.[38]

42

Divorce should be a final resort since Muhammad called it 'the most detestable of all lawful things in the sight of God'[39] According to Islamic law, every other possibility should first be explored. First, husband and wife should try to settle their disputes between themselves. If this does not work, two arbitrators should be called in, one from the husband's family and one from the wife's family. Only if this also fails should a divorce be considered.

After the pronouncement of divorce, there is a waiting period of three monthly cycles before the wife can remarry. During this time, the husband is responsible for his ex-wife's maintenance, and she has full right to remain in his house. This has two purposes: first that, should the wife be pregnant, the fatherhood of the child will be clear, and second, it is a 'cooling-off' period during which relatives can help the couple towards reconciliation or at least a better understanding.

Marriage relationships may be resumed any time during the waiting period, and the divorce will be revoked. If this does not work, the divorce can be pronounced a second time, and the waiting period started again. If there is then a third divorce, it becomes irrevocable, and the marriage can only be re-entered if the woman has first married and been divorced by another man.

Lemu (Heeren and Lemu, pp. 21–22) describes this procedure and then points out that, while this is for divorce at the husband's instigation, the wife can also be granted a divorce, provided she returns to her husband the dowry he gave her when they were married.

She then makes the interesting observation: 'Modern developments in marriage law in England and other western countries are tending towards the Islamic pattern, albeit unconsciously, in many ways, stressing guidance and counselling before divorce, privacy of divorce proceedings and speeding of the process of divorce once it has been established that the marriage has irretrievably broken down.' (ibid, p. 22)

Islamic divorce regulations are, at least in theory, much more complex and humane than is thought by Westerners; and Westerners are, it seems, moving towards the very system they have criticised.

In conclusion

It would be possible here to enter into detailed arguments on the various issues treated by the apologists. For example, I would like to ask S.M. Khan whether those he has quoted on pre-menstrual stress would agree with his conclusions about womens' testimony, and whether there are conditions that can make men's testimony unreliable. I would like to ask J.A. Badawi whether, if more women than men were killed in a particular war, Islam would then recommend polyandry. I would also like to ask whether it is right that women should be so dependent on men that polygamy becomes preferable to celibacy.

Yet I would also agree with Muslim writers on some points, for I too have been shocked by some of what I have seen in the West. Of course, segregation can be carried to extremes,[40] and the *hijab* can be misused, but I personally can agree with much of the Muslim challenge to western society. If we look at so much lawlessness and the results of sexual permissiveness, Christians should be saying, 'You may think that Muslim veiling is wrong, but does the Bible teach the endless choice and freedom of the West? Where is this freedom leading our society?'

It is right to ask what is the use of advocating monogamy if men are having relationships outside marriage. The institution of marriage has lost its sanctity for many people and there is an increasing number of children being born outside marriage. Single parent families have become a normal way of life. This situation in the West is indeed a matter of concern and cannot be justified.

There are, then, a number of assumptions made in the West about the condition of women in Islam. Some are, as Lemu claims, (see pp. 16–17 above) based on fantasy rather than reality, and one can sympathise with those Muslims who feel that their faith has been misunderstood. One can also understand their critique of some aspects of western culture, as it affects relationships between men and women.

However, I would want to observe that the situation in a non-western country like Pakistan is by no means perfect. Extra-marital relationships are more under cover and, taking place within the extended family, go unnoticed by society at large; but they occur. In spite of having the right to more than one wife, there are Muslim men who keep mistresses. All people fall short of God's holy standards, regardless of ethnic and religious background: there are much deeper questions here than which culture or system offers the 'best' order for gender relationships.

Yet the claims some Muslim apologists have made about Islam as the most progressive, humane and just system as far as women are concerned must be tested. There are other opinions.

2.2 Listening to Muslim women

Ida Glaser

Islam, say the apologists, liberates women. Some of the arguments, suggests some Muslim woman, merely serve to confuse. What are we, as outsiders, to make of this?

It is true that Christians and westerners have long accused Islam of oppressing its women, and that many of us have stereotyped pictures of what Muslim women are like. Lemu (see pp. 16–17 above) is not far wrong in her analysis that westerners have two pictures of Muslim women: the exotic and the oppressed. But, rather than simply criticizing these pictures, we need to ask on what they are based. Is it only that people are hostile to Islam and are deliberately misrepresenting it?

I think not. There is, of course, a measure of ignorance and misunderstanding; and misunderstandings need to be corrected. But some of the critique is based on actual relationships with Muslim women, and on what they themselves say. The apologetic is only one side of the story; and it is perhaps not without significance that the female Muslims quoted above as apologists are all westerners who have come to Islam having developed their sense of identity in non-Islamic cultures. Islam has, it seems to me, added a clarity of role and a security in depending on men that was missing from their previous experience, but they retain their basic western attitudes to individual rights and freedoms.

In contrast, many of us have met women brought up in Islamic cultures who suffer deeply because of their position in society and the way that Muslim men have treated them. This is amply documented in the writings of the women themselves. To some of these we seek to listen in this section.

Fatima Mernissi's analysis

A classic analysis comes from the Moroccan sociologist Fatima Mernissi in her *Beyond the Veil: Male-Female Dynamics in Muslim Society.* She recognizes that Islam affirms the potential equality of men and women, but her writing is based around the assertion that 'there is a fundamental contradiction between Islam as interpreted officially and equality between the sexes' (pp. 18–19). That is, there is an actual inequality that has been produced by the social and legal structures of Islam as it has been and is practised.

Her basic thesis runs thus:

> Sexual equality violates Islam's premise, actualized in its
> laws, that heterosexual love is dangerous to Allah's order.
> Muslim marriage is based on male dominance. The deseg-
> regation of sexes violates Islam's ideology on women's
> position in the social order; that women should be under
> the authority of their fathers, brothers or husbands. Since
> women are considered by Allah to be a destructive ele-
> ment, they are to be spatially confined and excluded from
> matters other than those of the family. Female access to
> non-domestic space is put under the control of males
> (p. 19).

Therefore, she adds: 'Men and women were and still are
socialized to perceive each other as enemies' (p. 20).

She goes on to argue that, from the time of Muhammad, sexual instincts have been considered natural and
good but powerful and potentially destructive. Islamic
society has therefore been organized so as to regulate
them.

In particular, she explores the ideas of Qasim Amin,
an early male Muslim feminist, who claimed that woman
are feared because they might be the cause of *fitna*,
disorder or chaos — the very word *fitna* can also mean a
beautiful woman, a *femme fatale*. There is a long tradition
of women being seen as dangerous to men because of
their irrestistible attraction and powers of intrigue (pp. 31–
3). Islamic marriage, with its pattern of male dominance,
polygamy and divorce, can then be seen as designed to
satisfy male sexuality while regulating dangerous female
sexuality.

Mernissi analyses various aspects of the system as seen
in Morocco.

Husband–wife relationships

The ideal wife, as described by the classical Islamic scholar Al-Ghazzali is

> Beautiful, non-temperamental, with black pupils, and long hair, big eyes, white skin, and in love with her husband, looking at no one but him (p. 108).

He also quotes Muhammad's saying that a woman who loves and obeys her husband is a gift from God. Mernissi comments, 'Such a woman would indeed be a miracle, given the conflict structure of the conjugal unit, based on a relationship of forces in which the most likely outcome is the woman's dislike of and rebellion against her husband' (ibid.).

She then quotes several women she has interviewed who see it as a miracle when their husbands love and respect them, because, she suggests, Islamic law does not suggest that women can expect love and respect. The 1957 Moroccan Code encapsulates a traditional Islamic understanding of the rights and duties of spouses. The wife's duties to her husband (Article 36) are:

1. Fidelity.
2. Obedience according to the accepted standards.
3. Breastfeeding, if possible, of the children born from the marriage.
4. The management of the household and its organization.
5. Deference towards the mother and father and close relatives of the husband (p. 109).

The husband's duties towards his wife (Article 35) are:

1. Financial support as stated by law, such as food, clothing, medical care, and housing.

2. In case of polygamy, the right to be treated equally with other wives.
3. The authorization to go and visit her parents and the right to receive them according to limits imposed by the accepted standards.
4. Complete liberty to administer and dispose of her possessions with no control on the part of the husband, the latter having no power over his wife's possessions (pp. 109–10).

49

Mernissi points out that this is a 'power relationship' (p. 110). The woman is to receive and obey orders, and some of her 'rights' are in fact restrictions. The right to be treated equally with co-wives implies restrictions in her claim on her husband, and the right to permission to visit and receive her parents implies restrictions on her freedom of movement. It is also striking that the man has no moral duties towards his wife: it is she and not he who is to be faithful.

As she explores such ideas, Mernissi asks why Moroccan society expects husbands to be masters rather than lovers. She suggests that, while sexuality is seen as positive and sexual satisfaction as necessary to the moral welfare of the Muslim, love between a man and his wife is seen as dangerous. This is because of the *fitna* that can be created by women. She then argues that Moroccan homes are so organised that intimacy between husbands and wives is discouraged.

First, she describes how the sexual act itself is surrounded by religious regulations and formulae: the couple should not have their heads pointing towards Mecca, and there are various Arabic phrases to be recited before commencing and at the moment of ejaculation (pp. 113–4). Major ablutions must then be performed before the partners can partake in ritual prayers. All this, says Mernissi, suggests that sexual intercourse is polluting, and the regulations can serve to limit the emotional bond formed between man and wife.

Further, love for a woman can be seen as competing with total worship of the one God. 'The Muslim god is known for his jealousy, and he is especially jealous of anything that might interfere with the believer's devotion to him' (p. 115).

Polygamy and divorce are then seen as devices that deliberately weaken the marriage bond. Polygamy produces competition between co-wives, and means both that the husband has less emotional investment in any one wife and that the wives have to invest less in their husband and more elsewhere. The ease of divorce by the husband also weakens the bond by reducing the wife's security: no reason need be given for the divorce; it need only be registered. It can also result in problems for the husband. Mernissi quotes several instances of husbands who pronounce the repudiation formula in anger or intoxication, and then regret what they have done. In fact, the Moroccan Code does not recognise such a rash repudiation as valid, but this is not widely understood.

In all, the system mitigates against secure, loving husband–wife relationships and this, says Mernissi, is a fundamental point of instability in her society, which is likely to increase with the tensions produced by the changing pressures of late twentieth-century life (p. 119).

She goes on to explore several aspects of the system which contribute to the problem.

Mother-in-law

The mother-son bond is perhaps the closest family tie in Islamic societies. It is fostered by many *hadith* and by the Qur'an itself. The son owes his mother life-long gratitude:

> We have enjoined on man kindness to his parents:
> In pain did his mother bear him, and in pain did she give him birth.
> The carrying of the (child) to his weaning is (a period of) thirty months.
> At length, when he reaches the age of full strength, and attains forty years, he says,
> "O my Lord, grant that I may be grateful for Thy favour which Thou hast
> bestowed upon me and upon my parents . . ."
>
> (Surah 46:15).

Mernissi sees this as one of the major factors preventing strong marital bonds. In most cultures, marriage marks the end of a man's close association with his mother and the beginning of a new relationship with his wife. In traditional Muslim cultures such as Morocco, the married couple remains in the husband's home. This pattern, says Mernissi, strengthens the mother-son bond and therefore 'institutionalizes the Oedipal split between love and sex in a man's life' (p. 123).

His main love is to be towards his mother, with whom he cannot have sexual intercourse. His sexual partner is his wife, to whom he cannot show too much affection without alienating his mother.

Mernissi documents the centrality of the mother's role in deciding who her son should marry, the dependency of the new bride on her mother-in-law, and the power of the mother-in-law in controlling the affairs of the household.

52

The older woman, says Mernissi, is expected to be asexual, and her husband perhaps to turn to a younger wife. Her power and identity are then found in running the household, from which men are absent at most times. She can be a blessing to her daughters-in-law, and they are dependent on her for much of their knowledge of manners and beauty techniques, as well as of household duties and matters of health and motherhood. Especially in the case of a child-bride, the mother-in-law may take the place of a girl's mother.

However, the power can be misused, and wife and mother end up by vying for a man's affections. Mernissi reports her interviewees:

- On a mother-in-law being in control of even the trivia of life:

    She had the power to decide what to eat, the quality and quantity, and she had the key . . . For example, on the eve of festivals we would spend nights making cookies. But we were not allowed to take any for our own use, not even for our own children . . . I could not even have a cup of tea if I felt like it aside from ritual meal times (p. 130).

- On a husband wanting to give a gift to his wife:

    He would say, 'Fatiha, I would like to see you in a red scarf, it will match your complexion.' I would answer that I would be very happy to have one. He would go to the store, but he would have to buy four scarves — one for his mother, two for his divorced sisters, and finally one for me. He couldn't give me the red scarf directly; he had to give them to his mother. She then chose what she wanted for herself and her daughters and gave me the last one (p. 131).

• Sometimes, the mother-in-law can even prevent husband and wife spending time alone together:

Often late in the evening, I felt very sleepy, but I could not leave the room to go to sleep in mine. Neither could my husband, even if both of us were dying of fatigue. We had to sit there with [my mother-in-law] and wait until she decided to go to bed. Then we would run to ours . . . We could not close our door in her face (p. 132).

It is not surprising that Moroccan proverbs describe older women in uncomplimentary terms:

• A man who reaches eighty becomes a saint: a woman who reaches sixty is on the threshold of hell.
• What takes Satan a year to do, is done by an old hag within an hour (p. 124).

While the younger woman is dangerous because of her fatal attraction, the older is dangerous because of her frustration and intrigue.

Mernissi concludes: 'The triangle of mother, son and wife is a trump card in the Muslim pack of legal, ideological, and physical barriers that subordinate the wife to the husband and condemn the heterosexual relationship to mistrust, violence and deceit' (p. 135).

Spatial boundaries

One of the main ways the Moroccan, and many other Muslim, societies, distinguish between genders is through strict spatial boundaries. That is, there is territory available to men, and territory available to women, and meeting across genders is carefully regulated.

Mernissi explores this territorialism as expressing the divisions discussed above:

> Boundaries are never established gratuitously. Society does not form divisions purely for the pleasure of breaking the social universe into compartments. The institutionalized boundaries dividing the parts of society express the recognition of power in one part at the expense of the other. Any transgression of the boundaries is a danger to the social order because it is an attack on the acknowledged allocation of power (p. 137).

She sees Moroccan society as divided between the public universe of the *umma* — the Muslim people — and the domestic universe of sexuality. The former comprises the believers, but women's place in it is ambiguous. God does not speak to them directly, so it seems that the *umma* comprises primarily the male Muslims, and that the public universe is their world. The domestic universe includes both men and women, primarily as sexual beings. However, because men spend little time in the home, Mernissi concludes that its members are, in practice, women only (p. 138).

Each universe runs according to its own principles. The *umma* is regulated by equality, reciprocity, aggregation, unity, communion, brotherhood, love and trust. The family is regulated by inequality, lack of reciprocity, segregation, separation, division, subordination, authority and mistrust.

Women, says Mernissi, are confined to the domestic universe, and any foray out of it is seen as an anomaly. But even within the world of the home, they are not in control: it is the men who have authority. In the house as well as outside it, men and women have different spaces and defined functions which necessitate little interaction. 'Men and women are supposed to collaborate in only one of the tasks required for the survival of society: procreation' . . . (pp. 139–40).

She then explores how this works out in the seclusion of women in Moroccan society and their veiling when they do go into the public domain, and describes again the need for men to be protected from temptation. However, she also points out that, where westerners may see seclusion as oppressive, many Muslims see it as a sign of privilege. Only the rich have been able to keep their wives covered and at home. This means that those who do venture outside can be subject to harassment.

Underneath this is the idea that the public domain is male territory, and that 'a woman is always trespassing in male space because she is, by definition, a foe. A woman has no right to use male spaces. If she enters them, she is upsetting the male's order and his peace of mind. She is actually committing an act of aggression against him merely by being present where she should not be' (p. 144).

This has particularly strong implications in the world of education and paid work, which necessitate womens' presence on the streets at least during travel between home and the place of work. Mernissi reflects on how women have moved into these spheres in recent decades, and how this has challenged many traditional ideas about gender dynamics and family structures. Her own writings are evidence of this.

56

Analyses from elsewhere

Egypt

The doctor Nawal El Saadawi writes out of anger at what she has seen in the women she has treated. In particular, she explores the idea that male honour is vested in female virginity before marriage. She remarks: 'A man's honour is safe as long as the female members of his family keep their hymens intact . . . He can be a womanizer of the worst calibre and yet be considered an honourable man as long as his womenfolk are able to protect their genital organs.'[41]

Why is this? El Saadawi's conviction is that, 'At the root of this anomalous situation lies the fact that sexual experience in the life of a man is a source of pride and a symbol of virility; whereas sexual experience in the life of women is a source of shame and a symbol of degradation.'[42]

Her book is full of examples of malpractice resulting from the system, including adverse medical results of female circumcision. She writes of what happens to girls who are judged to have lost their virginity but whose problem is medical rather than moral, and of males indulging in illicit sexual acts while women are wrongfully blamed and punished. One of her 'most gruesome' stories is, '. . . that of the uncle who was strongly attracted to his brother's daughter and had sexual relations with her. When the fact became known, the two brothers conspired together and poisoned the young girl to forestall the shame that threatened the family honour, were it to become known that she had lost her virginity' (pp. 19–20).

She then goes on to discuss the 'severe physical and psychological constraints' which surround the lives of Arab women, suggesting that, 'as a result, the mental and psychological development of a woman is greatly retarded, and she is unable to free herself from passive attitudes and the habit of depending on others. She remains like a child in the early stages of its life, but differs in the fact that her body has grown' (p. 44).

There are, she says, many ways of suppressing women: they usually rely on fear or on deprivation of knowledge. She speaks of a 'cult of ignorance' (p. 45), in which 'experience is looked upon almost as a deformity to be hidden, and not as a mark of intrinsic human value' (p. 44). This applies not only to sexuality and relationships with men, but also to other aspects of bodily function.

At the same time, a girl is brought up to be 'almost totally preoccupied with her body, her hair, her eyelashes, her clothes, at the expense of her mind and thoughts and her future as a human being.' She is being prepared for marriage. And that marriage when it comes will be determined by her parents. While Mernissi stresses the role of the mother in her son's marriage, El Sadaawi focuses on the role of the father in the daughter's marriage: 'The Arab family being highly patriarchal, both socially and legally,

the authority of the father over his daughters is absolute'
(p. 47).

She illustrates this from a newspaper story entitled,
'The court decides on divorce because the wife married
without her father's consent.'

58

> The bride was over twenty-one years old and had decided
> to marry the man she loved, without the prior consent of
> the father. The marriage contract and ceremony were
> presided over by a mazoun (religious dignitary), according
> to Islamic law, in the presence of two witnesses. The
> marriage was therefore regular in both its legal and
> religious aspects. Subsequently the father initiated juridi-
> cal proceedings in which he requested that the marriage
> contract be considered null and void because the daughter
> had not sought his consent (p. 48)

The court agreed, on the grounds that, according to
custom, the father's consent is essential to a marriage.

Egyptian law, as well as custom, devalues women:
'They have transformed women into merchandise, which
can be bought in exchange for a dowry and sold for the
price of an alimony. Sometimes she can even be sold for
nothing' (p. 51).

She quotes as evidence Article 67 of the Common
Law on Marriage, which sets out the conditions under
which a divorced wife is not entitled to alimony, including
'if she is suffering from any condition which might
prevent the husband from utilizing her as a wife.' El
Saadawi comments: 'The term 'not utilizable as a wife' lays
bare the true nature of the relationship that exists between
a man and a woman after marriage. It is a relationship
built on the utilization of the woman by the man, on her

exploitation by him, in a manner which is more inhuman than the exploitation by a land-owner of his labourers or a master of his slaves' (p. 51).

A wife, for example, works for her husband without pay, and her husband can return her to her parents with no further responsibility if she falls seriously ill. A labourer would be paid, and a slave would be treated at his master's expense.

Further, women are not considered trustworthy witnesses as are men, and are punished much more harshly than men in cases of adultery. As for prostitution, 'According to Egyptian law, if a man is caught in sexual intercourse with a prostitute he is not put in jail, but is used as a witness against her, whereas she is sentenced to a term of imprisonment' (p. 56).

El Saadawi notes that such oppression is not peculiar to Egypt or to Islamic systems, and some of the practices she discusses are also common amongst Egyptian Copts. However, she does think that Islamic law allows for — and even encourages — malpractice. Yet, like Mernissi, she theorizes that what underlies Islamic patriarchy is not the idea that women are inferior. 'To my mind, Islamic culture rests on the . . . premises . . . that woman is powerful and not weak, positive and not passive, capable of destroying and not easily destroyable, and that if anyone needs protection it is the man rather than the woman' (p. 100).

Such is not the impression given by the five Egyptian women whose stories have been collected in *Khul Khaal* by Nayra Atiya. Each of the four Muslim women (the Christian will be discussed in Ch. 4) gives the impression that life revolves around men — Om Gad's around her lost son, Suda's and Dunya's around finding the right husband, and Om Naeema's around her husband and her lack of a male child. Om Naeema has no doubt that 'boys are more precious than girls in our countryside', this being her explanation for the facts that midwives charge twice as much for delivering a boy as for delivering a girl and that the charge for circumcision is 50 percent more for boys than for girls (pp. 139–40).

Her account of her life highlights several problems faced by women. For example, they tend to get the blame for everything. She did not tell her husband when a man made illicit suggestions to her because, 'My people and my husband's people would have had to be involved. They would eventually have laid the blame on me, no matter which way things turned out . . . A woman has to be on her guard at all times. People will blame her no matter what happens or doesn't happen' (p. 162).

Her daughter's plight exemplifies the helplessness of an unloved wife:

> We have asked Naeema's husband to divorce her or support her. He will do neither. We have sued him in the court, but he fails to appear on the dates set. Nothing can be done in his absence. His only answer to our plight is this, 'I will neither divorce nor support her. Let her stew in her own juices.' His family tried to bring her back. She did go back last spring but again they treated her badly. She returned to us in the dead of night this last time, beaten and miserable . . . (p. 176)

The distraught mother asks, 'What can we do? Can we question the will of God?' and continues:

Her husband comes around and says to her, 'Supposing I shatter your nerves, my girl, and you die of grief? Who can claim your things? They'll be mine. You neither have a brother nor a sister to inherit from you . . .

Now she only says, 'I'll never marry again. I'll stay alone, fasting and praying. I've seen all I want to of marriage. I want nothing more to do with men' (p. 177).

Om Naeema's own experience of marriage was a good one, since her husband was kind and had no thoughts of taking a second wife. He wanted to stay with her even though her only surviving child was a girl, and she herself tried to provoke him into divorcing her so that she could find a husband who might give her more children.

However, she also had experience of bitterness and jealousy, especially that caused by polygamy. She was herself the daughter of a second wife, whose co-wife used magic practices to make her husband desert her when she was pregnant with her first child. Om Naeema starts her narrative with several hair-raising stories about jealousy and revenge in such marriages, including some of women murdering their step-children. Her story starts: 'Life in a family where there is more than one wife is bitter. A second wife is always subject to the hatred of her step-children, and we always say, "May God see fit to cut short her days among the living." Can one wife ever trust her husband's other wife or wives? It is not possible' (p. 129).

Iran

In the Eye of the Storm,[43] includes papers exploring various aspects of the life of women in post-revolutionary Iran. Fatemeh Moghadam's contribution, 'Commoditization of sexuality and female labour participation in Islam: implications for Iran 1960–90' (pp. 80–97) is of particular interest. Moghadam points out that 'Islam originated in the mercantile and exchange economy of Mecca' (p. 83) and asserts that, although it was influenced by other socio-economic systems, that of Mecca had a strong impact.

She goes on to describe Muslim marriage in terms of the sale of sexuality:

> The various passages of the Qur'an that deal with marriage in essence treat female sexuality as a tradeable object. In a Muslim marriage the buyer (the man) and the seller (the woman or her guardian) should agree voluntarily on the terms of the contract and the price for female sexuality, *mehr* (dowry) . . . The buyer is also responsible for the expenses related to the upkeep of the commodity in question, *nafaqeh*. Once the transaction is completed, the owner has complete and monogamous right to the object (p. 84).

She then discusses how, in Shi'ite marriage, the wife should always consent to her husband's demands for intercourse, which implies his entitlement to services if he pays for the woman's upkeep. This she relates to the Qur'anic analogy between wives and land (Surah 2:223): 'Just as an owner has unlimited rights to his holding, a man has unlimited rights over his wives' (idem). Injunctions to treat wives well are about looking after one's own property, and, of course, 'should the buyer find the commodity unsatisfactory, he can dispose of it — he can divorce his wife' (idem). The products of the marriage — the children — belong to the owner — the man: on divorce or widowhood, a woman has no rights over her children.

Further, a man can have more than one wife, and, in Iran, can undertake temporary marriages.[44] These entitle him to use the sexuality of a woman for any period of time agreed with her. 'The two categories of permanent and temporary marriage can be viewed as sale and lease options for the consumption of female sexuality' (p. 85).

Moghadam notes that women are not totally saleable: it is only sexuality that is treated as a commodity. Women are not reduced to the status of slaves, and have, at least in theory, many personal rights. However, she says, such rights are often based on assumptions of inferiority (for example, a woman has the right to inherit property, but her share is only half that of male co-heirs), and are often limited because of the husband's rights over his property.[45]

India

The British sociologist Patricia Jeffery records the comments of *purdah* women near Delhi in *Frogs in a Well: Indian Women in Purdah*. She reports that she did not start from the premise that *purdah* was oppressive: on the contrary, previous experience in Pakistan had 'neutralized her own distaste' for *purdah* (p. 2) because of the acceptance of it by the women she met there. She embarked on her study in India with no intention of focusing on the seclusion of women, but her experience led her to explore it further. Jeffery is not a Muslim, and I have said that this section would explore the writings of Muslim women. I include her material because it seems important to me that the women she met should be heard; and I shall limit myself to quoting her interviewees and omitting her analysis.

- From a woman who had spent some time in the West:

> Here there is nothing. I must stay within the zenana, keeping strict purdah, as becomes our rank, seeing no-one but the women and my husband. We see nothing. We know nothing. We have nothing to say to each other. We quarrel. It is dull. But they (nodding surreptitiously towards the oldest woman) will have it so . . . And they know how to make life horrible for us in each household, if we offer to relax an atom of the purdah law (p. 122).

- On the separation of women fostering ignorance:

> My own marriage was spoilt by my own ignorance and embarrassment. I knew nothing about marriage, about sex, about how to talk to men . . . No — I don't want my girls to be like myself (p. 125).
> What sort of a life was that? It is much better for people to be able to travel around and learn about other places and how people live in different countries . . . People only learn by going out (p. 126).

- From a girl restricted to studying at home:

> The problem for my father was that he wanted us educated but with izzat (honour) — in other words, preferably within the village, rather than having to go some distance, as we would have done. But on top of this, our grandmother used to come every day and make a fuss about us big girls going to school, and that was

what decided it. It seemed the only way to keep the peace (p. 127).

- On the difference between the treatment of boys' and girls' education:

  Our father tried to encourage the older (boys), but they just weren't keen. If only he'd been prepared to make such an effort with myself and my sister — we were keen enough to study! He wouldn't have needed to push us and cajole us into going to school and college. Our brothers have had all the opportunities they could wish for — and just look how they've wasted them (p. 129).

- On having to depend on men to arrange household matters (the woman quoted had watched the workman put in the tap, but *purdah* traditions made it impossible for her to speak to him):

  The workman has just put the tap in the easiest way for himself, with no thought for the convenience of us women who will be using it every day. My brother-in-law treats us as if we had the intelligence of dogs — he doesn't think we're worth consulting about things like that . . . his older brother wouldn't treat us like that (p. 132).

Marriage, in-laws, the strain of having to go on bearing children until the husband is satisfied with the number of sons produced, fear of going out, dependency on men, the sheer discomfort of the *burqa*, lack of facilities for women in public places, male harassment of women outside their houses, whether veiled or not . . . all the stereotypical problems of secluded women are reflected in Jeffery's findings.

The UK

Here too, several anthologies of women's experiences continue to confirm stereotypical western pictures of oppressed Muslim women.[46]

66
- The distress of a new immigrant entirely dependent on a fractious husband:

  > After I came here, all joy and dream disappeared . . . I started to realise my husband is very mean though he impresses the family back home with gifts. He helped me the first few days how to use gas, shops and laundry etc. He always talked about money how much someone can earn here. Because of my lack of English I started to feel very unhappy — I did not have a friend either. Whole day I cried, on top of it my husband came home and showed his temper and beat me up even (*Breaking the Silence*, p. 10).

- Tensions with parents over relationships with boys:

  > I've been going out with (my boyfriend) for 8 months now and during that time I had got caught twice. First time I got caught I got into a lot of trouble then when I got caught again me and my parents had a big fight you know what they said to me, they said I can't go to school anymore, I must stay at home and work. I pleaded with them and so in the end they had agreed with me so that I don't see that boy again. So now I am back at school and I am still seeing that boy (Ibid., p. 15).

- Restrictions on girls' education:

  > When I was 17 I came to England with my brother and mother because my father was here . . . Me and my brother knew English reading and writing but not speaking. So my brother joined ESL class but it was a mixed

class so I wasn't allowed to go although I loved to go there. Sometimes later I found a class only for women so I joined that class . . . Now my brother has been going to college. But I am still not allowed to go to college because of my culture (Ibid., p. 20).

- Shame, blame and strictness:

    The Muslim society is so strict towards the girls. Not that I don't agree with it but they do try and put them down all their lives. I understand the reasons. The biggest one is if the girl goes out with a boy it's really shameful for the parents and the community and her future marriage can be badly affected. So a girl gets blamed for doing all these things. Boys can do whatever they want from the age of ten. There are many problems for girls. (*Women Talking*, p. 10).

- Male domination:

    Most Muslim men want their own way because, in our religion, they are the boss! A woman can never be boss, a man can have his way but a woman cannot have hers, although we try (Ibid., p. 18).

- Lack of freedom:

    Women have a lot more choice and freedom in this country. They can be independent because they are working so they can make choices about their lives where in Pakistan they can't (Ibid., p. 33).

The positive side

Of course, this is not all there is to literature about the life of Muslim women. The UK anthologies record positive as well as negative aspects of life for Muslim women, and indicate some areas in which they see their Islamic cultures as better than western models.

- Pride in Islam:

  I am glad and pleased that I am a Muslim. I am proud of my culture. In some religions women are respected but many men don't understand that they should respect women. I think our religion is a very important one and I'm happy that I am a Muslim (*Women Talking*, p. 10).

- Community bonds:

  There is a strong bond between people . . . a strength that I think is more apparent among the Asian women I know as a community in England, than the white women I know (Ibid., p. 16).

- The strength of women:

  . . . an amazing woman from Bangladesh who was widowed and had four young kids and what she managed to do with what she had and what she was up against just leaves you standing there (Ibid., p. 33).

- Close family links:

  When I look at this country's family life I feel very strange and sad. Simply they don't know what they are missing and the love, affection, care and protection I was surrounded with by my parents, brother, sisters — now by my husband — the warmth and the peaceful secure feeling inside me is wonderful . . . (*Breaking the Silence*, p. 41).

Patricia Jeffery quotes women who are content with *purdah* as well as those who are not: 'You find it difficult to like our purdah. But we have known nothing else. We lead a quiet, peaceful and protected life within our own homes. And, with men as they are, we should be miserable, terrified, outside (p. 122).

The women she describes are full of life and humour, and can see the positive side of *purdah*.

> . . . the burqah hides what you're wearing underneath. If you have to go in a hurry, you can just change your shalwar and nobody will know about the dirty or torn dress which you were wearing for housework! The second benefit is that you can pass men in the street without being recognised. Sometimes I want to go to the cinema with my friend so I just tell my husband that we're going to the bazaar (which he does not question) and off we go. Sometimes we pass him on the way back home, but he's none the wiser (p. 153).

As well as her incisive analysis of male/female dynamics, **Fatima Mernissi** has produced a delightful book of autobiographical reflections which captures the warmth and fun of the *harem* world as well as its trials. *The Harem Within* (1994) describes her powerful paternal grandmother, her resourceful maternal grandmother, the fellowship between co-wives, and the creative pastimes of a houseful of women.

Yet even those content with their lot in India recognise that it depends on the defects of men. And why, we wonder, should they be put into a position in which they are frightened to go outside? Why cannot public as well as private space be made safe for women?

Mernissi's colourful, human world of women is discontented and subversive. Women plot and deceive to get their own way in the face of male vigilance, and their fantasies are woven around images of birds flying to freedom. Her book finishes with her realization, at the age of nine, that gender differences are going to separate her from her male cousin, Samir, who has been her constant playmate up till then. She discusses this with Mina, a freed slave who was kidnapped from Sudan as a child and has found refuge in her family's house.

> She listened with her back to the western wall, her yellow headdress as elegant as ever, and when I had finished she told me that life was going to be tougher from now on for both me and Samir. 'Childhood is when the difference does not matter,' she said. 'From now on, you won't be able to escape it. You'll be ruled by the difference. The world is going to turn ruthless.'

> 'But why?' I asked her, 'and why can't men and women keep on playing together even when they are older? Why the separation?' Mina replied by not answering my questions but saying that both men and women live miserable lives because of the separation. Separation creates an enormous gap in understanding . . . 'a cosmic frontier splits the planet in two halves. The frontier indicates the line of power because wherever there is a frontier, there are two kinds of creatures walking on Allah's earth, the powerful on one side, and the powerless on the other.'

> I asked Mina how I would know on which side I stood. Her answer was quick, short and very clear: 'If you can't get out, you are on the powerless side' (p. 254).

Notes

1. *Women in Islam versus the Judaeo-Christian Tradition: Myth and the Reality,* p. 11.

2. Ibid., p. 11.
3. Tertullian quoted in Muhammad, 1995, p. 4.
4. St Augustine quoted in Muhammad, 1995, p. 4.
5. St Paul quoted in Muhammad, 1995 p. 4.
6. This, he asserts, is part of the Catholic Bible. It is, in fact, part of the Old Testament Apocrypha. This is not accepted as part of the Bible by any of the Protestant churches. According to Article 6 of the Anglican 39 Articles of Religion, 'the (Apocrypha) the Church doth read for example of life and instruction; but yet doth it not apply them to establish any doctrine'.
7. *Islam in Focus*, p. 197.
8. Some commentators (e.g. Yusuf Ali) understand the 'scum' as anything in the individual's life that detracts from pure religion. More traditionally, the 'scum' is any falsehood or false system that is seen as an enemy of Islam (e.g. Usmani, Maududi).
9. Abdalati, ibid., p. 184–5.
10. For example, Mernissi (1991, see Ch. 3.2 below) depends very much on her perception of Muhammad as a man fighting for women's rights. Ahmed (1992, see Ch. 4 below) is not so sure that Muhammad improved life for women. Sarwar (1984, p. 167) also points to female infanticide in pre-Islamic Arabia.
11. 'Women in Islam', in *The Challenge of Islam*, p. 248.
12. Abd Al-Masih, *Islam under the Magnifying Glass*, pp. 97–8.
13. C.R. Marsh, *Share your Faith with a Muslim*, p. 69.
14. G.J.O. Moshay, *Who is this Allah?*, p. 89.
15. *Islam in Focus*, p. 184.
16. ibid., p. 184.
17. See, for example, Usmani N52 on this verse.
18. Heeren and Lemu, *Women in Islam*, p. 14.
19. In Arabic, as in Hebrew, the word for 'womb' has the same root as the word for God's mercy. Some Muslim writers have therefore seen the womb here as a symbol. Others say that the phrase, which is literally, 'and wombs', means that people should respect siblings who have been born of the same womb. P. Trible, *God and the Rhetoric of Sexuality*, Ch. 2, discusses the significance of

God's mercy being related to womens' wombs in a Christian context.

20. *The Status of Women in Islam*, p. 185.

21. H. Abdalati, *Islam in Focus*, p. 185.

22. Ibid. p. 184.

23. Sarwar, 1984, p. 167. He refers to *Encyclopaedia Britannica* Vol. 19 p. 909 1977 as the source of this information.

24. The Qur'an says that he was *ummi* (7:157; 62:2). There have been different opinions as to what this means, but the majority understand it to mean that he could not read or write.

25. See, for example, Abdalati, *The Family Structure in Islam*, pp. 84–97.

26. Maududi, *Purdah and the Status of Woman in Islam*, p. 178.

27. Jackie and Hodan, *Hijab — an Islamic Obligation*.

28. C. Mallouhi, *Mini-Skirts, Mothers and Muslims*, p. 34.

29. A.B.M. Al-Kanadi, *The Islamic Ruling Regarding Women's Dress*, 1991, p. 16.

30. See Ahmed, *Women and Gender in Islam*, 1992, Ch. 8.

31. Heeren and Lemu, *Women in Islam*, pp. 27–8.

32. I wonder whether, if more women were killed than men, Islam would then allow polyandry?

33. *Bible or the Qur'an*, 1988.

34. This he sees as better than the adoption system whereby a child may not even know the identity of his or her parents. He offers an extended critique of adoption on p. 171.

35. Heeren and Lemu, *Women in Islam*, pp. 41–2.

36. Heeren in Heeren and Lemu, *Women in Islam*, p. 42.

37. *Shari'ah: The Islamic Law*, p. 179.

38. *Islam in Focus*, pp. 180–1.

39. Ibid, p. 181. See also Lemu in Heeren and Lemu, p. 21.

40. Jung refers to one remarkably extreme Muslim tradition: 'A man once saw the Caliph Ummar rushing down the street with a cut on his head, bleeding. "What happened? You had gone visiting your daughter", the man asked. To which the Caliph replied that his daughter was alone in the house. "So what? Isn't she your daughter?" questioned the man. "She was alone", answered the

Caliph. The devil is with everyone. So I fled to protect myself and her." ' (*Night of the New Moon*, p. 17).

41. *The Hidden Face of Eve*, 1980, p. 31.

42. Idem.

43. M. Afkhami and E. Friedle (eds.), *In the Eye of the Storm*, 1994.

44. See Ch. 3 below, pp. 104–6. Such marriages are forbidden in Sunni Islam.

45. She, like Mernissi and some others (e.g. Ahmed), also sees some of the moves towards women's 'liberation' as being economically based.

46. The quotations below are taken from two local studies. *Breaking the Silence* is an anthology resulting from an Asian women's writing programme in Tower Hamlets, London, and is published by Centerprise Trust, 1984. *Women Talking* is a collection of quotations resulting from a research project conducted by Shimshad Iqbal for the West Newcastle Local Studies History Group, published 1992.

3
The Islamic Pattern

Ch. 2 presented two conflicting views of women in Islam. On the one hand, some Muslim writers complain that the negative pictures of Muslim women common amongst Christians and westerners distort and misunderstand Islam. A true picture, they say, would show that Islam is exactly what women need to achieve freedom and dignity. On the other hand, some Muslim women present Islam as systematically oppressing the whole female sex. What are we to make of this?

The answer is that neither of the sections of Ch. 2 presented the whole story. The apologists tend not to expound all that Islam has to say about women: there are negatives as well as positives, and it is very tempting to ignore them. At the same time, Ida has not presented all that the Muslim women writers she quotes have to say. She has focused so far only on their descriptions of the Islamic system *as it is*: the same writers have also much to say about *how it ought to be*. In exploring the other side of both sections, the key questions surround the person of Muhammad. How did he treat women? And how, therefore, should Muslims treat them?

In her autobiography, *Benazir Bhutto, Daughter of the East*, the Prime Minister of Pakistan says that Muhammad never taught that women were inferior to men. In homes where true Islam rules, there is no question but that girls and boys should be treated equally:

> There was no question in my family that my sister and I would be given the same opportunities in life as my brothers. Nor was there in Islam. We learned at an early age that it was men's interpretation of our religion that restricted women's opportunities, not our religion itself. Islam in fact had been quite progressive towards women from its inception (pp. 30–31).

Yet she also admits that her family is unusual and that women in general are looked down upon in her Muslim culture: boys are more valued than girls. An incident during a visit to India with her father in 1972 serves as an example.

Pakistan had lost its war with India, the former East Pakistan had become Bangladesh and West Pakistan (the present Pakistan) had lost some 5,000 square miles of land to India. Benazir's father, then President of Pakistan, went to India to meet the then Prime Minister, Mrs Indira Gandhi. As victor, she held all the cards, and more than 90,000 Pakistani prisoners. It was the final meeting of the two leaders and the situation was tense. The anxious Pakistani delegation needed a way of communicating without causing embarassment: 'Because no announcement could be made unless it was official, the Pakistani delegation devised a code to enable each other to know how things were going. If there is an agreement, we'll say a boy has been born. If there is no agreement, we'll say a girl has been born' (p. 57).

Like Benazir Bhutto, most Muslims think that the prophet and the book of Islam can have taught only good things about women. This view is held by many Muslim women who are denied equality with men as well as by apologists and religious leaders. Muhammad, they believe, taught that women should be treated equally and respectfully: it is the Mullahs and other men who have misinterpreted Islam. This, they suppose, explains the contradictions of Ch. 2.

The question underlying this chapter is whether this is so. Is the problem one of interpretation and application, or might its roots lie in the fundamental sources of Islam? Given the positive teaching about women explored in Section 2.1, is there also negative teaching that has given rise to women's subjugation? We shall take the question to the Qur'an, as well as to the *Hadith*. These are collections of reports about what Muhammad said and did[1], and are in some ways more important as sources of Islamic practice than is the Qur'an itself.

They are important for two reasons:

- First, there are many *hadith* that function as commentary on the Qur'an. They tell of the occasions when the different verses were given, and sometimes give Muhammad's own interpretations of verses. They also add many details of practice to the bare outline of Qur'anic injunctions.[2]
- Secondly, Muhammad is considered an inspired example, to be followed not only in his principles but in the

details of what he did. For example, if Muhammad ate with his right hand, all Muslims should eat with their right hand. If he greeted people by saying, 'As-salamu 'alaykum',[3] then Muslims should greet one another with the same Arabic words.[4]

The words and actions of Muhammad are considered to be inspired, and the *Hadith* are second only to the Qur'an in authority. The only question is whether they really date back to Muhammad. Thousands of *hadith* were tested for authenticity in the third Islamic century: those quoted below are all from collections that are widely accepted as genuine.

In what follows, we will explore the teachings of the Qur'an and the *Hadith* that have been used to oppress women. Napoleon will look at traditional ways of understanding them. Ida will reflect on how Muslim feminists — male as well as female — are proposing alternative interpretations.

2.1 Traditional understandings

Napoleon John

Islam brought reforms, and improved life for women in the Arabia of Muhammad's days. The problem lies in the way that the example of those days has been used.

There is, as explained by the apologists, some very positive material about women in the Qur'an. There are also sayings of Muhammad which are sympathetic and respectful towards them. But on balance Islam's attitude towards women and their sexuality has been far from positive. This negative attitude towards women has its foundations largely in the *hadith*. What has happened is that aspects of life which represented progress in sixth century Arabia have become the rule for all times and places.

As I read, I find negative teachings that affect every part of women's lives, from birth through to life after death. I do not want to suggest that all, or even most, Muslim men take advantage of these teachings: many respect and love their wives and families. But Islam does include rulings that allow for oppression of women, and, where such teachings are allowed to predominate over the positives explored in Ch. 2, it is not surprising that women feel they are 'second class citizens'.

One of the most disturbing *hadith* puts women in the same category as asses and dogs — and dogs are considered unclean animals in Islam. It suggests that the very presence of a woman can pollute a man's prayer:[5]

> Abu Huraira reported God's messenger as saying, a woman, an ass and a dog cut off the prayer, but something like the back of a saddle guards against that (*Mishkat Al-Masabih, The Sutra*, Vol. 1, p. 157).

This is an extreme case, but the sad fact is that there are many things in the Qur'an and the *hadith* that can be used to diminish women.

A. The creation of humanity

Behold, thy Lord said to the angels: 'I will create a vicegerent on earth.' They said: 'Wilt Thou place therein one who will make mischief and shed blood? — whilst we do glorify Thy holy (name)?' He said: 'I know what ye know not.'

And he taught Adam the nature of all things,[6] then he placed them before the angels and said: 'Tell me the nature of these if ye are right.

And behold, We said to the angels: 'Bow down to Adam': and they bowed down (Surah 2:30, 31, 34).

While the creation of Adam is mentioned frequently in the Qur'an,[7] there is little about the creation of the woman.[8] Usually, Adam's creation is coupled with God's command to the angels to prostrate before him. The word translated 'bowed down', is *sajada*, in Arabic. The same word is used for the worship of God.

Where the woman is mentioned with Adam, she is not named, but is referred to as his wife and then her presence is only indicated by dual word forms. Although they are together, God addresses Adam alone, except when he expels them to earth:

We said: 'O Adam! dwell thou and thy wife in the Garden; and eat of the bountiful things therein as ye will; but approach not this tree, or ye run into harm and transgression.

Then did Satan make them slip from the Garden, and get them out of the state (of felicity) in which they had been. We said: Get ye down, all (ye people), with enmity between yourselves (Surah 2:34–5).

It is then Adam who is given words to enable them to repent and receive forgiveness.

Then learnt Adam from his Lord words of inspiration, and his Lord turned towards him; for he is Oft-returning, Most merciful (Surah 2:36).

While it is clear that the Qur'anic stories cannot by themselves be used as have the Bible stories to suggest that Eve was responsible for Adam's sin, it is also clear that Eve is a secondary character. She is included, but the story is about Adam: it is he who is created as God's vicegerent[9] (the Arabic word is *khalifah*), and it is he who is considered a prophet by all Muslims. Eve is known to them, and receives the honorific title of *hazrat*, but it is her husband who receives words from God.

If Adam, and thus perhaps humanity in general, was created as God's vicegerent, why did God create the woman? The Qur'anic answer is similar to that of the Bible:

> And among his signs is this, that he created for you mates from among yourselves, that ye may dwell in tranquility with them, and that he has put love and mercy between your (hearts): verily in that are signs for those who reflect (Surah 30:21).

As in the Bible, human beings are made in two genders so that they can relate to each other. As with the Bible, this has often been understood as meaning that the woman was made for the sake of, almost as the servant of, the man. Another translation betrays this:

> And of his signs is this: he created for you helpmeets from yourselves that ye might find rest in them, and he ordained between you love and mercy. Lo, herein indeed are portents for folk who reflect (Surah 30: 21, Pickthall).

This is also affirmed by the *Hadith* and other traditional stories which have been used to expand on the brief Qur'anic account.

While the Qur'an has nothing of the creation of Eve from Adam's rib, the *Hadith* assume it, and it has long been used to denigrate women:

> Abu Huraira reported God's messenger as saying, Act kindly towards women, for they were created from a rib and the most crooked part of a rib is its top. If you attempt to straighten it you will break it, and if you leave it alone it will remain crooked; so act kindly towards women (*Mishkat Al Masabih*, Vol. 1, p. 688).

The Qur'an cannot be read as suggesting that Eve was responsible for the first sin: in fact, it has the Devil whispering to Adam and leading him to the tree (Surah 20:120). But the *Hadith* lay blame on Eve and on all women after her:

> He reported God's messenger as saying, had it not been for the B. Israel meat would not have gone bad, and had it not been for Eve a woman would never have acted unfaithfully towards her husband (*Mishkat Al-Masabih, The Book of Marriage*, Vol. 1, p. 688).

> Narrated Usama bin Zaid: The Prophet said, after me I have not left any affliction more harmful to men than women (*Sahih Al-Bukhari*, Vol. 7, p. 22).

The *Hadith* are supplemented with the *isra'iliyyat* — traditional stories probably gleaned from Jewish sources in the early years of Islam.[10] A typical commentator from the Indian sub-continent expands on the Adam story in Surah 2:36:

> It is said that Adam and Hawwa began to live in the paradise and Satan was thrown away from that place of reverence. His malignance was increased and at last with the help of the snake and the peacock he entered into

paradise and insinuated the mother Hawwa to eat of that tree. She was simple and easily caught in the net of the Satanic persuasions and ate of that tree and also caused Adam to eat it and assured him that by its eating he would become more favourite and nearer to God (Usmani).

A popular Sufi treatise comments:

> A woman was the cause of the first calamity that overtook Adam in paradise.[11]

B. Women's lives

The *Hadith* are comprehensive: they cover all aspects of life from the cradle to the grave — and beyond. While they are very positive about the value of women's roles as mothers (see Ch. 2), there are many points at which they are more negative.

Birth

It is quite normal for the people of the East to bring children to their priests or leaders to be blessed.[12] The early Muslim community was not different: they brought children to Muhammad. But it seems to have been only boys that were blessed:

> A'isha told that boys used to be brought to God's messenger, and he would invoke blessings on them and soften some dates and rub their palates with them (*Mishkat Al-Masabih*, Vol. 2, p. 884).

Many Muslims perform the *aqiqa* ceremony at the birth of a child: they sacrifice an animal in token of their gratitude to God. According to the most authentic collection of *hadith*, Sahih Al Bukhari, it is for baby boys that the sacrifice is necessary. A secondary *hadith* is quoted to show that the *aqiqa* can also apply to girls, but the requirement is half that for boys.

> Narrated Salman bin Amir Ad Dabbi: I heard Allah's Apostle saying, Aqiqa is to be offered for (newly born) boy, so slaughter (an animal) for him, and relieve him of his suffering. (Note: It has been quoted in Fateh-Bari that the majority of the Religious Scholars agree to the Hadith narrated in Sahih At-TIRMIZY that the Prophet was asked about Aqiqa and he ordered 2 sheep for a boy and one sheep for a girl and that is his tradition 'SUNNA' (*Sahih Al-Bukhari*, Vol. 7, p. 275).

Religious duties

Muslim apologists tell us that, in religious affairs, there is no difference between men and women: they are equal. When we look in the traditions of the prophet, however, a woman's religious freedoms are limited and can be further limited by her husband. This can be seen in the five pillars of Islam:

- *Shahada*, the Creed: There is no god but Allah and Muhammad is the Apostle of Allah.
- *Salah*, five daily prayers.
- *Zakat*, Almsgiving.
- *Sawm*, Fasting.
- *Hajj*, Pilgrimage to Mecca.

Prayer

> A'ishah told of Fatima daughter of Abu Hubaish coming to the Prophet and saying, I am a woman whose blood keeps flowing and I am never purified. Shall I therefore abandon prayer? He replied, no, that is only a vein and is

not menstruation; so when your menstruation comes on abandon prayer, and when it ends wash the blood from yourself and then pray (*Mishkat Al-Masabih*, Vol. 2, p. 112).

84 Menstruation is a natural part of a woman's life yet she should not pray during her periods. Some writers[13] see this as a privileged exemption from religious duties, but the following *hadith* sees it rather as a deficiency:

> Abu Sa'id al-Khudri said that when God's messenger went out to the place of prayer on the day of sacrifice, or on the day when the fast was broken, he came upon some women and said, give alms, you women folk, for I have been shown that you will be the majority of the inhabitants of hell. They asked, for what reason, messenger of God? He replied, you are greatly given to abuse, and you are ungrateful to your husbands. Among women who are deficient in intelligence and religion I have not seen anyone more able to remove the understanding of a prudent man than one of you. They asked, what is the deficiency of our religion and our intelligence, messenger of God? He replied, is not the testimony of a woman equivalent to half the testimony of a man? They said, yes. Remarking that that pertained to the deficiency of her intelligence, he asked, is it not the case that when she menstruates she neither prays nor fasts? When they replied, yes, he said, that that pertains to the deficiency of her religion (*Mishkat Al-Masabih*, Vol. 1, p. 9).

Women are also barred from reading the Qur'an and entering the mosque while menstruating:

> Ibn Umar reported God's messenger as saying, the woman who is menstruating and the one who is seminally defiled must not recite any of the Qur'an (*Mishkat Al-Masabih, The Book of Purification*, Vol. 1, p. 93).

A'ishah reported God's messenger as saying, turn these houses so as not to face the mosque, for I do not make the mosque lawful for a menstruating woman or one who is seminally defiled (Idem).

The Qur'an says:

Whoever works righteousness, man or woman, and has faith, verily, to him We give a new life, a life that is good and pure, and We will bestow on such reward according to the best of their actions (Surah 16: 97).

Any one doing right will inherit the good life; but such *hadith* teach that women are limited in the good they can do because of their nature and physical make up. This is particularly significant in a religion which teaches that rewards are given according to what is done, and not only by the grace of God.[14]

Fasting This is an important religious act in Islam and helps one to build credit for the future life. Again, the *Hadith* limit women, this time because they cannot fast without their husband's permission. This is because fasting includes abstinence from sexual intercourse, and women are to be available to their husbands.

Abu Sa'id told of a woman who came to God's messenger when he was with him and said, My husband, Safwan b. al-Mu'attal, beats me when I pray, makes me break my fast when I am observing it, and does not pray the dawn prayer till the sun rises. Safwan was present, so he asked him about what she had said and he replied, Messenger of God, as for her statement that I beat her when she prays, she recites two *suras* and I have forbidden her to do so. God's messenger said to him, if it had been one sura it would be enough for people. He continued: As for her statement that I make her break her fast when she is observing it, she keeps on fasting, and I am a young man who cannot contain himself. God's messenger said, a woman may fast only with her husband's permission (*Mishkat al-Masabih*, Vol. 1, p. 693).

Almsgiving Free will giving is a part of most religions. In Islam, such giving is called *sadaqah*. It is additional to the required *zakat* giving, but considered to be a source of much merit. Again, women are limited, this time by the fact that their roles are usually restricted to the home so that they cannot earn money.

> Abu Huraira reported the Apostle of Allah (may peace be upon him) as saying when a woman gives something her husband has earned without being commanded by him to do so, she has half his reward (*Sunan Abu Dawud, Kitab al-Zakat*, Vol. 2, p. 443).

A footnote explains:

> It is necessary for wife, slave and trustee to obtain the permission of the master or husband to spend the property. In case there is no permission from him explicitly or implicitly, there will be no reward for them (Ibid).

If, however, a woman is determined to give in charity, she can give some of her own food:

> Sa'd said: when the Apostle of Allah (may peace be upon him) took the oath of allegiance from woman, a woman of high rank, who seemed to be one of the women of Mudar, rose and said: Prophet of Allah, we are dependent on our parents, our sons. (Abu Dawud said: I think this version has the word and our husbands). So what part of their property can we spend lawfully? He said: Fresh food which you eat and give as a present (*Sunan Abu Dawud, Kitab al-Zakat*, Vol. 2, pp. 442–443).

Pilgrimage

> Abu Huraira told that God's messenger addressed them
> saying pilgrimage has been ordained for you people so
> perform it . . . He said that God's messenger was asked
> what action was most excellent and replied that it was
> faith in God and his messenger. He was asked what came
> next and replied that it was Jihad in God's path. He was
> asked what came next and replied that it was a pilgrimage
> which was accepted. He reported God's messenger as
> saying, if anyone performs the pilgrimage for God's sake
> without talking immodestly or acting wickedly, he will
> return (free from sin) as on the day his mother bore him
> (*Mishkat Al-Masabih, The Rites of Pilgrimage*, Vol. 1,
> p. 535).

The *hajj* is one of the most important and meritorious
actions in Islam, and believed to be a sure way to
forgiveness and a new start in life. Yet, according to the
Hadith, a woman's freedom is curbed even here because of
her dependency on men:

> Abu Huraira reported God's messenger as saying, a
> woman must not make a journey of a day and a night
> unless she is accompanied by a man who is within the
> prohibited degrees[15] (*Mishkat al-Masabih, The Rites of
> Pilgrimage*, Vol. 1, p. 536).

In each of these acts of piety, which lie at the heart of
Islamic practice, women are treated differently than men.
While some would say that the differences make life easier
for women, in that they are exempted from some of the
duties of men, they can also be seen as putting women at
a disadvantage. They are dependent on men in that they
cannot even carry out their basic religious duties without
male help and approval; and in some cases their very

physical make up means that they are prevented from building up the merit that can bring them God's blessing.

Marriage

Choice of spouse Muslim women, like those in many other cultures, are subject to marriage proposals. Some *hadith* indicate that a previously married woman has the right to make her own choice:

> Ibn Abbas reported the Prophet as saying, a woman without a husband has more right to her person than her guardian . . . in a version he said, a woman who has been previously married has more right to her person than her guardian (*Mishkat Al-Masabih, Book of Marriage*, Vol. 1, p. 665).

It is already implied that a virgin has fewer rights. It is true that the *Hadith* tell us:

> A virgin's permission must be asked about herself, her permission being her silence (*Mishkat Al-Masabih, Book of Marriage*, Vol. 1, p. 665).

If she objects at the marriage ceremony, it is not valid. However, she is dependent on her male guardian's choice:

> A'isha reported God's messenger as saying, if any woman marries without the consent of her guardian her marriage is void, her marriage is void, her marriage is void. If there is cohabitation she gets her dower for the intercourse her husband has had (*Mishkat Al-Masabih, Book of Marriage*, Vol. 1, p. 666).

All the great Sheiks of Islam such as Shafii, Malik, Ibn Hanbal, Ibn Timiyya and others are of the opinion that a virgin's father can force her into marriage, even if she is an adult woman.

There is also a tradition of fathers arranging marriages with older men while their daughters are still children. The example was set by Muhammad himself, in his marriage to the daughter of his closest friend:

> A'ishah said: The Apostle of Allah (may peace be upon him) married me when I was seven years old. The narrator Sulaiman said: Or six years. He had intercourse with me when I was nine years old (*Sunan Abu Dawud*, Vol. 2).

Several traditions record that Aisha was six or seven at the time of their betrothal.[16]

The marriage relationship Islam teaches that husbands are required to care for their wives, and have many duties towards them. But even the Qur'an itself says that one duty is that they discipline their wives: they are to some degree responsible for their wives' behaviour. The verse is a much-debated one, and its various interpretations will be discussed at length below. Pickthall's translation gives the flavour of how it has usually been understood.

> Men are in charge of women, because Allah hath made the one of them to excel the other, and because they spend of their property (for the support of women). So good women are the obedient, guarding in secret that which Allah hath guarded. As for those from whom ye fear rebellion, admonish them and banish them to beds apart, and scourge them. Then if they obey you, seek not a way against them. Lo! Allah is ever High Exalted, Great (Surah 4:34).

All the traditional expositors of the Qur'an agree on the meaning of this verse. For instance, al-Galaleen's commentary (p. 69) says that, if you are afraid of women's disobedience, threaten them, then banish them to beds apart and, if this does not work, scourge them. Maududi[17] explains:

90

> This does not mean that a man should resort to these three measures all at once, but that they may be employed if a wife adopts an attitude of obstinate defiance. So far as the actual application of these measures is concerned, there should, naturally, be some correspondence between the fault and the punishment that is administered. Moreover, it is obvious that wherever a light touch can prove effective one should not resort to sterner measures (Note 59 on Surah 4).

He points out that Muhammad permitted corporal punishment of wives only with distaste, and that he said that men were not to hit their wives in the face nor to beat them hard enough to scar them. Other commentators also discuss reasons for and levels of punishment: none disputes the husband's right and responsibility to punish his wife.

A *hadith* affirms Muhammad's reluctance to allow men to beat their wives; but it also teaches that women should beware of complaining of mistreatment:

> Ilyas b. Abd Allah b. Abu Dhubab reported the Apostle of Allah (may peace be upon him) as saying: Do not beat Allah's handmaidens, but when Umar came to the Apostle of Allah (may peace be upon him) and said: Women have become emboldened towards their husbands, he (the Prophet) gave permission to beat them. Then many women came round the family of the Apostle of Allah (may peace be upon him) complaining against their

husbands. So the apostle of Allah (may peace be upon him) said: Many women have gone round Muhammad's family complaining against their husbands. They are not the best among you (*Sunan Abu Dawud, Kitab al-Nikah*, Vol. 2, p. 575).

In contrast, the husband should not even be asked his reasons for beating his wife:

Umar reported the Prophet as saying, a man will not be asked about why he beat his wife (Ibid).

Some *hadith* say that the relationship of husband and wife should be that of mutual love, but many seem rather to encourage a relationship of domination and fear.

On the authority of Muhammad (peace and blessing of Allah be upon him), he said: Hang up your scourge in a place where your wife (or wives) can see it (*Al-Zamakhshari, Kash-shaf*, Vol. 1, p. 525).

Such is the husband's authority that, we are told, Muhammad said that, if it were possible, he would have commanded women to worship their husbands:

Abu Huraira reported God's messenger as saying, if I were to order anyone to prostrate himself before another, I would order a woman to prostrate herself before her husband (*Mishkat Al-Masabih, The Book of Marriage*, Vol. 1, p. 691).

One of the husband's prerogatives is access to his wife's sexuality. As we have seen, he can banish his wife to a separate bed if he finds her disobedient; but a woman can not remain away from her husband's bed of her own accord.

Narrated Abu Huraira: The Prophet said, if a man invites his wife to sleep with him and she refuses to come to him, the angels send their curses on her till morning (*Sahih Al-Bukhari* Vol. 7, p. 93).

The Qur'an does not suggest otherwise:

92

Your wives are as a tilth unto you; so approach your tilth when or how ye will . . .[18]

As well as *hadith* that give instructions to Muslims, there are many that recount the life of Muhammad. His marriages — both the monogamous one to Khadijah and polygamous ones of the Medinan period, are models for Muslims to follow. For example, a strong sexual appetite is encouraged, but only within the bounds of marriage:

Ibn Mas'ud said that God's messenger saw a woman who charmed him, so he went to Sauda who was making perfume in the company of some women. They left him, and after he had satisfied his desire he said, if any man sees a woman who charms him he should go to his wife, for she has the same kind of thing as the other woman (*Mishkat Al-Masabih, The Book of Marriage* Vol. 1, p. 662).

Divorce

Prophet! When ye do divorce women, divorce them at their prescribed periods (Surah 65:1).

Ibn Umar reported the Prophet (may peace be upon him) as saying: Of all the lawful acts the most detestable to Allah is divorce (*Sunan Abu Dawud, Kitab al-Talaq*, Vol. 2, p. 585–86).

A childless Muslim woman came to see my wife in some distress. She had just received a registered letter from her husband in Pakistan, announcing that he had divorced her. She could not believe that such a divorce, carried out without warning and without reference to herself, could possibly be legal; yet so it turned out. Divorce (Arabic *talaq*) to Allah is the most detestable thing; yet in actual practice, it can be remarkably easy. A man can divorce his wife at will, without being considered to have done anything wrong.

Although, as we saw in Ch. 2, there are some schools which think that three divorces cannot be declared at the same time, there are others who disagree:

> Sometimes a husband declares three talaqs at one and the same time, for example, the husband says, I divorce you, I divorce you, I divorce you or I divorce you three times. There is a difference of opinion about the fact that whether it amounts to three talaqs or only a single talaq. Its significance is manifest because of the fact that a triple talaq warrants the doctrine of Halala for remarriage between the same spouses while as a single talaq does not necessitate so.[19]

In sum: although it is recommended that there should be a time lag between the three declarations, a husband is free to pronounce all three at once, and a wife has no choice but to accept it. We are told that if the divorce was given in a moment of anger and the husband wants to get his wife back he has to face the penalty of *halala*. The argument is that, since *halala* is required even after the careless triple pronouncement of the divorce formula, such a divorce must be valid.

The word *halala* means making something lawful. In this context, it refers to the ruling that, once a husband has divorced his wife, he may not take her back until she has been married to someone else, even if only for one night. This law comes from the Qur'an itself:

> So if a husband divorces his wife (irrevocably), he cannot, after that, re-marry her until after she has married another husband and he has divorced her (Surah 2:230).

Some writers argue that the law was given to make divorce difficult, saying that, although permitted in the Qur'an, it was disliked by Muhammad. The following *hadith* is used to support their argument:

> Ali reported: (The narrator Isma'il said: I think al-Sha'bi attributed this tradition to the Prophet): The Prophet (may peace be upon him) said: Curse be upon the one who marries a divorced woman with the intention of making her lawful for her former husband and upon the one for whom she is made lawful (*Sunan Abu Dawud, Kitab al-Nikah*, Vol. 2, p. 555).

Despite this reported dislike, Muhammad upheld the law:

> Narrated Aisha: Rifa'a Al-Qurazi married a lady and he divorced her whereupon she married another man. She came to the Prophet and said that her new husband did not approach her, and that he was completely impotent. The Prophet said (to her), No (you cannot remarry your first husband) till you taste the second husband and he tastes you (i.e. till he consummates his marriage with you) (*Sahih Al-Bukhari*, Vol. 7, p. 182).

Many ordinary Muslims think that a nominal marriage is sufficient, but most of the commentators agree that the sexual act must take place.[20]

The triple divorce formula does not have to be said in Arabic, and can even be made conditional on a future event:

> And Ibrahim said: If someone said (to his wife), I am not in need of you, then the verdict is to be given according to his intention. And a divorce is valid when expressed in the language of the nation to which the person belongs. And Qatada said: If someone says (to his wife), if you become pregnant, then you are divorced thrice, he should have sexual intercourse with her once only every time she becomes clean after her menstruation, and if her pregnancy becomes apparent, she will be regarded as divorced irrevocably (*Sahih Al-Bukhari*, Vol. 7, p. 145–46).

The only thing that can make the pronouncement invalid is the husband's being either insane or drunk (*Al-Bukhari*, Vol. 7, p. 146).

A woman is unable to dispute a divorce instigated by her husband, but she does have the right to seek a divorce from him. A different Arabic word is used for such a divorce — *khul*, or 'self-redemption'. Aisha Lemu explains the origin of women's right to divorce by telling the story of a woman who came to Muhammad,

> . . . saying that although her husband was a good man and she had no complaint against his treatment, she disliked him greatly and could not live with him. The Prophet directed that she should return to the husband a garden which he had given to her as her dowry, as the condition of her divorce. This procedure is sanctioned in the Qur'an where Allah says: 'And if you fear that they may not be able to keep the limits of Allah, then there is no sin for either of them, if the woman redeems herself with that 2:229 (Heeren and Lemu, 1978, p. 22).

Maududi gives the following explanation of this verse:

> Whatever settlement is made between a husband and a wife should come into effect. If the matter is referred to the court, however, it will investigate only whether the wife has really become too disgusted with the husband to put up with him. Once this is determined, the court is entitled to fix the amount of payment incumbent on the wife as compensation for the repudiation of her marriage, and the husband will be bound to accept that amount and divorce his wife.

Usually, the maximum payment required will be the value of the *mehr*, the dowry given to a bride by her bridegroom.

Maududi's explanation indicates that the woman is still disadvantaged:

- First, a woman cannot divorce her husband but only buy herself back from him: it is still he who has to divorce her.
- Secondly, self-redemption can sometimes be very costly, as is clear from the *hadith*:

> Nafi quoted a client to Safiya daughter of Abu Ubaid to the effect that she got a divorce from her husband in return for everything she possessed and that Abdallah b. Umar made no objection to that (*Mishkat al-Masabih: Book of Marriage*, Vol. 1, p. 698).

Another *hadith* serves to discourage women from seeking *khul* except for the most serious reasons:

> Thauban reported God's messenger as saying, if any woman asks her husband for divorce without some strong reason the odour of paradise will be forbidden to her (*Mishkat Al-Masabih, Book of Marriage*, Vol. 1, p. 696).

There is no doubt that husbands have much more power over the continuation of their marriages than do wives.

C. The power of men over women

A friend of mine brought an English man who had embraced Islam to visit me. As we sat in my study I asked him the question I have always asked such converts, 'Friend, what attracted you to Islam?' One thing he found particularly attractive was Islam's strong stand for law and order, and its ways of dealing with criminals. He insisted that, with Islamic rule, crime in the UK would disappear. The problem, he said, was that people had lost the will to enforce law and order.

I asked him to explain further, and he asked me a question: 'Suppose you came home and found your wife in bed with a man, what would you do?' I explained that, since both my wife and I are committed Christians, such a situation was unlikely. But for argument's sake, according to the Bible I could choose to divorce her without sinning against God's holy will. This is only permissible, and not a command from God: it would be best to forgive and be reconciled. He then offered his verdict: 'As a man in such a situation, you should kill your wife.'

So I asked him a question, and his answer stunned me. I said, 'But let us reverse the case, suppose it is not my wife but I who is the guilty party and she finds me in bed with a woman. Would you suggest the same punishment for me? 'No, she has no right to take your life. You are a man!' he replied. This he saw as part of the new faith which he had embraced, and he was proud of it.

Adultery is certainly considered a great sin in Islam, as it is in Christianity. The Qur'an calls for severe punishment, but, although some passages deal primarily with women who are unchaste,[21] others specify that it should be for both male and female:

98

> The woman and the man guilty of adultery or fornication — flog each of them with a hundred stripes; let not compassion move you in their case, in a matter prescribed by God, if ye believe in God and the Last Day: and let a party of the believers witness their punishment.[22]

Where, then, did this young convert get his ideas? Few Muslims would share such extreme views, but there are *hadith* which give a man more power over his wife than she over him. Perhaps he concluded from these that men are more valuable than women.

We heard in Ch. 2 the apologists' claim that Islam improved the lot of women; and there is certainly some truth in it. Yet some *hadith* show us that this is not the whole story: some women found their freedoms restricted by the new Islamic system. In parts of Arabia women were powerful figures at the advent of Islam:

> . . . Then Umar went on narrating the Hadith and said . . . We, the people of Quraish used to have the upper hand over our wives, but when we came to the Ansar, we found that their women had the upper hand over their men, so our women also started learning the ways of the Ansari women. I shouted at my wife and she retorted against me and I disliked that she should answer me back (*Sahih Al-Bukhari*, Vol. 7, p. 87–88).

Now, as testified by the women quoted in the second part of Ch. 2, there are many restrictions imposed upon women. She should veil her face even in the presence of a blind man:

> Umm Salama said: I was with God's messenger along with Maimuna when Ibn Umm Maktum approached and came in to visit him, so he told us to veil ourselves. I said, Messenger of God, is he not blind and unable to see us? He replied, are you blind and unable to see him? (*Mishkat Al-Masabih, The Book of Marriage,* Vol. 1, p. 663).

Men, on the other hand, have great freedoms relative to women. In particular, Islam has allowed the following sexual freedoms to men:

- More than one wife: Islam allows polygyny but not polyandry.
- Concubines: as can be afforded
- Slave women, who can be used for sexual pleasures
- In Shi'a Islam, *Mut'ah*: contracting temporary marriages

More than one wife

> If ye fear that ye shall not be able to deal justly with the orphans, marry women of your choice, two or three or four; but if ye fear that ye shall not be able to deal justly (with them), then only one, or (a captive) that your right hands possess. That will be suitable, to prevent you from doing injustice (Surah 4:3).

This does not mean that Muslim men are limited to having four wives, but that they cannot be wedded to more than four women at one time. In practice, if a man wants to marry other women, all he needs to do is to divorce one or more among the four and replace them with others.

The example of Muhammad's Companions suggests that it was common practice amongst them to have more than four wives in their life times.[23] Umar Ibn al-Khattab, the second Caliph, wedded seven wives in the course of his life; Uthman, the third Caliph, eight; and Ali, the third Caliph, after the death of his first wife, Muhammad's daughter Fatima, married ten women. Muhammad's own grandson Hassan (Muhammad said about him that he is the master of the youth of paradise) surpassed all of them: he had a total of seventy wives in his life time.

There is no suggestion in the records that any of the wives were unfaithful: divorce and remarriage was simply the husbands' choice. They were able to replace their wives because of the freedom Islam had given to them and, the records say, they had concubines and female slaves as well as wives.

The Qur'an ensures that divorced women should keep the marriage gift given to them by their husbands, but in doing so it permits the exchange of wives:

> But if ye decide to take one wife in place of another, even if ye had given the latter a whole treasure for dower, take not the least bit of it back (Surah 4:20).

Surah 4:3 quoted above makes it clear that men should treat all their wives with complete equality. Some modern writers acknowledge how difficult this is: so difficult that some suppose the verse to be recommending monogamy.[24] Even Muhammad himself was not able to prevent jealousy in his own household. A dispute arose that was so strong that people thought that he had divorced all his wives (*Sahih Al-Bukhari* Vol. 7, p. 89).

This is how the tradition says Umar advised his own daughter Hafsa, who was one of Muhammad's wives:

> The Prophet smiled and then I said to him, will you heed what I say, O Allah's Apostle? I entered upon Hafsa and said to her, do not be tempted to imitate your companion (A'isha), for she is more charming than you and more beloved to the Prophet. The Prophet smiled for a second time (*Sahih Al-Bukhari*, Vol. 7, p. 90).

Muhammad had a favourite wife: it seems unlikely that other men should be different. Perhaps it was his awareness of this, and the pain of the conflict in his own home, that led him to forbid his son-in-law, 'Ali, a second wife:[25]

> Narrated Al-Miswar bin Makhrama: I heard Allah's Apostle who was on the pulpit, saying, Banu Hisham bin Al-Mughira have requested me to allow them to marry their daughter to Ali bin Abi Talib, but I don't give permission, and will not give permission unless Ali bin Abi Talib divorces my daughter in order to marry their daughter, because Fatima is a part of my body, and I hate what she hates to see, and what hurts her, hurts me (*Sahih Al-Bukhari*, Vol. 7, p. 115–116).

Abdalati says that non-Muslims misunderstand the system when they say that it is easy for Muslim men to change wives: 'As easy as shifting from one apartment to another, or even as changing one's suit.' No doubt, many Muslim men love their first wives dearly. But, in my country of origin, a country with an Islamic culture, there is a saying, *Aurut to mard ke pano ki juti hoti hai, jab chaha badal li*:

'Woman is like a man's shoes: when he wants to, he can change them.'

Concubines and slave-girls

Islam has allowed concubines. War bounties were made permissible for all Muslims. In fact, according to the *Hadith*, it is only Muslims who have a God-given right to the spoils of war:

> Abu Huraira reported God's messenger as saying, spoils were not lawful for anyone before us, that being because God saw our weakness and incapacity and made them allowable for us (*Mishkat Al-Masabih, The Book of Jihad*, Vol. 2, p. 848).

> Abu Umama reported the Prophet as saying, God has given me superiority over the prophets, or as saying, he has given my people superiority over other peoples and made spoils lawful to us (p. 852).

The Qur'an frequently affirms that a man has sexual rights over any women included in his share:

> The believers must (eventually) win through — those who humble themselves in their prayers; who avoid vain talk; who are active in deeds of charity; who abstain from sex, except with those joined to them in the marriage bond, or (the captives) whom their right hands possess — for (in their case) they are free from blame (Surah 23: 1–6[26])

Any booty from the holy wars — be it women or children, garments or money — was distributed among Muslim fighters after deducting one fifth for Allah and his Apostle. The *Hadith* confirm the Qur'anic suggestion that women were taken as captives and used as Muslim warriors chose:

> Jabir said that in the period when the Qur'an was coming down they used to withdraw the penis . . . the Prophet heard of that and did not prohibit it. He told of a man who went to God's messenger and said, I have a slave-girl who is our servant and I have intercourse with her, but do not want her to conceive. He replied, withdraw your penis from her if you wish, for what is decreed for her will come to her (*Mishkat Al-Masabih, The Book of Marriage*), Vol. 1, p. 677).

103

> Abu Sa'id al-Khudri said: We went out with God's messenger on the expedition to the B. al-Mustaliq and took some Arab women captive, and we desired the women, for we were suffering from the absence of our wives. We liked withdrawing the penis and wanted to do so, but we asked ourselves whether we could do it when God's messenger was among us before asking him. So we asked him about that and he replied, it does not matter if you do not do it, for every soul that is to be born up to the day of resurrection will be born (p. 677).

Muslim warriors were encouraged to use these captive women even if their husbands were still alive:

> Abu Sai'd al-Khudri said the Apostle of Allah (may peace be upon him) sent a military expedition to Awtas on the occasion of the battle of Hunain. They met their enemy and fought with them. They defeated them and took them captives. Some of the Companions of the Apostle of Allah (may peace be upon him) were reluctant to have intercourse with the female captives in the presence of their husbands who were unbelievers. So Allah, the Exalted, sent down the Qur'anic verse: And all married women (are forbidden) unto you save those (captives)

whom your right hands possess (*Sunan Abu Dawud, Kitab al-Nikah*, Vol. 2, p. 577).

Mut'ah: the marriage of desire

Mut'ah is a temporary marriage: a personal contract between a man and a woman to cohabit for a limited period of time in return for an agreed payment for the woman. Sunni Muslims reject this practice, although they recognise that it was used during the time of Muhammad. It remains valid in Shi'ite law.

All the primary sources of Islam tell us that Muhammad allowed *mut'ah* during his life time, and that the practice continued even in the era of the first Caliph, Abu Bakr. It was the second Caliph, Umar bin Khitab who, perhaps, stopped it.

> Narrated Abdullah: We used to participate in the holy battles led by Allah's Apostle and we had nothing (no wives) with us. So we said, shall we get ourselves castrated? He forbade us that and then allowed us to marry women with a temporary contract and recited to us: O you who believe! Make not unlawful the good things which Allah has made lawful for you, but commit no transgression.[27] (*Al-Bukhari*, Vol. 7, p. 8–9).

Other traditions question whether permission for *mut'ah* applied to all men:

> Narrated Jabir bin Abdullah and Salama bin Al-Akwa: While we were in an army, Allah's Apostle came to us and said, you have been allowed to do the Mut'a (marriage), so do it. Salama bin Al-Akwa said: Allah's Apostle said, if a man and a woman agree (to marry temporarily), their marriage should last for three nights, and if they like to continue, they can do so; and if they want to separate,

they can do so. I do not know whether that was only for us or for all the people in general (*Al-Bukhari*, Vol. 7, p. 37).

It was certainly not permitted at all times:

Abu Abdullah (Al-Bukhari) said: Ali made it clear that the Prophet said, the Mut'a marriage has been cancelled (made unlawful) (idem).

It seems that there were certain periods when *mut'ah* became permissible, for example when men were away from home on expeditions.

Jabir b. Abdullah and Salama b. Aal-Akwa said: There came to us the proclaimer of Allah's Messenger (may peace be upon him) and said: Allah's Messenger (may peace be upon him) has granted you permission to benefit yourselves, i.e. to contract temporary marriage with women (*Sahih Muslim, Kitab Al Nikah*, Vol. 2, p. 705).

The nature of these marriages is described thus:

Sabra Juhanni reported: Allah's Messenger (may peace be upon him) permitted temporary marriage for us. So I and another person went out and saw a woman of Banu Amir, who was like a young long-necked she-camel. We presented ourselves to her (for contracting temporary marriage), whereupon she said: What dower would you give me? I said: My cloak. And my companion also said: My cloak. And the cloak of my companion was superior to my cloak, but I was younger than he. So when she looked at the cloak of my companion she liked it, and when she cast a glance at me I looked more attractive to her. She then said: Well, you and your cloak are sufficient for me. I remained with her for three nights, and then Allah's Messenger (may peace be upon him) said: He who has

any such woman with whom he had contracted temporary marriage, he should let her off (*Sahih Muslim, Kitab
Al-Nikah,* Vol. 2, p. 706).

There are various opinions as to when such marriages
were stopped. Some say it was during the life time of
Muhammad, others that it was stopped by Umar, the
second Caliph. *Hadith* are quoted in favour of both, and
also by Shi'ites to show that *mut'ah* is still valid.[28]

It seems that in fact Muhammad allowed and forbade
the practice of *mut'ah* a number of times. A footnote in
Sunan Abu Dawud confirms this view:

> Mut'ah (temporary marriage) was forbidden by the
> Prophet (may peace be upon him) on six
> occasions . . . Al-Thawri said: What is correct is that
> temporary marriage was made lawful twice and pro-
> hibited twice . . . Henceforth it remained forbidden
> eternally. This is the view held by all Companions and
> scholars. Some of the Companions thought it lawful but
> later on they withdrew their opinion. The present posi-
> tion is that temporary marriage is eternally forbidden
> according to all the Sunnis (orthodox Muslims) (*Sunan
> Abu Dawud, Kitab Al-Nikah,* Vol. 2, p. 554).

It seems to me that it is not easy to tell from existing
sources whether Muhammad forbade this practice eternally or not. Even contemporary Sunni Muslim writers
agree that the information is obscure.[29] The Shi'ites,
however, think *mut'ah* not only permissible but meritorious.

> It should be noted that in Shi'ite religion Mut'ah is not
> only permissible but, also an act of worship of a high
> order. We have, already, seen the Shi'ite tradition that the
> holy Prophet said: He who does Mut'ah once is equal in

rank to Imam Husain, he who does it twice is equal in rank to Imam Hasan, he who does it three times attains the status of Hazrat Ali, and a person who does it four times, he will attain my station[30] (p. 56).

D. The world to come

The reward of an after life for the faithful is very much a part of most religions. Christianity and Islam are especially clear about it. In Christianity, it is described in terms of spiritual wholeness, happiness and relationship. It is a life in a perfect world, without the ills of the present life, without suffering and pain. People will live with their Lord for ever and ever. This heaven of Christians is their heavenly Father's Kingdom and is not related to the pleasures of this world. Both men and women are co-heirs of this Kingdom.[31]

The Islamic heaven, as described in the Qur'an and the *Hadith*, is different: it is a place of sensual delights as well as of the nearness of God.[32] The Qur'an speaks of gardens, of beauty, of food and drink and of beautiful companions.

God hath promised to believers, men and women, gardens under which rivers flow, to dwell therein, and beautiful mansions in gardens of everlasting bliss. But the greatest bliss is the good pleasure of God: that is the supreme felicity (Surah 9:72).

Therein will they recline (at ease); therein can they call (at pleasure) for fruit in abundance, and (delicious) drink; and beside them will be chaste women restraining their glances, (companions) of equal age (Surah 38:51–52).

There will even be wine,[33] which is totally prohibited to Muslims in their lives before death.

> Truly the righteous will be in bliss: on thrones (of dignity) will they command a sight (of all things): thou wilt recognise in their faces the beaming brightness of bliss, and their thirst will be slaked with pure wine sealed . . . (Surah 83:22–5).

The *Hadith* elaborate on this picture, describing the sensual delights in great detail. For example:

> Abu Musa reported God's messenger as saying, in paradise the believer will have a tent of a single hollowed pearl whose breadth (a version saying, whose length) is sixty miles, in each corner of which there will be a family out of sight of one another, each of which the believer will visit in turn. He will also have two gardens whose vessels and contents will be of silver and two gardens whose vessels and contents will be of gold. The only thing intervening to hinder the people from looking at their Lord will be the mantle of grandeur over his face in the garden of Eden (*Mishkat Al-Masabih, The Book of Fitan*, Vol. 2, p. 1196).

There is a heavenly market place:

> Anas reported God's messenger as saying, in paradise there is a market to which they will come every Friday. The north wind will blow and will scatter (fragrance) on their faces and their clothing, and they will be increased in beauty and loveliness. They will then return to their families, having been increased in beauty and loveliness, and their families will say to them, we swear by God that you have been increased in beauty and loveliness since leaving us, to which they will reply, you also, we swear by God, have been increased in beauty and loveliness since

we left you (*Mishkat Al-Masabih, The Book of Fitan,* Vol. 2, p. 197).

If you want to ride a horse, one will be provided:

> Buraida told that when a man asked God's messenger whether there were any horses in paradise he replied, if God brings you into paradise you will not wish to be conveyed in it on a horse of red ruby which will fly with you in paradise wherever you wish without doing so. A man asked God's messenger whether there were any camels in paradise and he did not give him the same reply as he gave the other, but said, if God brings you into paradise you will have what your soul desires and your eyes take pleasure in (*Mishkat Al-Masabih, The Book of Fitan,* Vol. 2, p. 1201).

Who will inherit this bountiful place? Many Qur'anic passages tell us that heaven is open to all those who believe and do righteous acts. Surah 33:35 and Surah 9:72 quoted above specify that women as well as men are included. But, when we read further, we wonder if this is in fact so. The Muslim heaven often seems more like a kingdom for believing Muslim men than a dwelling place for both sexes. This I say because of the sexual rewards which are described.

The Islamic harem which began with four wedded wives and a number of concubines at the time of Muhammad will expand in the world to come and Muslim men will have frequent honeymoons in Muhammad's Paradise:

> As to the righteous, (they will be) in a position of security, among gardens and springs; dressed in fine silk and in rich brocade, they will face each other; so; and We shall join

them to Companions, with beautiful, big, and lustrous eyes (Surah 44:51–54).

The Arabic word translated 'companion' is *hur*, from which we get the word, 'houri'. Who are they? Are they their worldly wives or are they some otherworldly creatures? Some insist that these companions of paradise are the women who remained faithful to their husbands while on this earth:[34] that is, men will be wedded to their earthly wives in heaven. But let us examine the evidence of the Qur'an and sayings of Muhammad, and see whether this is true.

> Abu Sa'id reported God's messenger as saying, 'The lowliest of the inhabitants of paradise will be he who has eighty thousand servants, seventy-two wives . . .' (*Mishkat Al-Masabih* Vol. 2, p. 1204).

> Anas reported the Prophet as saying, 'In paradise the believer will be given such and such power to conduct sexual intercourse.' He was asked whether he would be capable of that and replied that he would be given the capacity of a hundred men (p. 1200).

It is only oil-rich Arabs who have many wives nowadays: most Muslims could not afford many wives even if they wanted them. Suppose, on average, every Muslim man had five wives in his lifetime and all of these women entered heaven:[35] there would still be a surplus of 67 wives per man. Whence this surplus of wives?

Some Muslim scholars make the whole issue of these ladies a spiritual one (Yusuf Ali, N5058, p. 1436), but the evidence to the contrary is so widely distributed through Islamic sources that it cannot be ignored.

- They cannot be earthly wives, because the one is said to speak to the other:

  > Mu'adh reported the Prophet as saying that no woman annoys her husband in this world without his wife among the large-eyed maidens saying, you must not annoy him. God curse you! He is only a passing guest with you and is about to leave you to come to us (*Mishkat Al-Masabih*, Vol. 1, p. 691).

- It appears that the men will not have previously known them:

  > Abu Sa'id reported God's messenger as saying, a man will recline in paradise on seventy pillows before he turns round. A woman will then come and strike him on the shoulder and he will see his face in her cheek clearer than a mirror. The smallest pearl she wears will illuminate the space between the East and the West. She will give him a salutation to which he will respond, and when he asks her who she is she will reply that she is some of the extra. She will be wearing seventy garments through which his eyes will pierce so that he will see the marrow of her leg through them . . .[36] (p. 1204–5).

- According to the Qur'an, they will be virgins:

  > In them will be (maidens) chaste, restraining their glances, whom no man or jinn before them has touched (Surah 55: 56).

What, then, happens to men's earthly wives? Where will the Muslim women go? In Pakistan there is a saying: 'Whereas out of every thousand men only one will go to hell, yet out of every thousand women only one will be found in heaven.'

Such sayings have not sprung up out of nothing. A *hadith* says:

> Narrated Usama: The Prophet said, I stood at the gate of
> Paradise and saw that the majority of the people who
> entered it were the poor, while the wealthy were stopped
> at the gate (for the accounts). But the companions of the
> Fire were ordered to be taken to the Fire. Then I stood at
> the gate of the fire and saw that the majority of those who
> entered it were women (*Sahih Al-Bukhari*, Vol. 7, p. 94).

112

Such was the attitude of Muhammad towards women that
even his very close companions were fearful to talk freely
to their wives during his life time:

> Narrated Ibn Umar: During the lifetime of the Prophet
> we used to avoid chatting leisurely and freely with our
> wives lest some Divine inspiration might be revealed
> concerning us. But when the Prophet had died, we
> started chatting leisurely and freely (with them) (*Sahih Al-
> Bukhari*, Vol. 7, p. 81).

The Islamic sources I have quoted in this chapter have
shown, I think, that the apologists' contention that traditional Islam gives men and women equal rights and equal
(though dissimilar) roles is questionable. This, however, is
not to denigrate all Muslim men, or to say that in every
part of the Muslim world women are just a suffering
symbol and their role is nothing more than to satisfy the
sexual appetites of men. On the contrary, there are many
examples where I would say Muslim men have treated and
still do treat women more according to the biblical
standards than do many western men. But I would want
to say that this is because of our common humanity, and
not because of Islam.

The *Hadith* considered in this section do not give
freedom and equality to woman, nor make her a co-heir
with man of eternal life.[37] In her present life she is the

victim of a religion and in the life to come she will remain a victim of the same religion. In this world, she is abused and looked down upon. In the world to come she is in danger of the everlasting fires of Allah.

113

2.2 Feminist interpretations

Ida Glaser

The traditional interpretations of Islamic sources have certainly resulted in women being put into a secondary position; and the Muslim women of Ch. 2 have witnessed and documented this. Yet they remain Muslims. The reason is that they see alternative possibilities: it is all a matter of interpretation.

Leila Ahmed, in her seminal work *Women and Gender in Islam: Historical Roots of a Modern Debate*, asserts that there are two competing voices on gender issues in Islam. The first, the 'ethical voice', insists that women are of equal status to men in moral and spiritual terms: the second, the 'pragmatic voice', is expressed in the out-working of Islamic law which oppresses women.

The 'ethical voice' is found in the Qur'an itself, which frequently asserts the equality and partnership of women with men. It is implied in some of the passages about the creation of women presented above (pp. 22, 80), and is epitomized in verse 35 of Surah 33:

> For Muslim men and women, for believing men and women,
> for devout men and women, for true men and women,

for men and women who are patient and constant,
for men and women who humble themselves
for men and women who give in charity,
for men and women who fast (and deny themselves),
for men and women who guard their chastity,
for men and women who engage much in God's praise
— for them God has prepared forgiveness and great
reward.

The implications, says Ahmed, are far-reaching, since the ethical qualities described have political and social dimensions. She then refers to Qur'anic teaching about the equal worth of male and female labour (Surah 3:195), and the equal contributions of men and women to the conception of children, and concludes that,

> The unmistakable presence of an ethical egalitarianism explains why Muslim women frequently insist, often inexplicably to non-Muslims, that Islam is not sexist (p. 66).

Egalitarian as Islam may be in this 'ethical voice', Ahmed recognises that it has been anything but egalitarian in practice. This she traces back through the whole of Islamic history.

In the time of Muhammad, she argues, there were various models of gender dynamics amongst the Arabs. These included matriarchal as well as patriarchal models.[38] For example, there were women warriors, and Muhammad's first wife was a business woman who first employed him and then proposed marriage to him. There were even polyandrous marriages.

Muhammad's new community at Medina needed practice which would bring unity to the diverse followers of Islam. Family practice, according to Ahmed, moved towards a single, patriarchal model, in which women's sexuality and their children belonged not to them but to their husbands or other male guardians. The 'ethical voice' is found in the Qur'an, but the statements about equality are made in the context of an increasingly patriarchal society: the 'pragmatic voice' is there too.

> Islam placed relationships between the sexes on a new footing. Implicit in this new order was the male right to control women and to interdict their interactions with other men. Thus the ground was prepared for the closures that would follow: women's exclusion from social activities in which they might have contact with men other than those with rights to their sexuality; their physical seclusion, soon to become the norm; and the institution of internal mechanisms of control, such as instilling the notion of submission as a woman's duty (p. 62).

As Islamic ideas developed through the Abbasid and Sasanid empires, the patriarchal model continued and was intensified. Throughout Islamic history, says Ahmed, the 'ethical voice' has been 'virtually unheard by rulers and lawmakers' (p. 66). In earlier times, there were groups who focused on ethical issues and, for example, rejected concubinage, the marriage of very young girls and polygamy.

> However, throughout history it has not been those who have emphasized the ethical and spiritual dimensions of religion who have held power. The political, religious and legal authorities in the Abbasid period in particular, whose interpretative and legal legacy has defined Islam ever since, heard only the androcentric voice of Islam, and they

> interpreted the religion as intending to institute andro-
> centric laws and androcentric vision in all Muslim soci-
> eties throughout time (p. 67).

Such androcentric ideas, contends Ahmed, are not the
only possible ways of understanding Islam. If it was
differently understood by some early Muslims, can it not
also be differently understood now?

116

This is the challenge that Muslim feminists — male
as well as female — have been bringing to the Muslim
world for more than a century. 'Do we have to accept the
regulations developed by men in the Middle Ages?' they
ask. 'Can we not re-read the Qur'an and the *Hadith*? Are
there not ways of understanding Islam that liberate
women?' An Iranian woman writes:

> The goal is to contest the right and legitimacy of Iran's
> patriarchal clerical order to be the sole interpreters of the
> values, norms and aesthetic standards of Shii Islam . . . The
> truth is that there is nothing sacred about a limited and
> highly protected discourse, developed over centuries by a
> society of zealous men in order to produce and maintain a
> regime of control, a major function of which is to keep
> women in bondage — for ever.[39]

Can we re-read the Qur'an?

There are two options open to people who accept the
Qur'an as coming from God. The first, which is taken by
apologists surveyed in Ch. 1, upholds traditional ways of
reading the sources, but argues that they do not make
women inferior. Feminist writers choose a second strategy: they challenge traditional interpretations.

We take as an example the interpretation of that notorious verse, Surah 4:35. It begins:

> Men are the protectors and maintainers of women, because God has given the one more (strength) than the other, and because they support them out of their means.

The key words are those translated 'maintainers and protectors' (*qawwamun*) and 'has given the one more (strength)' (*faddala*). The range of interpretation can be seen by the range of translations and explanatory notes given by different commentators.

Usmani, a traditional commentator, translates, 'men are made lords over women for that Allah gave greatness to one over the other', and says in his notes that the degree of man is greater than the degree of woman, that the woman is to be given different responsibilities because she is weaker and has a different capacity, and that man is superior to woman because of his superior knowledge and power, and because he spends his wealth looking after her.

Maududi, a more recent commentator, has, 'men are the protectors and maintainers of women because Allah has made one of them to excel over the other.' He argues that it is biological differences which underly a divine role-division, but that this does not imply male superiority or differences in honour and dignity. God has given men certain qualities which he has not given to women, at least not to an equal extent. Thus the male is qualified to function as the head of the family, and the female is so constituted that she should live under his care and protection.

Azad, a modernist writer concerned for female equality, translates 'men are a little higher in rank than women on account of the qualities with which God hath gifted them and on account of what they spend (for women) from their substance.' He puts the verse into the context of a society which discounted women and saw them as instruments for the satisfaction of men. He sees the Qur'an as restoring female dignity, but recognising differences in gender roles:

> The male is very often the means of the fulfilment of the needs of the female, particularly in the field of material living. That is why man is normally called upon to look after the material well-being of the woman. The women-folk should not on that account feel humiliated and rue over the fact that they were not born as men so that they might discharge the functions discharged by men. The Qur'an assures them that even as for men the avenues of distinction in the field of knowledge and goodness are open to them.

There is, then, a range of interpretation from the more traditional who happily affirm male superiority to those who want to affirm gender equality. Much apologetic follows Maududi in affirming a difference in gender roles, but denying that this implies difference of status. For example, Suzanne Haneef, a western convert to Islam, has been quoted in Ch. 1 (pp. 29–30), as affirming the role division as entirely positive, and in no way reducing the dignity of women. She does not, however, quote the rest of the verse:

> Therefore the righteous women are devoutly obedient, and guard in (the husband's) absence what God would

have them guard. As to those women on whose part ye fear disloyalty and ill-conduct, admonish them (first), (next), refuse to share their beds, (and last) beat them (lightly); but if they return to obedience, seek not against them means (of annoyance): for God is Most High, Great (above all) (Surah 4:34).

119

Traditional discussions on this verse, as mentioned in the first part of this chapter, are about the nature of disloyalty or misconduct, the meaning of the refusal to share beds, and the type and amount of beating allowed. Feminists want to question the right and responsibility of a husband to discipline his wife.

How, then, do Muslim feminists deal with the verse? We illustrate from one male and one female who are concerned about the equality of women. The key for both writers is an attempt to read the verse in its historical context. Both look at *hadith* that say when it was given, and use the Qur'an to look for principles rather than legal prescriptions.

Asghar Ali Engineer is the director of the Institute of Islamic Studies in Bombay. In *The Rights of Women in Islam*, he admits that according 'dignity and freedom to women as much as to men' 'cannot be done if one rigidly follows the orthodox reading, interpretation and meaning of the Qur'anic intent' (p. 5), and calls for a new interpretation in the modern context. For him, such an interpretation starts from the premise that all readers and therefore all readings are affected by the attitudes prevailing in the society to which the reader belongs. With respect to women,

Male-dominated societies often harnessed even just and egalitarian norms laid down for women in divine scriptures to perpetuate their hold. The Qur'an, which is comparatively liberal in its treatment of women, also suffered the same fate (p. 1).

120 Not only is the effect of context seen in the interpretation of the Qur'an: it can, says Engineer, be found even within the Qur'an itself. There is therefore a need to distinguish between what he calls the normative and the contextual in the Qur'an. That is, he considers that some injunctions are for all times and places, while others depend on the particular situation into which the verses were spoken.

For example, the Qur'an relates the establishment of the *hijab*, and this has grown into various forms of *purdah*. The orthodox interpretation has led to the idea that men are superior and women are weak, so that men have to seclude their women in order to protect their chastity. Engineer suggests that, at the time of Muhammad, women's chastity needed to be protected by some sort of veil, but that it is now possible for women to protect her own chastity without observing *purdah*. It is chastity that is normative: *hijab* was merely contextual. For our days, the question is what new situational forms might best encourage the norm of chastity.

Next, Engineer describes how the development of Islamic law was influenced by its context. He challenges the assumption of many Muslims that the *shari'ah* is totally divine and immutable. In fact, the law developed over two centuries before the classical formulations were reached, and even then there were many points on which there was no consensus. For example, the Caliph 'Umar sometimes used *ijtihad* — his own judgement — to justify going against specific Qur'anic injunctions, because, he said, the situation had changed.[40] In other words, *shari'ah* is a situational, not a transcendental law, and it must be creatively applied in the changed circumstances (p. 9).

Qur'anic interpretation is, and always has been, affected by the consciousness of the interpreter and his or her times.

As a modern example, Engineer discusses the abolition of slavery. In medieval times, the Qur'an was used to show that Muslims had a divine right to slaves if they could afford them. Now that slavery is 'regarded as intolerable by all civilised societies' (p. 2), no Islamic teacher, he says, uses the Qur'an in this way. Modernist interpreters dismiss the idea of intercourse with slave girls discussed by Napoleon above (pp. 99, 102–103), or read the relevant verses as permitting marriage to slaves as well as to free women. Therefore, he concludes:

> If the 'Ulama still resist change in certain *shari'ah* edicts concerning women such as polygamy, evidence, divorce etc., it is not because they are based on the Qur'an and *sunnah*[41] (slavery was also based on the Qur'an and *sunnah* yet it was abolished when the time came for it) but because societies are still male-dominated and it hurts the pride of men to accept change (p. 11).

Engineer elsewhere lays down another foundation for interpreting the Qur'anic teaching about women. He considers the position of women in pre-Islamic society and concludes that, while the Qur'an reflects much of the practice of its time, it limits or challenges misogynist behaviours. Thus, for example, where women could be inherited as property, the Qur'an rules that they can inherit property of their own. Where polygamous marriages were unlimited, the Qur'an allows only four wives. Where there were many different forms of marriage contract, the Qur'an retains the idea of marriage as contract but lays down one form of mutual responsibility.

The pre-Islamic situation was not so bad for women, he says, as some writers suggest. However, the Qur'an brought improvements by rejecting practices that were obviously unjust, and gave 'a definite and normative shape to women's rights and duties' (p. 37). The high status it gave to women was later compromised as religious leaders and jurists tried to adapt to 'harsh practical realities' (p. 37). The modern reader needs to remember that the Qur'an's movement towards justice is the norm.

It is on the basis of these principles that Engineer considers Surah 4:34, in his third chapter, on sexual equality. He starts with a survey of verses that clearly teach the equality of women, including Surah 4:1 and Surah 33:35, and concludes that:

> There is no doubt that there is a general thrust towards equality of the sexes in the Qur'an . . . Unlike in other religions there is absolutely no distinction between men and women in religious matters either (p. 44).

The full equality of the sexes is normative, and it is in this light that anything 'contextual' must be understood. He concedes that 'the Qur'an does speak of man having a slight edge and social superiority over women' (p. 45), but asserts that this is a social phenomenon of the time and not normative. It is in support of this assertion that he introduces Surah 4:34.

The verse, he argues, shows that any male superiority was because of the context in which men provided for women economically. That is, the superiority is purely functional, and has nothing to do with intrinsic superiority of one sex over the other. It is only by virtue of the fact that the men earned and supported the women that they had the upper hand. He then points out that the women were also working, in their homes, and sympathises with the idea that domestic work is of commercial value. He quotes the Qur'an (Surah 45:22) to show that all work should be justly rewarded.

The question, then, is why the Qur'an should assign men superiority because of their earnings. This, he says, is a matter of 'social consciousness and proper interpretation' (p. 46). In those days, the social situation was such that women were confined to domestic work, and men saw themselves as superior because they were the providers. The Qur'an reflects this, by saying that the men are *qawwamun* (maintainers and protecters). It does not say that they should be *qawwamun*. This, together with the verses that specify just rewards for all work, makes it clear that this is not a normative statement.

However, the verse is very important for understanding the gender question. For centuries, it has been 'obvious' to most Muslims that *qawwamun* could be translated 'rulers' or 'overseers', and that men were by nature superior to women. When we now see it as contextual, it is no longer obvious what it offers as normative. To understand it, it is necessary to read it in its historical context.

Engineer recounts the traditional 'occasion of revelation': a woman called Habibah was slapped by her husband for disobedience, and complained to her father. He took her to lodge her complaint with the Prophet. Muhammad told the woman to retaliate, was opposed by some of the men, and then the verse was given.

This throws a new light onto it: rather than affirming the right of Habibah's husband to beat her, it appears as a concession to the times and a limitation on violence: corporal punishment is to be a last resort. The *hadith* ends with Muhammad saying that he wanted things one way, but God wanted them another way. Engineer concludes:

> Maybe the Prophet realised that his advice would have created an uproar in a society where man was completely dominant. The verse was revealed as soothing advice to control the violence of man towards woman and advising them to adjust themselves in a man-dominated society . . . We see from available evidence that the idea was not to encourage the beating of wives but to discourage it and gradually abolish it (p. 47).

Such an interpretation is, he says, in line with several *hadith* which discourage wife-beating and exhort men to improve their treatment of women. He goes on to consider a range of recent understandings of the rest of the verse, all of which challenge ideas of male superiority. In particular, he points out that the Arabic does not say that God has given men more than women, but that he has given some more than others. This is then a general assertion of differences between human beings, and not necessarily between men and women (p. 51). He concludes:

> The difficulty arises when Muslim jurists see this verse as a normative prescription. Then they tend to prove the superiority of men over women. This verse seen in its proper social context does not advocate male superiority (p. 52).

125

Fatima Mernissi the Moroccan sociologist whose writings we explored in Ch. 2, also seeks to interpret Islamic sources on the basis of context, but gives far more attention to historical details and to the particular personalities who interacted with Muhammad. In her *Women and Islam: An Historical and Theological Enquiry*, (1991), she looks at Surah 4:34 in a chapter (8) entitled '*Umar and the men of Medina*. 'Umar was a close and much valued companion of Muhammad, and became the second Caliph. He was an exemplary leader, living in simplicity, but with great charisma and a passion for justice. However, he also had some faults, including 'his fiery, violent character with women' (p. 142). He became 'the spokesman for the men's resistance to the Prophet's egalitarian project' (idem).

When the Muslims arrived in Medina, they found that women had greater freedom than in Mecca. It was 'Umar who complained to Muhammad about the effect of this on the Meccan wives (see p. 90 above). He is also reported as having exhorted Muhammad's wives to submit to their husband when he judged them to be insubordinate, and as having represented male interests on a number of occasions. The giving of Surah 4:34 was one of these.

126 Mernissi paints a picture of the 60-year-old Prophet, peace-loving but harassed by conflicts within his community and having to deal with threats from without. There had just been a great controversy over sexual positions which had caused much tension between men and women, and now a new problem arose. Mernissi's judgement is that, 'This time, God judged against his own prophet, for the very survival of monotheism was at stake'[42] (p. 145).

In discussing Surah 4:34, Mernissi first points out the affirmation of the equality of women in the following verse, and wonders why most interpreters prefer verse 34, which is, she says, 'in flagrant contradiction' to verse 35, which was given during an earlier controversy (p. 154). The need is to explain the contradiction — the 'retreat from the initial egalitarian message' (idem).

She then tells the story of Habibah, Muhammad's advice and God's overruling. Her major concern is not so much the detailed meaning of the verse, as the conflict between Muhammad's desire to stop the beating of women, and the verse that permits it. The key is, she suggests, the disagreement on the subject in the Muslim community, especially as represented by 'Umar. She quotes the authority Ibn Sa'd:

> The Prophet said: 'Do not beat women.' And in fact people renounced it. And then 'Umar came looking for the Prophet and said to him: 'Messenger of God, women are rebelling against their husbands.' The Prophet authorised them to beat them, but he ('Umar) said: 'A crowd of women is gathered together around Muhammad's family. There are seventy women who have come to complain about their husbands' (p. 156).

This dangerous rebellion was, according to the classical commentators, not infidelity but a refusal to submit to their husbands' sexual demands.

Mernissi then turns to the much respected classical interpreter Tabari, who was also aware of the Prophet's repudiations of violence towards women. She points out what a problem Surah 4:34 was for him — to the extent that he listed 200 conflicting opinions on it (p. 156). She presents his discussions about a number of intricate linguistic and legal problems in order to show that, although at that time there was no question but that the husband had authority over his wife, Tabari was at pains to retain Muhammad's opposition to violence. She concludes (p. 159):

127

> This gives us an idea of the difficulty that the interpretation of verse 34 of sura 4 poses and of why modern politicians, who have not succeeded in assimilating the concept of democracy, use it to legitimize their fanaticism, never stopping for a moment to consider the enormous difficulty it has posed, and still poses, to those who make some effort to respect the divine will. They use it to affirm male supremacy, as if this were a verse without ambiguity, without differences in interpretation, without conflict.

She concludes her chapter: 'The Prophet, beset by Companions of both sexes and their contradictory demands, troubled by divine revelations that went counter to his aims, influenced by 'Umar, who represented tradition, deep-seated reflexes, and customs, knew that he had to use his influence in the most reliable manner — that is, the one least likely to be challenged' (p. 160).

Mernissi has, then, pointed out the difficulties in the verse, and done it on the best possible authority, but she has refrained from giving her own interpretation. She has, however, challenged all uses of it to assert male superiority, and suggested that it was only given because of a stiff-
128 necked insistence on superiority by some of the men at the time of Muhammad.

What about the *Hadith*?

Napoleon has observed that many negative Islamic attitudes to women have their origin in the *Hadith* rather than the Qur'an. Both apologists and feminists tend to stress the more positive *hadith*, such as those which affirm mothers or tell of Muhammad spending time teaching women or helping his wives. But the difficult ones remain.

Mernissi is particularly aware of this. She introduces *Women and Islam* (1991) with a story:

> 'Can a woman be a leader of Muslims?' I asked my grocer, who, like most grocers in Morocco, is a true 'barometer' of public opinion.
>
> 'I take refuge in Allah!' he exclaimed, shocked, despite the friendly relations between us. Aghast at the idea, he almost dropped the half-dozen eggs I had come to buy. 'May God protect us from the catastrophes of the times!' mumbled a customer who was buying olives, as he made as if to spit (p. 1).

Why this strong reaction?

> A second customer . . . hit me with a Hadith that he knew would be fatal: 'Those who entrust their affairs to a woman will never know prosperity!' Silence fell on the

scene. There was nothing I could say. In a Muslim theocracy, a Hadith is no small matter (p. 1).

Mernissi determined to find out about this *hadith*, so that she could understand why it had such a powerful effect on ordinary people. As she says, 'a *hadith* is no small matter.' Its authority goes unquestioned, and, in this and many of the other cases concerning women, there is no way of re-interpreting it to make it less misogynist.

There is, however, another avenue of research. As observed earlier, the only question is whether the *hadith* dates back to Muhammad. For a Muslim, a *hadith* must be accepted if it is genuine: there is no choice about this. But not all *hadith* are considered genuine by all Muslims, and many are classified as 'weak' — that is, their Muhamma-dan origin is not certain.

Engineer can dismiss misogynist *hadith* on two grounds. The first is that Muhammad as example was acting in his historical context. Much of what he said and did can therefore be regarded as situational rather than normative. The second is that many *hadith* do not date back to Muhammad at all, but reflect 'the cultural and socio-religious prejudices of the first and second centuries of the Islamic calendar' (Engineer, p. 13). If a *hadith* contradicts the Qur'anic norm of gender equality, it need not be taken seriously.

Mernissi also rejects misogynist *hadith*, but justifies this through the methods of traditional *hadith* study.

Every *hadith* has two parts: the *matn* or content, and the *isnad* or chain of transmission. During the process of collection, scholars travelled extensively to find people who would relate *hadith* to them. They then asked from whom the relater had heard it, and from whom that person had heard it, until they reached someone who had themselves been with Muhammad. The resulting chain of transmission, as well as the content, was tested before the *hadith* was accepted. The scholar had to ensure that adjacent transmitters could have met, and also that every link in the chain was a person of integrity. It is Mernissi's contention that the very inclusion of the *isnad* means that every Muslim can (and, perhaps, should) question the validity of any *hadith* (p. 35).

130

She is fully aware that, since the Middle Ages, Muslim scholars as well as ordinary people have over-whelmingly accepted the *hadith* classifications of such classical collectors as have been quoted by Napoleon: if, for example, al-Bukhari says that a *hadith* is sound, it is sound. It might be deemed impious to question it. Yet Mernissi insists:

> Islam was, at least during its first centuries, the religion of reasoning, responsible individuals capable of telling what was true from what was false as long as they were equipped to do so, as long as they possessed the tools of knowledge . . . The fact that, over the course of centuries, we have seen believers who criticize and judge replaced by muzzled, censored, obedient, and grateful Muslims in no way detracts from this fundamental dimension of Islam (p. 35–6).

So, on the *hadith* of the grocer's shop, and on others that denigrate women, she exercises her right.

She focuses on the career of al-Bukhari, in whose collection the *hadith* of the grocery can be found. She describes his struggles, his travels, his rigorous methods and his piety. He interviewed 1,080 persons and collected from them 600,000 *hadith*. Of these, after thorough investigation, he retained only 11,275 as authentic, and of these 4,000 are repetitions. As well as his collection of *hadith*, al–Bukhari wrote *Al-tarikh al-kabir*, The Great History, which recounts the lives of the transmitters; and the study of such lives became an important part of Islamic scholarship. The transmitter had to be a person of unquestionable piety and integrity to be trusted.

131

Mernissi comments: 'The most astonishing thing is that the skepticism that guided the work of the founders of religious scholarship has disappeared today' (p. 45).

She is then ready to discuss specific *hadith*. Her method is to ask who first reported the *hadith*, in what situation he did so, what might have been his motivation, and whether there had been any further debate about its content. We consider her results for two *hadith*.

Those who trust their affairs to a woman will never know prosperity. This was first reported by Abu Bakra at a time of great political stress. Abu Bakra had been a slave who converted to Islam and to freedom after the Muslim armies laid siege to his town. He reported the *hadith* twenty-five years after the death of Muhammad, during the first civil war between Muslims.

'A'isha, Muhammad's favourite wife, was leading the rebellion against Ali, the reigning caliph and Muhammad's cousin. She needed to find a sizeable city to occupy as headquarters for the next stage of the campaign, and chose Basra, where Abu Bakra was a leading citizen. Mernissi observes that such citizens were in a difficult position.

> Should he take up arms against 'Ali, the cousin of the Prophet and the caliph, challenged maybe but legitimate, or should he take up arms against 'A'isha, the 'lover of the Beloved of God' and the 'wife of the Prophet on earth and in paradise'? (p. 50–51).

132 With a number of others, he decided not to fight with 'A'isha. There followed the famous 'Battle of the Camel', named after the camel on which she led her troops out from Basra to fight 'Ali. She was defeated, and 'Ali retook Basra. It was then, according to Abu Bakra, that he said to her:

> It is true that you are our *umm* (mother, alluding to her title of 'Mother of Believers' which the Prophet bestowed on his wives during his last years); it is true that as such you have rights over us. But I heard the prophet say: 'Those who trust power to a woman will never know prosperity' (Quoted on p. 56–57).

This, it seems, is the only misogynist comment recorded in the extensive accounts of the Battle of the Camel; yet it has affected popular thinking right up to the present, and has even been used to blame 'A'isha's action in leading her army for all subsequent inter-Islamic bloodshed (p. 5–7).

Having shown how convenient was Abu Bakra's 'memory' and how isolated his sentiments, Mernissi goes on to question his integrity. She quotes Imam Malik, the founder of one of the major schools of Islamic law:

> There are some people whom I rejected as narrators of Hadith, not because they lied in their role as men of science by recounting false Hadith that the Prophet did not say, but just simply because I saw them lying in their relationships with people, in their daily relationships that had nothing to do with religion (p. 60).

Abu Bakra was, it seems, once flogged for false testimony: he was one of four witnesses to adultery, and another of the four admitted to being unsure of what he had seen. Following Islamic law, all four were then flogged as false witnesses. Therefore, concludes Mernissi, 'Abu Bakra must be rejected as a source of Hadith by every good, well-informed Malikite Muslim' (p. 61)

133

As if that were not enough, she goes on to observe that, accepted as authentic by al-Bukhari though it was, the actual *hadith* was 'hotly contested' by Muslim scholars. Even the great authority al-Tabari 'was one of those religious authorities who took a position against it, not finding it a sufficient basis for depriving women of their power of decision making and for justifying their exclusion from politics' (p. 61).

Abu Bakra is thus totally discredited as a reporter of *Hadith*.

The dog, the ass, and women interrupt prayer if they pass in front of the believer, interposing themselves between him and the qibla.

Mernissi reports that, as a child, she was very shocked by this *hadith*. It did not accord with her picture of her Prophet: 'I hardly ever repeated it, hoping that by dint of silence it would be erased from my memory . . . Why would the Prophet have said a *hadith* like that which does me harm? . . . How could Muhammad, 'The Beloved', so hurt a young girl who, in the bloom of youth, had transformed him into a pillar of her romantic dreams?' (pp. 64–5).

She recalls another *hadith* in which, when asked whom he loved most in the world, Muhammad replies,

"A'isha'. His questioner was surprised that he named a woman, and not, say, a soldier, so he asked which man was most beloved. The answer was, 'Abu Bakr' — the father of 'A'isha. Mernissi comments:

134

> In an Arabia where power predominated, where the sabre was king, this prophet, who publicly stated that he preferred women to men, was preaching a very unusual message. Apparently Abu Huraira, that Companion who put woman in the same category as the ass and the dog as disturbances for the believer, did not at all understand his *risala* (message) (p. 64).

She then rubs in the seriousness of the *hadith* by explaining the history and importance of the *qibla* — the direction of prayer — '. . . labelling her as a disturbance amounts to saying that there is a fundamental contradiction between her essence and that of the divine' (p. 70).

She proceeds to demolish Abu Hurayra, the narrator of this *hadith*, as a transmitter of *hadith* just as she did Abu Bakra. This she does by describing him as a weak and misogynist character, who narrated several *hadith* that denigrate women. For example, the reported saying of Muhammad, 'I do not leave after me any cause of trouble more fatal to man than woman', comes through Abu Hurayra. Eight of the *hadith* quoted above by Napoleon also come from him.

Mernissi recounts how Abu Hurayra reported *hadith* about Muhammad's practice of ritual purification after sexual intercourse that were questioned by Muhammad's wives, and even one occasion on which he eventually admitted that what he reported was not directly from

Muhammad. There were many occasions on which he reported something that was challenged by 'A'isha herself. For example,

> They told 'A'isha that Abu Hurayra was asserting that the Messenger of God said: 'Three things bring bad luck: house, woman and horse.' 'A'isha responded: 'Abu Hurayra learned his lessons very badly. He came into our house when the Prophet was in the middle of a sentence. He only heard the end of it. What the Prophet said was: 'May Allah refute the Jews; they say three things bring bad luck: house, woman and horse' (Quoted on p. 76).

In contrast to other companions who were conscious of their fallibility and reluctant to report *hadith* in case their memories were faulty, Abu Hurayra recounted 5,300 *hadith* from his three years with Muhammad. Mernissi implies that Abu Hurayra's memory was as fallible as anyone's, and suggests that, anyway, the reason he had access to so many of Muhammad's sayings was that he was too lazy to work, and so could spend as much time as he liked following the Prophet.

All of his *hadith*, and especially those about women, are thereby called into question.

Can such interpretations gain common acceptance within Islam?

Did Muhammad teach and do things detrimental to women? Both Engineer and Mernissi answer, 'No!', but on different grounds. Engineer dismisses negative *hadith a priori*, since they contradict his understanding of the Qur'an's teaching on the equality of women. Mernissi enters the classical arguments, and thence dismisses negatives on historical grounds. Both imply radical questioning of some of the foundations of Islamic law. They suggest that some of the most widely accepted *hadith* are invalid, and criticise classical interpretations. They are therefore liable to be rejected as lacking in authority.

136

Although re-interpretations are gaining some acceptance, it seems more popular to affirm traditional understandings, to add an emphasis on the husband's responsibility towards his wife, and to say that this is the way that God has made us. Perhaps the reason for this is that Mernissi and Engineer represent quite new ways of handling the Qur'an and *Hadith*: they both begin by insisting that interpretation must be done in the light of historical context, and both imply that particular rulings, even within the Qur'an, are valid only in particular situations. What Muhammad did in Medina might not be what all Muslims should do in every place and at every time.

There is a long tradition of studying the history of early Islam and the occasions of revelation of verses in order better to understand the Qur'an, and their approaches might be considered a natural development of this. However, such extensive study of the human context is done in the belief that the Qur'an is God's eternal Word which has been with him from eternity, and quite literally 'came down' via the angel Gabriel to Muhammad. It was in no way the product of Muhammad's own mind, but was dictated word by word by the angel. To be sure, it was sent down bit by bit, as required by the particular situations, but the book itself is in no way determined by those situations.

It is therefore considered authoritative for all times and places, and to suggest that some of it might have been different in a different cultural situation is, for many, unthinkable.[43] This is so not only for matters of principle, but for details of practice. It is just as divinely ordained that, for example, all women at all times and in all places should 'draw their veils over their bosoms' (Surah 24:31) as that God's eternal rewards are for both males and females (Surah 33:35).

The approaches of Engineer and Mernissi imply that the contents of the Qur'an depends to some extent on the situation into which it came, and that Muhammad was sometimes pushed into allowing things which he thought were wrong and in fact might be wrong in a different situation. This is revolutionary, and perhaps even sacrilegious.

Although Muhammad is believed to have been a human being, most Muslims believe him to have been without sin and offer him the highest respect. To suggest that he might have weakly given in to pressures from his Companions is questionable, to say the least.

Thus, for example, Usmani quotes the *hadith* about the wife complaining about her husband as the occasion of revelation of Surah 4:34, but comes to quite a different conclusion than Engineer or Mernissi. He adds to Muhammad's comment that, 'We desired something and God willed something else', 'and what God willed is all goodness.' That is, he has the Prophet affirming God's ruling, and willingly submitting to his will. The implication is that this ruling is to be followed at all times, even if we don't like it. Usmani goes on to discuss the details of how men should discipline their wives.

As if this were not enough, Mernissi and Engineer have challenged traditional interpretations, and Islam has historically based its legal rulings on the accepted rulings of former scholars. Mernissi has even challenged the traditional classifications of *Hadith* which, next to the Qur'an, are the sources of Islamic law. The whole system of *shari'ah* has had *ijma'*, or consensus, as one of its foundations; and the consensus cannot be valid without reference to the classical scholars.[44] One of the things to be shunned, in both belief and law, has been *bida'ah*, which can be translated 'innovation'. That is not to say that the law is not to be re-applied in new situations, but that new interpretations which have no precedent are in danger of being heretical.

Both writers are acutely aware of what they are doing, but justify themselves in different ways.

Engineer acknowledges that he will be accused of *tafsir bi-r-ra'y* — interpretation according to one's own opinion. Traditional scholars view such interpretation with suspicion, unless the opinions are firmly based on what has already been said by accepted authorities and made by people uf unimpeachable piety and religious education. Doi (*Shari'ah: the Islamic Law*, 1984, p. 31) warns: 'It is very risky to undertake the interpretation of the Holy Qur'an on the basis of a personal opinion without reference to the authorities stated above.[45] The Prophet (S.A.W.) has warned: "Whosoever said anything in the matter of the Qur'an according to his own thoughts or anything about which he did not know, he is making his residence in the fire of hell.'"

Over against this, Engineer works on the premise that the classical commentators were affected by their own social milieu, and that much of their interpretation is therefore situational and not applicable in the present context. However, he insists that he is not questioning the wisdom that they exercised in their times or the value of their work (p. 15). He is only questioning its universal validity.

Further, there is a difference between following a personal opinion and undertaking a careful re-reading in the light of a changed situation. He cites the well-known and respected scholar Abu Kalam Azad as someone who offered new readings of the Qur'an but was 'second to none' in his commitment to Islam (p. 4), and points out that the Qur'an itself calls its readers to reflect (e.g. Surah 47:24). If we are not supposed to think through its meanings for ourselves, he asks, why are we called to study the Qur'an?

He admits that the line between following one's own desires and seeking a true opinion in a new context is a fine one, which demands all possible integrity and honesty. Yet the attempt must be made, and he finds plenty of evidence from all periods of Islamic history to show that it always has been made.

Mernissi chooses a rather different strategy. She is careful to use the methods of respected orthodox scholars, and to ask questions rather than overtly to propose her revolutionary alternatives. This can be seen from her treatment of *hadith* described above.

Despite this, it is clear that she is offering innovation, and her very questions imply the need for radically new methods of interpretation.

> One cannot trap Fatima Mernissi on the charge of heresy, or incompetence. As wise as a *faqih* (expert in religious studies) she knows her authors, the references, the besetting weaknesses of the times and the men. How difficult to say to her: 'Put on your *hijab* (veil) and be silent!' Better to keep quiet oneself before such a pitiless indictment. One of her countrymen said to me: 'One would think she was going to knock down all the walls, but she doesn't go quite that far.' How wrong he is![46]

Given the current popularity of movements towards more traditional understandings of women's roles, and the strongly conservative nature of traditional Islamic thinking, it might seem unlikely that such views as those of Engineer and Mernissi will soon gain acceptance amongst the majority of Muslims. However, the questions are much broader than those of interpretation of the Qur'an and the *Hadith*. As Engineer has pointed out, all interpretations depend on the context of the interpreter, and decisions about the meaning of the scriptures are likely to be more affected by current social concerns that the interpreter might think.

This is particularly so with reference to women. Their position has become symbolic of a much wider struggle: they have become visible symbols of the ethos of their societies.

From Egypt, Leila Ahmed (1992) shows how they first became the symbol of backwardness during colonial times. Middle Eastern men campaigned for the abolition of the veil because they saw it as a source of shame in the face of western criticism. Remove the veil, they thought, and westerners will see us as progressive. Let our women be educated and work, they thought, and we will be able to catch up with western technologies.

141

In the post-colonial era, governments first sought to follow western patterns, but disillusionment set in as economic systems changed traditional roles and relationships but did not bring the desired prosperity. There was therefore an anti-western reaction, and a turning back to Islam as the way to peace and wealth. As part of this, many Arabs started to return to modified traditional understandings of women's roles, which included the need to veil but did not keep women secluded in the domestic world. Veiled women in public places have therefore become a visible sign of a return to Islam, and the *hijab* became a political and ideological symbol.

In quite a different context, Farhat Haq, in *Women, Islam and the State in Pakistan*, recounts the interaction between goverment and women's roles in Pakistan. Women were given many freedoms under Ayub Khan, the first president of Pakistan, but later 'Islamization' under Zia Ul Haq theatened to reverse these. Women's movements throughout Pakistan's history have struggled to obtain freedoms and correct injustices, and have largely been opposed by the *Jamaat-i-Islami* — the Islamic party founded by Maududi.

However, when Fatima Jinnah, the sister of Pakistan's founder, stood for the presidency in opposition to Ayub Khan, the *Jamaat-i-Islami*, opposed as it was to women in leadership, supported her. Ayub Khan, despite his concern for women's rights, exploited the question of whether a woman can lead an Islamic state by obtaining a *fatwa* to the effect that her candicacy was un-Islamic.

Tensions over internal politics, reactions to the West, commercial interests and social expectations are, then, just as likely to influence understandings of Islamic teachings about women as are ideas about the nature of the Qur'an and how it should be interpreted. All the different factors interact and affect each other. How the debate will continue, and what will be its outcome, has yet to be seen.

Whatever one makes of the conservatism of traditional Islam and its resistance to 'innovation' in theory, the fact is that Islam is changing all the time and has always adjusted to different times and places. Current political Islamicism, for all its rhetoric about return to basics, is a new phenomenon which diverges in many ways from the Islam of, for example, the early Caliphs. As Engineer points out, there have been deep changes of attitude throughout the world of Islam even this century, for example over the question of slavery.

No system can or does remain static. The question is not whether Islamic attitudes to women will change, but how they will change. Will they move in the direction of re-affirmation of the traditional views defended by the apologists, or will they move in the direction of the radical re-interpretations advocated by the feminists? The answer must surely be that they will move, as they are already moving, in both directions amongst different groups and in different places; and that there may be other directions yet to emerge.

Notes

1. There are also *hadith qudsi*, which report words of God, but the vast majority of the many thousands of *hadith* are about Muhammad.

2. For example, the Qur'an commands prayer at different times of the day: it is the *hadith* that give details of words, postures and times for prayer.

3. 'Peace be with you.'

4. Christian readers may find this idea difficult: there is no parallel to the *Hadith* in Christian tradition. When we talk about following Jesus, we mean devotion to him as a person and following his spiritual and moral lead. We would never think of copying his mode of dress or of trying to find out how he ate or washed or slept. The Jesus pattern, which will be explored in Ch. 5, is not only different from the Muhammad pattern in content: it is quite a different sort of pattern.

5. Another version of this *hadith* indicates that it is a woman, a dog or an ass passing between the devotee and the *qibla* — the direction of prayer — that spoils the prayer.

6. Literally, 'He taught Adam the names'.

7. See Surah 15:26–28, 18:51, 20:115–116, 38: 72.

8. See the verses discussed in Ch. 2.

9. Most commentators would see Adam as standing for all human beings here.

10. These are needed to explain many of the stories in the Qur'an, because the Qur'an often refers to stories rather than telling them. Extra details are needed to make the references comprehensible.

11. Al-Hujwiri, *Kashful Mahjub*, p. 364. It is interesting that this is part of an argument in favour of celibacy. Islam is generally against celibacy, and Muslims can be very critical of what are seen as Christian denials of the importance of sexuality. The argument of *Kashful Mahjub* has much in common with early Christian arguments for the celibate life.

12. The Gospels record children being brought to Jesus for blessing (e.g. Matthew 19:13).

13. E.g. Abdalati, *Islam in Focus*, p. 189.

14. Islam certainly teaches that all are dependent on God's mercy, but this is a different concept from the Christian idea of grace. The one is about God's sovereign choice to forgive: the other is about his undeserved love.

15. That is, either her husband or a male relative who is so close that she could not marry him were she divorced or single.

16. Some writers, including westerners and Christians, have sought to justify such a marriage on political grounds (e.g. W. M. Watt, *Muhammad: Prophet and Statesman*, p. 102), or even to suggest that the relationship must have been more parental than marital (e.g. E. Challen, *To Love a Muslim*, p. 114). I find these unconvincing, since Aisha's father was Muhammad's closest friend even before the marriage, and the girl herself says that the marriage was consummated when she was nine years old.

17. Maududi (1903–79) was a journalist and founder of the Jamaat-I-Islami in Pakistan.

18. Surah 2:223. This verse is said to have been given in answer to a controversy about sexual positions. It is traditionally interpreted as teaching that the man is at liberty to choose his mode of intercourse so long as it is vaginal, i.e. it can result in the sowing of the seed in the 'tilth'. See *Usmani* N367 on this verse.

19. A. Qutb, *A Treatise on Competing Faith Oriented Family Norms*, p. 82.

20. I have a friend who was a Muslim Mullah and became a Christian in Pakistan (now he lives in the UK). One day a well educated Pakistani Muslim man came to him with his wife and said that in his anger he had divorced his wife three times. But now he was sorry and wanted to go back to his wife but the law of *halala* prohibited this. He asked my friend if he would become the temporary husband? He said that he absolutely trusted my friend and knew that he would not touch his wife. In the past my Mullah friend had performed *halalas* but now he lived according to the law of Christ which forbade him to do such an evil act. He

advised the man just to say sorry to his wife and be reconciled to her. My friend further advised the man not to be fooled by anyone. Whoever would take the woman to his bed would not take her there just for a ritual *halala*. He must have intercourse with the woman to make her lawful for her previous husband. This is the demand of Islamic law.

21. E.g. Surah 4:15, Surah 24:3–10. The latter discusses how a wife can defend herself against her husband's accusations. **145**

22. Surah 24:2. There are also *hadith* which recommend stoning to death as a penalty for married adulterers, and a Qur'anic verse that suggests that the punishment can be remitted if both parties repent (Surah 4:16). For a fuller discussion, see Doi, *Shari'ah: The Islamic Law,* pp. 236ff.

23. The following are recorded in Suyuti's *Chronicles of the Caliphs.*

24. See for example Yusuf Ali's note 509 on this verse.

25. There is no suggestion in Islamic law that a man needs the permission of his first wife's father in order to take a second wife.

26. Similar sentiments are found elsewhere, for example in Surah 4:3 and Surah 70:19–30.

27. Surah 5:90. Sunni commentators do not understand this verse as referring to *mut'ah*, since they no longer consider the practice lawful. However, Muhammad's uses of the Qur'an are usually taken as normative.

28. For example, see *Sahih Muslim: Kitab Al-Nikah*, Vol. 2, page 706 for a *hadith* that tells of *mut'ah* at the time of Umar, and p. 708 of the same book for one that says it was stopped by Muhammad at the Battle of Khaibar.

29. See Abdalati, *The Family Structure in Islam,* p. 104.

30. Mohammed Manzoor Nomani, *Khomeini, Iranian Revolution and the Shi'ite Faith,* 1988, p. 56.

31. See Revelation 21; Matthew 13:38–43; Romans 8:17; 1 Peter 3:7.

32. Such writers as Abdalati (see *Islam in Focus,* p. 13) and Yusuf Ali (see his commentary on any of these verses) see these delights as

metaphorical rather than literal: they are earthly descriptions of spiritual bliss.

33. This wine does not produce drunkenness or hangovers. (See 37:47).

34. A. Muhammad, *Marne ke ba'd kiya ho ga*, (*Life After Death*), undated p. 341.

35. And this seems unlikely judging by the *hadith* recorded on pp. 111–12 below.

36. What a contrast to life on earth, where Muslim men are prohibited from looking at the private parts of even their wives!

37. Compare 1 Peter 3:7.

38. Scholars vary as to how significant they consider the various models to have been. While Ahmed concludes that matriarchal models were important, for example, Al-Hibri (1982, p. 207) asserts that matriarchy had almost died out by the time of Muhammad, and that most of pre-islamic Arabia was 'viciously patriarchal'.

39. M. Afkhami, 'Women in post-revolutionary Iran: A Feminist Perspective', p. 18.

40. Engineer uses the example of the payment of a share of *zakah* to new converts to Islam. This was practised in the time of Muhammad, but Umar ruled that it was no longer necessary when the Muslim community was stronger, and embracing Islam did not have negative financial implications.

41. The practice of Muhammad as recorded in the *Hadith*.

42. This is the situation that gave rise to Surah 2:233, that permits free choice of sexual positions for men. Mernissi describes the preceding controversy, as the women of Medina refused to submit to some of their husbands' demands (pp. 145–148).

43. This is excepting the doctrine of abrogation, whereby a later ruling can cancel an earlier one. Al-Hibri ('A study of Islamic herstory', in Al-Hibri, A. (ed.), *Women and Islam*, pp. 213–4) cites this doctrine as a justification for her similar handling of women's issues in the Qur'an.

44. See, for example, Doi *Shari'ah: The Islamic Law*, p. 35 on the requirements for writers of Qur'anic commentaries, and p. 77 on

the conditions for the exercise of *qiyas*, the analogical reasoning
by which the *shari'ah* is to be applied in new situations.
45. He has listed most of the classical commentaries under standard
classifications.
46. Review from *Le Monde*, quoted on the back cover of *Women and
Islam*.

147

4

After Eve: A biblical diagnosis

4.1 Our common predicament

'How did we get into this mess?' asks Al-Hibri in the title of her paper.[1] And that is the question. It may be that Islam improved conditions for women; it may be that it is possible to interpret the Qur'an in ways amenable to twentieth-century feminist thinking; it may even be that the apologists are right when they suggest that the traditional roles assigned by Islam to women can be truly liberating. The problem is that, in practice, women across the Muslim world have been subjected to oppression and indignity throughout Islamic history, and many continue to be so. However we argue about the theory, whoever we blame for its misappropriation, we have to admit that there is a 'mess'.

The 'mess' is not only in the world of Islam

Kuhl Khaal, the collection of women's stories from Egypt quoted in Section 2:2 above,[2] has one Christian contributor. Alice does not have to face the agonies caused by polygamy and easy divorce, but she shares much with her

Muslim sisters, and even sees a positive side of Islamic divorce rules:

> I see the wisdom of our Muslim sisters who give their husbands their due so that they may not seek for their needs outside the home. Among the Christians because divorce is so difficult, women don't make enough of an effort. They neglect themselves and the sexual aspects of their marriage (p. 49).

Although she is in many ways more free than the Muslim contributors to the book, having received some education and chosen her marriage partner, she reports,

> It is true that I married a man I loved. But that love was soon crushed. Now I have a blind hatred for men in general although I don't show it. They are nothing, mean nothing to me, and I dislike them with all the energy which I possess. Man is without fail disloyal. I have faith in no man. The experiences of others, as well as my own, serve to reinforce this opinion (p.40).

Barton, a Bangladeshi Christian, observes that problems are also common to Hindus and Buddhists.[3] In her country, women of every religion are liable to marriage without consultation, domination by husbands and mothers-in-law, separation from their own mothers, lack of rights, hard manual labour, frequent child-bearing and all the blame if anything goes wrong.

> If anybody is asked, Why is (she) so badly treated? The answer would be, she is after all a woman, she is created to remain under the authority of a husband and to serve (p. 13).

If Christian as well as Muslim women in Egypt, and women from all religions in Bangladesh, experience oppression, does the problem therefore lie in non-western cultures? And does the answer lie in the West?

150 A cursory reading of the literature on western women would make us answer a resounding, 'NO!' The Muslim apologists are right when they criticise the West, and point out that, for example, women were not counted as citizens in England until 1850, and only achieved the vote this century. Perhaps the English system developed from the biblical idea that husband and wife should be so united that they are 'one flesh' (Genesis 2:24), and could therefore be treated as one unit: perhaps it simply indicates that households were important units and that husbands were the 'heads' of these. Neither of these ideas is in itself demeaning to women, but the system became so. Women may have been marginalised in different ways in western than in eastern societies, but marginalised they were.

Leila Ahmed (1992) examines the relationship between western and Middle Eastern cultures in her *Women and Gender in Islam*. She points out that many early Arab feminists were pro-western men, who argued for, for example, unveiling, primarily on the basis that it made them look uncivilised in western eyes. They still considered that it was up to them, as men, to discuss how 'their' women should be treated: there was no necessary concern for female welfare.

Further, the westerners who encouraged women's liberation in the Middle East did not necessarily encourage it in the West. Ahmed develops the thesis that,

> the Victorian colonial paternalistic establishment appropriated the language of feminism in the service of its assault on religions and cultures of other men, and in particular on Islam, in order to give an aura of moral justification to that assault at the very same time as it combated feminism in its own society (p. 152).

151

For example, Lord Cromer, the British Consul General in Egypt at the turn of the century, argued that, while Europeans elevated women because of their Christianity, Islam degraded them; and he regarded this as evidence of the inferiority of Muslim men. However, some of his policies — particularly in education — placed restrictions on Egyptian women, and he was a founder and president of the Men's League for Opposing Women's Suffrage in England.

Ahmed comments:

> Feminism on the home front and feminism directed against white men was to be resisted and suppressed; but taken abroad and directed aganst the cultures of colonized peoples, it could be promoted in ways that admirably served and furthered the project of the dominance of white men (p. 153).

She is adamant that freedom for women will not come by exchanging one culture for another, but by developments within each culture.

> The idea (which still often informs discussions about women in Arab and Muslim cultures and other nonwestern world cultures) that improving the status of women entails abandoning native customs, was the product of a particular historical moment and was constructed by an androcentric colonial establishment committed to male dominance in the service of particular ends. Its

absurdity and essential falseness become particularly apparent (at least from a feminist point of view) when one bears in mind that those who first advocated it believed that Victorian mores and dress, and Victorian Christianity, represented the ideal to which Muslim women should aspire (p. 165–6).

152

It is not only in Muslim societies that women are angry about how men have treated them. To every account of the plight of women under Islam, we could match an account of the plight of women in the West. To every analysis of the use of the Qur'an to oppress women, we could match an analysis of the use of the Bible to oppress women.[4] The 'mess' for women permeates all cultures as well as all religions. It may take different forms at different times and in different places, but it is shared by us all.

Common problems of interpretation

Christians and Muslims, because both have authoritative Scriptures, share the 'mess' as it affects the interpretation of their Books.[5] In Ch. 3, we saw how the Qur'an and the *Hadith* can be interpreted in different ways. Traditionally, the interpretations that give rise to male supremacy have been favoured. Christians too have interpreted their Scriptures in different ways. The Bible as well as the Qur'an has often been used to denigrate women. The Bible as well as the Qur'an can be seen as having two 'voices' on gender.

The first, like Leila Ahmed's 'ethical voice' (see pp. 113–15 above), gives women full equality with men. It starts with the creation, when,

God created man in his own image,

in the image of God he created him;
male and female he created them (Genesis 1:27).

The word for 'man' is *adam*, a general term that can mean male man but is also the word for a human being. The verse tells us that, as human beings, we all share the dignity of being made in God's image. It also tells us that there are two kinds of humans: males and females. These two kinds are together blessed and together commanded to manage the earth and to fill it with people:

> God blessed them and said to them, 'Be fruitful and increase in number; fill the earth and subdue it. Rule over the fish of the sea and the birds of the air and over every living creature that moves on the ground' (Genesis 1:28).

This voice is heard loudly in the New Testament. An oft quoted passage proclaiming equality between all human people is Galatians 3:26–8:

> You are all sons of God through faith in Jesus Christ, for all of you who were baptised into Christ have clothed yourselves with Christ. There is neither Jew nor Greek, slave nor free, male nor female, for you are all one in Christ Jesus.

All the traditional barriers of status are broken down: the only qualification for the privilege of being considered God's children is faith in Jesus Christ. And, in a culture that considered boys more valuable than girls, the equal status in Christ is that of sons — whether we are male or female.

But there is another voice. The Bible was written into cultures that were patriarchal, and, because it is a human book as well as a divine book, it reflects those cultures.[6] This means that many of the practices it records treat women as inferior. The question is then, 'To what extent do these practices simply describe what was going on at the time, and to what extent do they prescribe what we should do now?' Christians, like Muslims, have problems in interpretation.

With descriptive passages, we have less of a problem. We do not believe that we are bound to follow the example of any prophet except Jesus, and, even with him, we follow his principles rather than the details of what he did. The other prophets and biblical characters we believe to be just as imperfect as any other human being. Many of the things that they did were wrong, and often they were just acting as people of their own times and within their own cultures. Stories about the mistreatment of women can therefore be regarded as stories about the mistreatment of women. They are not examples to be followed, but warnings to learn from. Some such stories will be explored below.

Most of what the Bible has to say about women is in story form; but there are a few passages which discuss how women ought to behave. In the New Testament, these are all found in the epistles (letters): that these were written to specific groups of people in specific situations underlines their situational character. Some deal with the role of women in public worship (1 Cor. 11:3–16; 14:33–6; 1 Tim. 2:11–15), and others with marriage (1 Cor. 7; Eph. 5:21–33; Col. 3:18–4:1; 1 Pet. 2:18–3:7). They have been hotly debated throughout the Christian centuries, a major question being where they are offering advice for their immediate readership and where they are laying down principles for future generations.

Here, we consider one passage, which raises issues parallel to those raised by the Qur'anic example considered in Ch. 3.2: how is the husband–wife relationship to be ordered?[7]

Ephesians 5:21–33: submission and headship

Submit to one another out of reverence for Christ.

Wives, submit to your husbands as to the Lord. For the husband is the head of the wife as Christ is the head of the church, his body, of which he is the Saviour. Now as the church submits to Christ, so also wives should submit to their husbands in everything.

Husbands, love your wives, just as Christ loved the church and gave himself up for her to make her holy, cleansing her by the washing with water through the word, and to present her to himself as a radiant church, without stain or wrinkle or any other blemish, but holy and blameless. In the same way, husbands ought to love their wives as their own bodies. He who loves his wife loves himself. After all, no-one ever hated his own body, but he feeds and cares for it, just as Christ does the church — for we are members of his body. 'For this reason a man will leave his father and mother and be united with his wife, and the two will become one flesh.' This is a profound mystery — but I am talking about Christ and the church. However, each one of you also must love his wife as he loves himself, and the wife must respect her husband.

The classic interpretation has been that the headship of the husband implies his authority over the wife, and that the submission of the wife to the husband implies her subordination to him. This is balanced by his duty to love her to the point of giving his life for her, which means that the difference between man and woman is one of role rather than one of worth. There is a mutuality of self-giving love, within which the husband is to take the leadership role. This accords with the nature of men and women as God made them, and is to be the basis of secure and godly family life.

156

However, the duties are to be carried out without coercion. The wife is voluntarily to put herself under her husband, and there is no suggestion either that he should enforce his wife's submission or that she should enforce his self-giving. There is not even a hint of the Qur'anic idea that the husband should discipline his wife.

Recent debate has challenged aspects of this interpretation by questioning the meanings of 'submission' and 'headship'. We shall explore two ways of dealing with this.

1. James B. Hurley: a traditional position

Hurley, in *Man and Woman in Biblical Perspective*, parallels the Muslim apologists by affirming the basic traditional interpretation, but does it in a way that emphasises the value of women and criticises historical misuses of male authority. He affirms male authority in his understanding of both 'submission' and 'headship'.

'Submit'

means 'put in order', 'arrange', 'put in place', and is best translated by forms such as 'to make subject' or 'to subdue' in active uses and by forms such as 'to submit oneself' or 'to be obedient to' in passive or reflexive uses. Each of the more than forty New Testament uses of the verb carries an

overtone of authority and subjection or submission to
it. . . . There can be no question of the sort of submission that Paul has in view here. It is that of a subordinate
to one placed over him (p. 142).

On 'headship', he comes to similar conclusions:

> . . . it is a great mistake to try to remove any sense of
> submission from (Paul's) use of 'head' in verse 23, which
> verse presents the model of Christ's headship as the reason
> for a wife's submission. . . . There can be no escaping the
> idea of rule and authority (pp. 145–6).

Hurley goes on to discuss the reason for the authority —
as Christ's rule is *for the sake of* the church, so the husband's
headship is to be for the sake of his wife. Similarly, the
husband is not told to make his wife subject: rather, the
wife is to subject herself to him; and this is 'not for
the sake of the superior wisdom of their husbands, but for
the sake of Christ' (p. 147). There follows a long discussion on the exercise of authority, which assures us that
Hurley is well aware of its possible misuse, and cites the
example of Jesus Christ himself as the ruler who made
himself servant.

The exposition of this passage from Ephesians is part
of an extensive study of what the Bible teaches about
women, and reflects his overall conclusions about husband–
wife relationships: that

> The marriage relationship entails the self-sacrificing head-
> ship of the husband and the responsive submission of the
> wife (p. 244).

Headship implies authority, but,

> It is . . . a major mistake to restrict the biblical teaching
> to 'the right to command' or to be 'top of the chain of

command'. If so, it is quickly dehumanizing and also unworkable. *Biblical headship and authority are for the sake of building others up* (p. 240).

158 How this works out, however, depends on the particular marriage, and must be worked out between husband and wife according to each's needs and abilities. He cites the extensive description of wifely activities in Proverbs 31, to show 'the extent to which authority may be delegated without challenge to 'headship' (p. 240–1). He insists that,

> there are *no particular tasks* which the New Testament assigns as 'men's work' or as 'women's work' within the marital sphere . . . This suggests that it is not the husband's tasks but his initiative, example, leadership and responsibility which are in view. Each home and culture must relate the husband's and wife's role to specific tasks — and be wary of 'canonizing' certain traits or tasks as exclusively male or female when the Scripture does not do so (p. 241).

Like the Muslim apologists, Hurley upholds an essentially traditional understanding of gender relationships, but sees this as entirely positive. He challenges misuse of male authority, but he does not challenge the basic idea: rather, he expounds it and explains it, in the belief that this is what God has ordained, and is therefore for the good of all humankind.

Unlike the Muslim apologists, he restricts his exposition of marriage to relationships, and refrains from discussing roles. This is because he simply does not find any New Testament teaching about such roles. The Old Testament has plenty of pictures of women's roles, but these he sees not as prescriptive but as descriptive of that particular culture, in which, he says,

> women were not chattels and had rights that were closely guarded by the law. Although inheritance was passed through the male line, women could inherit in the absence of a male . . . Women participated in worship including the taking of vows and offering of sacrifice . . . women were free to participate in social and commercial life, although they were subordinate authorities in the sense that their contracts were subject to their husbands' ratification (p. 243).

159

He notes that, by the time of Christ,

> the subordinate role of women had led to their being viewed as inferior beings as well as subordinate ones (p. 235).

This is why both Jesus and the New Testament writers challenge prevailing norms. It is, perhaps, also why Hurley refrains from extrapolating teaching about authority to its implications about roles. This difference from the Muslim apologists will be further discussed in Ch. 6.

2. Mary Evans: a different view

Mary Evans' approach in *Women in the Bible*, pages 73–7, is more closely parallel to that of the Muslim feminists than to that of the apologists: rather than defending traditional interpretations, she challenges them. In particular, she challenges the idea that the Bible teaches that authority should always be male. Like Hurley, her book presents an extensive study of what the Bible has to say about women, and she largely agrees with him in his analysis of Old Testament culture, the situation at the time of Jesus, and

Jesus' challenge to it. However, even in the context of church leadership, she comes to the conclusion that: 'No function or activity within the church was specifically or absolutely barred to women: they could, and apparently did, play a full part in the life and worship of the churches. Senior leaders were almost always males, but women could and did exercise leadership within the churches, and where female leadership did exist it appears to be no different in kind from male leadership' (p. 132).

160

It is not surprising, then, that she does not see our Ephesians passage as teaching male rule and authority. She understands it in the context of the first verse quoted above: 'Submit to one another out of reverence for Christ' (v. 21).

She acknowledges that some commentators see this verse as part of the previous passage, she points out that verse 22 omits the verb, 'submit', and therefore needs to be linked to verse 21 if it is to make sense. Submission of wives to husbands is therefore a particular example of the submission that all Christians are to show to each other:

> Verse 21 makes it clear that for Paul the idea of mutual submission was not a contradiction in terms and warns us to beware of interpreting the relationship in hierarchical terms (p. 74).

Submission she understands as involving 'a deliberate decision to give priority to the other person' (p. 74).

On the subject of headship, she first notes that the passage itself points to what it means by the idea at the end of verse 23, when it says that Christ is the saviour of the Church. This, she says, shows that Paul is thinking of Christ's total self-giving rather than his rule and authority.

She acknowledges that, in Ephesians 1:22–23, his head-ship is clearly about his rule over everything (including the Church), but notes that, in 4:15–16, it is described in quite different terms as being about love, support and nourishment of the Church in particular. From this she concludes that:

> A man is said in Ephesians 5 to be head of his wife not in the way that Christ is sovereign of all (including the church) but in the particular way that Christ is head of the church. 'In short, a headship qualified, interpreted and limited by Christ alone is proclaimed, not an umlimited headship that can be arbitrarily defined and has to be endured.[8]

The description of Christ as saviour of the church she sees as supporting this idea: while no human being can be the saviour of his wife, there are some aspects of Christ's saving work that a husband can imitate. If the comparison between husband and Christ must be a limited one where 'saviour' is concerned, surely it must also be limited where 'headship' is concerned. We must follow the context of the passage to find out what these limitations are, and not make unwarranted extrapolations from one word.

Evans notes Hurley's contention that verse 23 'pre-sents the model of Christ's headship as the reason for a wife's submission' (Hurley, p. 145), but rejects this inter-pretation on the grounds that the Greek begins verse 24 with *alla*, 'but'. The New International Version quoted above translates this, 'now', but many translations ignore it. It makes sense, says Evans: 'if we take it as meaning that even though the husband as 'head' of the wife is to serve her and give himself fully on her behalf, nevertheless the wife must not think that places her in a special position without responsibilities, for just as the church is subject to Christ, she too is to be subject to her husband in everything' (p. 75).

162 She further underlines her understanding by pointing out that , although the husband is to love his wife 'as his own body', the wife is never called his body as the Church is called the body of Christ. Rather, he refers to the idea of their being 'one flesh' found in the creation narrative.

She concludes: 'This passage as a whole indicates then that both the subjection of the wife and the love of the husband are in fact to be expressions of different ways of the mutual subjection called for in verse 21. Both can be seen in terms of a readiness to subordinate one's own will and advantage for the benefit of the other' (p. 76).

That is not to say that the roles of husband and wife are the same:

> While it is true that these exhortations, to the wife to be subject to her husband and to the husband to love, do not take away the responsibility of the wife to love her husband or of the husband to be subject to his wife, nevertheless Paul's deliberate choice of different terms and in fact his use of the parallel relationship show that he was very much aware that just as the roles of Christ and the church are not interchangeable, so neither are the roles of husband and wife (p. 76–7).

Both Hurley and Evans see men and women as equal in status, and both emphasise the balanced mutuality of the husband–wife relationship: the question is about their different natures and roles. Either's view could be the basis of a society in which men and women respect one another and work in complementary ways to serve God and their fellow human beings. The problem is that both views can also be misused.

The traditional danger has been that of the oppression of women.

> The distribution of power can be badly skewed in the Christian home. Fortified by preaching that accepts all sorts of cultural assumptions about what 'headship' means, abusers often use Scripture as ammunition for their misuse of power. One battered wife noted: 'After marriage my husband treated me as a nonperson with no value other than through him. He cited Scripture passages in support of his treatment of me. Any time I objected to his behaviour or to his decisions, he told me that I was to submit to him just as if he were Jesus Christ. He firmly believed that if I were obedient and submissive, God himself would take care of me. Therefore he was free to behave as irresponsibly as he liked . . .'[9]

It is all too possible to insist on a particular meaning of 'submit', and to ignore the context of mutual submission and the husband's responsibility of self-giving love. The husband can then see it as his role to enforce submission, and use this as an excuse to give rein to his most violent tendencies.

The contemporary danger is, perhaps, the opposite: that women so claim their freedom that they seek to take over their husbands' roles. It is, perhaps, because some women in New Testament times were misusing their new-found freedoms that Paul included the 'but' in verse 24 of Ephesians 5, and that he gave so much space to discussing how women could take part in public worship with propriety in 1 Corinthians 11 and 1 Timothy 2.[10]

Misuse of women's freedom is not to their advantage, any more than it is to the advantage of a man to become the sort of husband who cannot control his violence towards his wife. Suzanne Haneef, 'A'ishah Lemu and Fatima Heeren, the western women quoted in Ch. 2, have found something in Islam that they missed in contemporary western society: clear roles in marriage and a mutual dependency between husband and wife.

It seems that, with the advent of western feminism, women have so succeeded in their struggle that they have changed the power balance. In doing so, they have often lost the distinction between the genders and therefore find their own identity in question. In the struggle, men have tended to be seen as the enemy, so that the idea of interdependence has been weakened. In some extreme cases, we are even seeing women reject males completely, to the extent of deliberately choosing to bring up children apart from their fathers.

Getting out of the 'mess' is not as easy as it might seem. Replacing male domination with female domination is not, I would suggest, the answer. As the diabetics' motto acknowledges, 'Balance is life': the question is how we can attain the fine balance of mutual love and service envisaged in Ephesians — however it is interpreted.

Christians and Muslims alike have systems that have oppressed women. Both have scriptures that can offer hope to women, but both also have scriptures which have been used to belittle and imprison women. We could continue by comparing our scriptures, and asking which has been most used to oppress, and which has the most potential for liberation, but that would not help us to see how to avoid the ubiquitous misuses. It seems to me that the key question is Al-Hibri's: 'How did we get into this mess?' It is only if we know how we got into it that we can find a way out of it.

Al-Hibri's question is asked in the context of Islam, and in the belief that, while Islam as it is today is utterly patriarchal, true Islam is not (p. 207). Her answer is a historical analysis. Like many others, she notes that there were some matriarchal practices in pre-Islamic Arabia, but asserts that these were even then fading away. Most of Arabia was 'viciously patriarchal' (p. 208) because, she suggests, fighting was the most important task in bedouin society and women, when weakened by childbirth, could not fight.

165

She further hypothesises that this was a relatively new phenomenon, brought about by the influence of neighbouring patriarchal Byzantine and Persian societies, and by the introduction of more sophisticated weapons. There are earlier records of fierce and valiant women warriors, but it seems that they fought with tent posts (p. 211). This changed: while the women were organising their families and herds, the men entered into trade that gave them access to swords, and so the balance of power shifted. By the time of Muhammad, Al-Hibri suggests, the patriarchal take-over was almost complete.

Islam countered some of the worst injustices, but its great significance was, in her judgement, its replacement of the tribal — and therefore patriarchal — bond with the bond of religion, under which all people were equal. The problem was the strength of the partiarchal interest. By the death of Muhammad, women had not yet gained a sufficent power base so that, little by little, patriarchalism took over again.

Even so, argues Al-Hibri, women were not considered inferior, but a capable and dangerous force. The system that developed sought to restrain their power, not deny it. It took another historical accident to bring the idea of male superiority: the introduction of western ideology with the rise of colonialism. This, she says, led to real oppression and the greatest mess for women.

Al-Hibri's analysis is interesting, and there is much that might be debated in it. However, it seems to me that we need to go deeper in order to find the origins of the 'mess'. The use of historical method suggests that we are looking at the result of a particular set of circumstances that occurs in a particular place; but we have seen that the 'mess' is not so confined. It can be found in any time and place: the problems are of humanity and not of particularity.

Women from many backgrounds have carried out historical studies on the 'mess', but it seems to me that they have solved very little. Such studies have served only to increase feelings of anger and indignation, and to provoke power struggles. Those who feel they have been dominated are in danger of becoming the dominators. If the Ephesians passage is correct in seeing submission to others as the key to right human relationships, power struggles are in themselves wrong and will therefore not clear up the 'mess'. The deeper problem has to do with why human beings seek power over one another in the first place.

As a Christian woman, I want to take Al-Hibri's question to the Bible, and to the earliest chapters of its first book, Genesis, which describe the nature of human beings and their relationships with God and each other. I shall start with the story of Eve, which has long been used to belittle women, to blame them for the wrongs of the world, and to justify male domination over them. I want to argue that this is a wrong interpretation but that, rightly understood, the story teaches us to expect just such distorted readings.

4.2 Eve's mess

Many Muslim apologists rightly point out that the Qur'an does not tell of Eve's creation from Adam's rib, nor of her temptation, fall and 'curses'. Again rightly, they report hair-raising conclusions that have been drawn from these stories at various times in history. These are not the only conclusions that can be — or have been — drawn. Currently, many Christian readers insist that the stories, rightly interpreted, teach a mutuality between men and women that has been marred through the sin of *both*.

The Bangladeshi Christian woman quoted above (p. 149), aware that women in all religious communities in her country suffer similar oppression, writes:

> People from the Biblical tradition do quote from Genesis stories to justify maltreatment of women. We women who have deep love for the Bible and for our faith, and at the same time love for our suffering sisters, have no choice but to discover the redeeming good news for women in our own scriptures.[11]

That the biblical story has been used to teach female inferiority for ages past is beyond question, just as it is beyond question that Surah 4:35 has been used to teach male domination. What is in question is whether such teaching is faithful to the story and to the rest of the Bible. 168 I think that it is not: as what is done with Qur'anic material depends on interpretation, so what is done with Biblical material depends on interpretation.

Parallel to the range of interpretations of Surah 4:35, there are traditional interpretations that see the story in Genesis 2 and 3 as teaching male superiority, and a whole spectrum through to interpretations that would use them to assert female superiority. The problem is that what Genesis gives us is a story, and well-told stories do not tell their readers what to think. They leave tantalising gaps which are filled by the readers' imagination, and pose more questions than they answer. Readers tend to answer the questions out of their own experience and prejudice: it is a strict discipline to interpret any one of the Bible's stories in the light of the rest of the book.

I want here to explore the biblical story of Eve in the light of our question, 'How did we get into this mess?' These chapters of Genesis are generally agreed to be teaching us about how our world was established, and therefore to be offering important insights into what human beings are, and how they relate to God, to his creation and to each other.

Christian commentators agree that they teach us very clearly that God made the world (including us) good, but that things went wrong because of human disobedience towards God. Genesis 1, which describes creation, is punctuated by the comment, 'And God saw that it was good' (vv. 4, 10, 12, 17, 21, 25), and the last verse concludes, 'God saw all that he had made, and it was very good' (v.31). By the end of Genesis 3, things have changed. The serpent and the ground have been cursed (3:14, 17), the human beings have been told of the suffering that they will have to endure, and they have been expelled from the beautiful Garden of Eden. The 'good' world has been spoilt.

I want to suggest that the very focus on Adam and Eve as male and female tells us that gender relationships have also been spoilt. The original relationship between male and female was good, but things have gone wrong. It seems to me that this is one of the main messages of the story, and that this message is confirmed by the examples of male-female relationships discussed in the rest of Genesis.[12]

A 'good' relationship

In Genesis 1, the creation of human beings 'in the image of God' is described as creation as male and female:

> So God created man in his own image,
> in the image of God he created him;
> male and female he created them (Genesis 1:27).

It is helpful here to note that there are two Hebrew words used in Genesis 1–2 that can be translated 'man'. The above passage has *adam*, which can refer either to a human-being or to a male man. It is not clear at what stage in the story this word first becomes the name of an individual. The other word, *îsh*, always refers to a male human being. It appears first in 2:23, when the man (*adam*) recognises the woman as 'bone of his bones and flesh of his flesh'. The word for 'woman' is *ishshah*.

170 In Genesis 1, nothing is said about how the male and the female are different, nor about their roles. They are made together, blessed together and told to fill and rule the earth together. This unity and equality are part of the creation that God saw as 'very good'(v. 31).

Genesis 2 describes the creation of human beings in more detail, and 'zooms in' on 'male and female he created them'.

First, the *adam* is created out of the *adamah*, the ground:

> When the Lord God made the earth and the heavens — and no shrub of the field had yet appeared on the earth and no plant of the field had yet sprung up, for the Lord God had not sent rain on the earth and there was no man to work on the ground . . . the Lord God formed the man from the dust of the ground and breathed into his nostrils the breath of life, and the man became a living being.
>
> Now the Lord God had planted a garden in the east, in Eden; and there he put the man he had formed . . . The Lord God took the man and put him in the Garden of Eden to work it and take care of it (vv. 4–8, 15).

The *adam* is made because the *adamah* needs him (v. 5), and the related names imply a fundamental relationship between the human-being and the ground. Genesis 1 has the plants given to the humans for food: Genesis 2 has the human given to the ground so that the plants can grow. The mutuality and interdependence of *adam* and *adamah* are unmistakable.

Next, and in parallel, the woman is made because the man needs her. The words of God, 'It is not good for the man to be alone' (v. 18) contrast sharply with the repeated, 'it was good' of Genesis 1. The completion of his good creation requires two kinds of human being. As the earth could not fulfil its purpose without the man, the man could not fulfil his without the woman. As God made the man out of the ground, he now makes the woman out of the man. Again, the names reflect this. The man is now *îsh*, and the woman is *ishshah*.

> The Lord God said, 'It is not good for the man to be alone. I will make a helper suitable for him.' Now the Lord God had formed out of the ground all the beasts of the field and all the birds of the air. He brought them to the man to see what he would name them; and whatever the man called each living creature, that was its name. So the man gave names to all the livestock, the birds of the air and all the beasts of the field.
>
> But for the man (*adam*) no suitable helper was found. So the Lord God caused the man to fall into a deep sleep; and while he was sleeping, he took one of the man's ribs and closed up the place with flesh. Then the Lord God made a woman from the rib he had taken out of the man, and he brought her to the man.
>
> The man (*adam*) said, 'This is now bone of my bones and flesh of my flesh; she shall be called 'woman' (*ishshah*) for she was taken out of man (*îsh*).'
>
> For this reason a man will leave his father and mother and be united to his wife, and the two will become one flesh (vv. 19–24).

Genesis 1 makes the ruling and filling of the earth the joint responsibility of human beings. Genesis 2 shows that neither ruling nor filling can be done by the male alone.

The word 'helper' (Hebrew *ezer*) suggests dependence — that the man needs the woman if he is to perform his responsibilities.[13] The man's recognition of the woman as of the same kind as himself suggests their equality.

172 Verse 24 brings the chapter to its conclusion by pointing forward to the good, God-ordained marriage relationship which results from the God-given nature of male and female. On the one hand, the man is dependent on the woman, as he leaves behind his parents to be joined to her. On the other hand, the man is now given to the woman as the woman has just been given to the man. Equality is then affirmed by the statement that the two become 'one flesh': they were separated when the flesh of the woman was taken from the flesh of the man, and now they are to be joined again in marriage. The mutuality and interdependence of *îsh* and *ishshah* are, one would have thought, unmistakable.

The relationship gone wrong

Genesis 3 has the famous story of the temptation and disobedience of Adam and Eve, and their expulsion from the Garden of Eden.[14] It has often been interpreted as teaching that the main cause of evil in the world is women, that men should be in authority over women, and that the woman's role is in the home with the children. I want to suggest that this is a wrong interpretation, and it is because things have gone wrong that we interpret the story wrongly. In fact, we interpret it as people who have gone wrong, and our interpretations reinforce the wrongness.

If this sounds like a circular argument, it is because it describes a circle — a vicious circle in which the predicament of women is re-inforced by interpretations which come out of the predicament and actually teach that what has gone wrong is right.

The first thing that happens after Adam and Eve's disobedience is that they hide from each other (by trying to cover themselves with leaves) and from God (by sheltering behind the trees). Most interpreters recognise that human beings have continued to hide from God ever since — that we shrink from his holiness and try to pretend to ourselves that we have done nothing wrong. It is also recognised that human beings have a tendency to hide from each other — that we conceal the things of which we are ashamed, and try to let people see only what we deem to be good about ourselves. But the fact that Adam and Eve are male and female suggests that men and women hide from one another — it is a signal that the mutual recognition and union of Genesis 2 has gone wrong.

As the story unfolds, some of the consequences of this become clear:

The man blames the woman God calls Adam to account, and he replies, 'The woman you put here with me — she gave me . . .' In Genesis 2, he recognises her with joy: here, he seeks to distance himself from her. This is a signal that men are going to see themselves in a different category of humanity than women, and are going to blame them for much that goes wrong in the future. The history of interpretation of the story confirms this:

we remember the oft-quoted passages in Tertullian and Augustine:[15]

> Do you not know that you are each an Eve? The sentence of God on this sex of yours lives in this age: the guilt must of necessity live too. You are the devil's gateway: you are the unsealer of the forbidden tree: you are the first deserter of the divine law: you are she who persuaded him whom the devil wasn't valiant anough to attack. You destroyed so easily God's image, man (Tertullian).

> What is the difference whether it is a wife or a mother, it is still Eve the temptress that we must beware of in any woman (St Augustine).

The story is used to re-inforce the very thing that has gone wrong: to blame women for something that is a joint responsibility.[16]

Male and female roles become separated The sentences given by God to the man and the woman in vv.16–19 show that their basic relationships have gone wrong. To the man (*adam*), it is said that the ground (*adamah*) will be cursed, and that his work on it will be accompanied by pain. To the woman (*ishshah*), it is said that the pattern of relationship with her husband (*îsh*) will be changed, and that her bearing of children will be accompanied by pain.

The basic relationships — the man's towards the ground and the woman's towards the man — are described in terms of role — of agriculture and of childbearing. The responsibilities of subduing the earth and filling it with people which were given to male and female together in Genesis 1 now appear to have been separated — the first is the man's job, and the second the woman's.

174

In the story, this separation is the result of human disobedience, and it is nowhere said that the man ought to focus on the ground and the woman on children. Rather, it is said that when they focus on these roles they will both suffer. There is no indication that the man now has no need of the woman to be his 'helper' in the garden, and the first verse of Genesis 4 reminds us that the woman needs the man if she is to produce children.

Despite all this, Christians and Jews down the centuries have separated the roles of men and women, and have used this passage to justify their actions. The sentences have been read as prescribing how things ought to be, and not as describing a world gone wrong. Again, the story has been read by people who have gone wrong, and has been used to teach that the wrongness — the separate functioning of male and female who should work together — is right.

Women become dependent on men, and dominated by them This can be seen in the woman's sentence. The relationship between male and female, *ish* and *ishah*, is described thus (v. 16):

> Your desire will be for your husband, and he will rule over you.

There has been much discussion about the nature of the desire and of the rule.[17] The important thing is that there is a change in the balance of the relationship — from mutuality to dependence and domination. Whereas the man was unable to manage without the woman, the woman is now driven by a desire for the man. Whereas they were both to rule over the living creatures, the man will now rule over the woman. Even Calvin, who considers that part of the woman's disobedience was moving away from subordination to her husband, sees a change here:

176

> The woman, who had perversely exceeded her proper bounds, is forced back to her own position. She had, indeed, previously been subject to her husband, but that was a liberal and gentle subjection; now, however, she is cast into servitude.[18]

The man's move towards domination is demonstrated in v. 20, when he names his wife Eve.

Men are likely to exert their authority over women and to treat them as a means of reproduction It is generally agreed that, for the Hebrews, the act of naming something implies taking authority over it. That the man named his wife therefore shows his authority over her. The name given means 'life', and indicates the woman's great role in bringing new life into the world. However, it also focusses on one particular function, and suggests that Adam sees the main identity of his wife to be found in her motherhood.

Some commentators see this as similar to Adam's saying that the being that was taken out of him would be called *ishshah* in 2:23. Naming, they say, is a mark of authority over the person named, and these two verses show that the man was to have authority over the woman.[19] A closer reading suggests otherwise: that the first 'naming' is not a naming at all, but a recognition of the woman as the same kind of being as the man. The second naming comes after the 'fall', and is therefore part of the world-gone-wrong.

Let us consider these verses in detail:

> The man said, 'This is now bone of my bone and flesh of my flesh; she shall be called 'woman' because she was taken out of man (2:23).

> Adam named (lit. 'called her name') his wife Eve, because she would become the mother of all the living (3:20).

There are three important differences between the two 'namings':

First, the word 'name' is missing from 2:23. Secondly, 'called' is passive in 2:23 and active in 3:20. Thirdly, *ishshah* in 2:23 is simply a feminine form of *îsh*, and is not a proper noun. Eve in 3:20 is the name of an individual.

We see that the dimension of the man actively naming the woman is missing from Genesis 2. Rather, he is announcing his recognition of the woman as a creature like himself, and therefore having the same name as him. As one of the rabbinic commentators explains:

> She is bone of my bones and flesh of my flesh and therefore, of all the creatures to whom I have given names she is worthy of being called by the same name as mine (Ramban, quoted in Scherman and Zlotowitz, *Bereishis*, 1980, p. 110).

In contrast, the 'naming' in Genesis 3 uses the standard Hebrew formula for naming, and can be taken as indicating the authority of the namer. As pointed out above, this comes after things have gone wrong. It signals that men in fact take authority over women, and that women are in fact identified by motherhood, but tells us nothing about whether these things ought to be. Rather, as part of this chapter which describes the results of the 'fall', it is likely to show us an aspect of life-gone-wrong. The interpretation that links the two namings and uses them to teach that male authority is right is, then, yet another example of using a description of something that is wrong 178 as a prescription about what is right.

It is interesting that, throughout history, one way in which men have exerted their authority has been in interpreting their Scriptures — whatever their faith. Men in the world-gone-wrong have used their authority-gone-wrong to reinforce their authority over women, and women, in their dependency, have often colluded. No wonder we are in a mess!

Genesis 4: signs of hope

The good news is that the Bible does not end with Genesis 3: the mess is not total, and there are ways forward. With its description of Eve as mother, the very next chapter offers insights which balance the picture of what women are and ought to be.

First, while most genealogies in the Bible focus on the male line and on the men as begetters,[20] the births of both Cain and Abel and of Seth (Adam and Eve's sons) focus on the woman.

Secondly, it is Eve who names Seth, and, by implication, she who also names Cain and Abel. If the naming is a symbol of authority, this gives a balance to Adam's naming of Eve in Genesis 3, and to Seth's naming of his son in 4:26. The surprising thing is that most commentators ignore this.[21]

Thirdly, there is a parallel between Eve's cry of 4:1 and Adam's cry of 2:23. Eve's statement *qanîthî 'îsh 'eth-YHWH* (N.I.V. 'with the help of the Lord I have brought forth a man') in 4:1 presents difficulties in every word. There are, however, several things that are clear, and that can give insight, in any translation:

- *Qanîthî*, 'I have brought forth', is very unusual in describing a birth, more usually meaning 'I have bought' or 'I have obtained'. This is the first recorded birth, and the word can therefore indicate a response to a new and perhaps unexpected event.
- The word 'man' (*îsh*) is not used elsewhere for a baby. The idea of the woman bringing forth the man then reminds of the previous use of the word in 2:23–4, where the woman comes from the man.
- The words for 'with the help of the Lord' (*'eth-YHWH*) are perhaps the most difficult, since it is not clear whether *'eth* marks a direct object or acts as a preposition meaning 'with'. In either case, the meaning is obscure. What is clear, however, is that the involvement of God is recognised.

If the strangeness of the language is taken as a pointer to the significance of the event rather than as a reason for consigning it to obscurity, all this suggests a parallel with 2:23. Eve's cry of recognition of the birth of her son then echoes Adam's cry of recognition of his wife, and we have the man coming from the woman as we had the woman coming from the man.

So we have:

- God takes the *ishshah* from the *îsh* (Adam): He takes the *îsh* (Cain) from the *ishshah*.
- The man shares with God in creation by naming the animals: the woman shares with God in creation by bearing a child.
- The man names his wife: the woman names her sons.

180

While Genesis 3 teaches us that male-female relationships are in a mess, Genesis 4 gives hope that women are still full human beings, made in the image of God. Eve's and Adam's sons immediately exhibit the fact that they are part of a world gone wrong, as the elder murders the younger, but God is still at work, using human beings to bring new life into the world. To define a woman by her function as child–bearer may be demeaning, but the function itself is not so: it is a wondrous sharing in the creative activity of God himself.

In summary

The Genesis stories can, and, I would say, should, be read as teaching mutuality, partnership and equality of dignity between males and females. Taken as a whole, they exhibit fine balances to ensure this. The problem is that, as in every other aspect of life, the balance has gone wrong; and the fact that the man and the woman are treated separately suggests that this wrong balance is a central factor of life after the fall. From the details of Genesis 3, we can expect that:

- women are likely to be blamed by men, as, being human, they are likely to blame other people for their own mistakes.

- women are likely to become dependent on men, and to be dominated by them.
- far from women working together with men as their necessary 'helpers', male and female roles are likely to be separated.
- men are likely to exert authority over women, and to treat them as means of reproduction.
- the joy of child-bearing will be marred by pain.

These details are symptoms of a ruptured relationship. At the point of temptation, the woman was thinking about gaining power for herself, and not about her responsibilities towards God or husband. At the calling to account, the man was thinking about saving his own face, and not about how he had disappointed his Maker or about his unity with his wife. So that unity was shattered, and the pattern of both male and female looking to their own interests was begun. The door was opened to rivalry: to the jealousy and power struggle that replace love and service.

It is therefore only to be expected that both Muslims and Christians, in their shared humanity, will tend to interpret their scriptures according to the false balance. All readings, whether patriarchal or feminist or struggling for an intermediate balance, are readings in the world-gone-wrong, and should therefore be viewed with suspicion. The problem in both faiths is that the interpretations have often become more authoritative than the scriptures themselves. But, even were the scriptures entirely positive about women and the interpretations perfect, we could still expect the above pattern to emerge. If human beings have gone wrong in this way, they must be unable to follow even the best of precepts.

Genesis 6: The mess continued

182

The next time we meet women in Genesis is in the strange passage that describes the world before Noah's flood:

> When men began to increase in numbers on the earth and daughters were born to them, the sons of God saw that the daughters of men were beautiful (good), and they married any of them they chose. The Lord said, 'My Spirit will not contend with man for ever, for he is mortal; his days will be a hundred and twenty years.'
>
> The Nephilim were on the earth in those days — and also afterwards — when the sons of God went to the daughters of men and had children by them. They were the heroes of old, men of renown.
>
> The Lord saw how great man's wickedness on earth had become, and that every inclination of the thoughts of his heart was only evil all the time. The Lord was grieved that he had made man on the earth, and his heart was filled with pain (Genesis 1–6).

This is the background to God's announcement of the flood which unmade his world. It is a difficult passage to translate, and commentators spill much ink discussing it; but it has some important things to teach us. It will help us to know that the word used for 'men' is always *adam*.

No-one knows who the 'sons of God' were. Some think they were angels. The word translated 'God' can also mean 'rulers', and some prefer this translation. Whoever they were, these people were male, and they were powerful.

Everyone agrees that the 'daughters of men' were ordinary human women, the descendants of the *adam* who was made in the image of God. They were 'beautiful': the word used is *tov*, 'good', which reminds us that they were part of God's creation that he saw to be good (Genesis 1:10, 12, 18, 21, 24, 31).

It is also clear that these powerful males were exploiting the good daughters of *adam*. They were taking any of them that they wanted. The results of these unions were the Nephilim. Again, no-one knows who these were, but they are treated as monstrosities elsewhere in the Old Testament.[22] They seem to have been even more powerful than the 'sons of God'. Their appearance is linked with God's perception that the whole earth had become wicked, which leads to his grief, pain and judgement.

What is happening here? Simply this: that one of the most serious aspects of the mess in the world was that powerful males were exploiting powerless females, and this was resulting in a distortion of God's good creation. He had made it good, and it had become wicked.

The judgement of the flood shows God's reaction to this. He is grieved. He is deeply sad. The words used echo those in the sentences of Genesis 3. God feels the pain of his good creation going wrong. And he does something about it. He unmakes his world by sending a great flood, and then re-starts it with Noah and his family.

After the flood, it is clear that the world is not going to be perfect; but it is also clear that God has his purpose for us with all our problems. Noah offers a sacrifice to God, and God says:

> Never again will I curse the ground because of man, even though every inclination of his heart is evil from child-hood. And never again will I destroy all living creatures, as I have done. As long as the earth endures, seedtime and harvest, cold and heat, summer and winter, day and night will never cease (Genesis 8:21–22).

184

God is committed to this imperfect world; and the Bible acknowledges that the exploitation of women is part of the imperfection. We can expect to see the pattern of women being blamed, dependent, dominated and ex-ploited repeated throughout human history. But we can also expect to see God's indignation at this pattern, his rulings to limit its effects, and his intervention to enable us to change things.

4.3 The other women of Genesis

Genesis is mostly about men. Following the first eleven chapters, which are about the beginnings of the world, it is about Abraham and his sons, grandsons and great grandsons. It is not even about all of these: it focuses on those who become the forefathers of the Jewish people: on Abraham's son Isaac, and Isaac's son Jacob who is later called 'Israel'. It is his twelve sons after whom the twelve tribes of Israel are named, and it is the origins of Israel with which the Genesis writer is concerned.

However, a number of women come into the stories — you can't have sons without mothers. Islamic tradition also knows of these women, but the Qur'an mentions only two of them — Sarah and Potiphar's wife — and names neither. Despite its origins in a patriarchal society, Genesis gives attention to them, and much can be learnt from their stories. In what follows, I shall explore how they show that what went wrong for Eve has also gone wrong for other women.

Yet they also show that women matter: their stories *are* included, and not only as they affect the men. They are named, and many of their agonies are vividly described. In some cases, their stories are told with little comment; but sometimes we get a glimpse of what God thinks of their predicament, and see him — and sometimes even human males — intervening on their behalf. The women depicted are not just helpless victims: they are real human beings who matter to God. And they are not only victims: they are capable of being just as sinful as men, if only they are given the chance.

Sarah (Genesis 11–23)

Sarah, the wife of Abraham, is perhaps the most rounded female character in Genesis. Sometimes, she is exploited by her own husband, and sometimes her husband obeys her against his own will. Sometimes we are moved with pity for her as a barren wife, and sometimes we see her exploiting another dependent woman. In all this, God blesses her and carries out his plan for her life, and the New Testament records only good things of her. 1 Peter 3:6 refers to her as a model wife, 'who obeyed Abraham and called him her master.'

The first we learn of her is that she is barren (11:22–30). We are immediately faced with the fact that women were expected to bear children. They find their identity in motherhood, and Sarah[23] was denied this. Her predicament is the subject of much of what follows.

The next incident that affects Sarah is in 12:10ff. She has, as a matter of course, accompanied her husband in his journey from Ur to Canaan, but then there is a famine. Abraham takes his people to Egypt, where food is available, but is fearful because Sarah is beautiful. He thinks that the Egyptians might kill him in order to take her, so he tells her to say she is his sister, not his wife. She agrees.

As expected, Sarah's beauty is observed, and she is taken into the Pharoah's palace. Because she is thought to be Abraham's sister, he is treated well, and given great wealth because of her. Sarah, it seems, has been the dutiful wife. She has aquiesced to her husband's fear that she will be treated as an object to be taken as desired, and he has gained by trading her with Pharoah.

> But the Lord inflicted serious diseases on Pharoah and his household because of Abram's wife Sarai (12:17).

Human beings follow their own way, *but God* steps in. He will not allow Sarah to be so mistreated; neither will he allow Pharoah to suffer from the misconception authored by Abraham. Pharoah recognises what is going on, and sends Abraham and all his people away.

Sarah does not appear again until Genesis 16, where we are reminded that she is barren (v.1). She decides to do something about it. She has an Egyptian slave called Hagar, and suggests that Abraham impregnates her.

186

According to custom, Hagar's child will be considered Sarah's offspring.

In Genesis 15, God has reassured Abraham that he is going to give him an heir. Now, as Sarah agreed to Abraham's strategy in Egypt, he agrees to Sarah's strategy to gain a child. Perhaps he thinks that this will be God's way of fulfilling his promise. He sleeps with Hagar, and she conceives.

187

But there are problems. Hagar begins to despise Sarah, Sarah blames Abraham, and Abraham just tells Sarah to do whatever she likes. Sarah ill-treats Hagar, and Hagar runs away. Hagar eventually returns and gives birth to Ishmael.

It is not a nice story. None of the characters appears in good light. Sarah may be a dependent woman, under great pressure to have a child, but she seems not to sympathise with the dependent position of Hagar. Just as she has been treated as a commodity, she treats her servant as her property, and even seems to be surprised when Hagar reacts like a human being. Jealousy between the women ensues.

In the next chapter, God renews his promise to Abraham, and re-names him as 'father of many'. He tells him that the 'many' will come through a son who will be born to Sarah. Abraham laughs at the idea, since both he and Sarah are old; but God repeats the promise again.

Genesis 18 contains the only story of Sarah that is included in the Qur'an. Three angels come to Abraham, to tell him about the impending judgement on Sodom and Gomorrah, but also to re-affirm the promise of a son in Sarah's hearing. Sarah, like Abraham, laughed.[24] According to the Genesis version, the angel asks why Sarah laughed, and she denies it.

There is an interesting domestic cameo when the angels arrive. Abraham does not realise they are angels, and invites them to eat. He tells Sarah to make some bread, and then himself runs out to select a calf which he gives to a servant to prepare. It is then Abraham's job to serve the meal. In amongst the wheeling and dealing, it seems that Abraham and Sarah had a good partnership in household matters. Is this, we wonder, why the New Testament commends Sarah as an obedient wife?[25]

The next stage in Sarah's story, in Genesis 20, is almost a repeat of the Pharoah story, and many commentators think it refers to an earlier stage in her life. It is, perhaps, told here to emphasise Abraham's fallibility before the promise of a son is fulfilled in Genesis 21. This time, Abraham has moved south to an area called Gerar, and the king is called Abimelech. Sarah is presented as Abraham's sister, and the king takes her.

> But God came to Abimelech in a dream one night and said to him, 'You are as good as dead because of the woman you have taken; she is a married woman' (20:3).

Once again, God intervenes in a situation where a woman is being exploited and a man deceived. Once again, Abraham gains from the transaction, as Abimelech listens to God and gives Abraham great riches. Once again, Abraham is rebuked as he realises that the king, whom he thought an unbeliever, can be spoken to by God and can also obey.

Then comes the climax:

> Now the Lord was gracious to Sarah as he had said, and
> the Lord did for Sarah what he had promised. Sarah
> became pregnant and bore a son to Abraham in his old
> age, at the very time God had promised him (21:1–2).

Sarah called her son Isaac, which means 'he laughs', for she
said, 'God has brought me laughter, and everyone who
hears about this will laugh with me.'

189

So, was turbulent Sarah a reformed character? Did
she treat everyone with consideration and respect? Did she
give up being jealous, and behave like a contented old
woman? No! The very next thing we read is that Hagar's
son, Ishmael is teasing Sarah's son, Isaac and, instead of
rebuking Ishmael, Sarah gives way to a fit of jealousy and
demands that Abraham get rid of both mother and son.

Abraham is, understandably, distressed — not, apparently, for Hagar, but for his son Ishmael. God tells him,

> Do not be so distressed about the boy and your maid-
> servant. Listen to whatever Sarah tells you because it is
> through Isaac that your offspring will be reckoned. I will
> make the son of your maidservant into a nation also,
> because he is your offspring (21:12–13).

God sees the tensions and, it seems, recognises that they
will inevitably continue if both mothers and sons stay
together. He reassures Abraham of his concern for all, but
tells him to let Sarah have her way. Hagar is thrown out
again, and no more is heard of Sarah until her death
(23v1–2). Her burial ground is the first piece of land that
Abraham actually owns in Canaan.

In all, Sarah's life shows us the continued dependency
of women on men, but never allows us to suppose that
women are blameless. Both women and men are to blame

for the mess that women — and men — find themselves in. Yet there is hope: God is able to bless and to work despite our mess. He sees and acts when Sarah is being exploited, and, through all the human wranglings, gives her the promised son through whom his purposes will be fulfilled.

190

Hagar (Genesis 16, 21)

Hagar is not mentioned in the Qur'an, but she is well known to Muslims because of the teaching that links her and Ishmael with Mecca and Medina.[26] In Genesis, she is a slave and a foreigner, and an example of a woman who was treated as a commodity.

We have already recounted some of her story in Genesis 16: Sarah's assumption that she could dispose of her maid's sexuality as she wished, Abraham's sleeping with her, the ensuing pregnancy and her consequent triumphing over her mistress. She has a human reaction, although she has not been treated as having full human dignity. Sarah seems to be surprised at this, and so ill-treats her that she runs away.

As so often in Genesis, there is thus far no clue as to what God thinks of the actions of any of the protagonists; but then we read that, 'the angel of the Lord found Hagar near a spring in the desert.' He told her to go back to her mistress, but reassured her that God would bless her with many descendents. Her son would be called 'Ishmael' — 'God hears' — because the Lord had heard her misery.

> She gave this name to the Lord who spoke to her: 'You are God who sees me.' For she said, 'I have now seen the one who sees me.' That is why the well was called Beer

Lahai Roi (well of the living one who sees me) (16:13–14).

The pattern is repeated in Genesis 21, when Sarah sends Hagar away with her son. Once again, Sarah solves her domestic problems by getting rid of a piece of property that was longer useful. Once again, God hears — this time, he hears the distressed child. He reassures Hagar of the present and of the future, and provides water for them both. He does not leave them but 'God was with the boy as he grew up' (v.20).

Devalued and used and blamed though this dependent woman was, God heard her, he saw her, he found her and he spoke to her. He did not remove her from her difficult situation, but sent her back into it — not least, perhaps, because that was the only place where she could be secure until her child was born.

The most important thing to her was just this: that God saw *her*. He did not see a slave to be used, a piece of female humanity that could function as a baby machine, a disruptive element in the home . . . He saw *her*, a weak and needy human being. He communicated with her in all her human dignity as a person made in his image.

Rachel and Leah (Genesis 29–30)

Here we come to the two sisters who married the same man. The story is well known. Jacob, son of Isaac, went to his father's homeland to find a wife. He fell in love with his cousin Rachel, but, when it came to the wedding, her father Laban substituted her older sister Leah as bride. According to their customs, we suppose that the bride was veiled, and had little choice in the matter. The Scripture does not explain the details, but we are told that it was only the following morning that Jacob was able to look at his new wife, and to discover that it was Leah, who he considered ugly because of her weak eyesight.

192   Laban then gave him Rachel as a second wife, and trouble ensued. As there had been jealousy between Sarah and Hagar, now there was jealousy between Rachel and Leah. But this time it was worse: Leah was not a servant, but a full wife and the sister of Rachel. Moreover, she was older than Rachel, and the first wife. Yet Jacob loved Rachel more than Leah, and they both knew it.

The story is told in Genesis 29, and up to this point there is no mention of God. The human protagonists continue on their way without any reference to him. But God sees. In verse 31 we read what he saw: that Leah was unloved. So he intervened and gave her what would give her status in her culture: she became pregnant and bore three sons.

Leah recognised this as God's blessing to her, but Rachel simply became jealous (30:1). Like her grandmother, she offers her maid to her husband, and thence ensues a competition between Rachel and her maid and Leah and her maid to see who can have the most children. The outcome of the unsavoury rivalry is that Jacob has twelve sons and one[27] daughter, and when they grow up, there is jealousy between the sons of Rachel and the rest of the brothers.

We see that the Bible faithfully records some of the hazards of marriage contracts, the pressures on women to bear sons and the tensions of polygamous households. In the midst of the human wranglings, God sees the unloved woman and gives her the blessing that she needs. As far as we know, Leah never gains the love of her husband, but she does learn to trust God. When her last son is born, she calls him Judah, from the word for 'praise' and she says, 'This time, I will praise the Lord' (29:35)'

Dinah (Genesis 34)

Dinah is not a well-known character, and she is not even mentioned in the Qur'an. In Genesis, she is the only one of Jacob's daughters who is mentioned, and that is only because she had problems. She was raped:

> Now Dinah, the daughter Leah had borne to Jacob, went out to visit the women of the land. When Shechem son of Hamor the Hivite, the ruler of that area, saw her, he took her and raped her. His heart was drawn to Dinah daughter of Jacob, and he loved the girl and spoke tenderly to her. And Shechem said to his father Hamor, 'Get me this girl as my wife (Genesis 34:1–4).

What Dinah thought of the matter is not mentioned: her brothers, we are told, 'were filled with grief and fury'. When Hamor came to ask for Dinah as a wife for his son, they agreed, but on condition that Hamor and all his family and townsfolk be circumcised. They, in turn, agreed; but, while they were still in pain from the operation, Dinah's brothers attacked the town, killed every male in it and took their sister from Shechem's house, where she was, it seems, staying. Their father, Jacob, admonished them, but they felt justified. They said, 'Should he have treated our sister like a prostitute?' (v.31).

The story stands on its own in Genesis, with no apparent connection to what precedes it or what follows it. Dinah is not mentioned again in the Bible, except as a name in a genealogy (Genesis 46:15). What can we learn from the unpleasant account?

First, since this story is recorded in Scripture, we learn again that God sees, and it matters. He sees this abused, apparently insignificant woman, and he sees the men who desire her, abuse her, and fight over her.

Dinah is, I would suggest, treated more as an object than as a person. Perhaps Shechem did genuinely love her. Perhaps he recognised her personhood after he had raped her. Yet such recognition would surely have led to repentance, and repentance is not mentioned. Rather, having grabbed her, he wanted to keep her, and seems to have kept her in his home during the marriage negotiations. There is no record of him or anyone else asking her what *she* wanted.

The brothers might appear to be more caring towards her: they fought for her, didn't they? Yet there is no mention of concern for her as a person. They do not go to her and comfort her, but wait until they can take their revenge on the rapist. Whence, then, their wrath? The clue is in verse 7:

> They were filled with grief and fury, because Shechem had done a disgraceful thing in (or against) Israel by lying with Jacob's daughter — a thing that should not be done.

Israel was the name given by God to Jacob, and only then the name of the nation that sprang from his descendants. The outrage was not so much the hurt done to Dinah as the disgrace brought to the family. The question is that of family honour being invested in the chastity of its females;

194

and this far outweighs the honourable (or dishonourable) behaviour of the males. Jacob's sons, it seems, felt justified in defending their family honour even by deceit and murder. Their sister's welfare was only incidental: her significance was as a piece of family property which had been violated. In the world-gone-wrong, Dinah is yet another woman who is dominated by men, and whose personhood is submerged in a male-dominated society.

195

Tamar (Genesis 38)

Tamar also had problems. She was the daughter-in-law of Judah, one of Jacob's sons:

> Judah got a wife for Er, his firstborn, and her name was Tamar. But Er, Judah's firstborn, was wicked in the Lord's sight; so the Lord put him to death. Then Judah said to Onan (his second son), 'Lie with your brother's wife and fulfill your duty as her brother-in-law to produce off-spring for your brother. But Onan knew that the offspring would not be his; so whenever he lay with his brother's wife, he spilled his semen on the ground to keep from producing offspring for his brother. What he did was wicked in the Lord's sight; so he put him to death also. Judah then said to his daughter-in-law Tamar, 'Live as a widow in your father's house until my son Shelah grows up.' For he thought, 'He may die too, just like his brothers' (Genesis 38:6–11).

Already we see the world-gone-wrong pattern. Tamar is not consulted, and there is no record of what she thinks. Rather, she is to be used as her father-in-law sees fit, following the custom that a man who dies without offspring should have his line continued through the union of his wife and his brother.[28] As the story continues, it seems that Tamar was compliant, and that she expected to marry the younger son in due course. Women were, after all, dependent on male relatives in that society, and widowhood was only expected to be a temporary condition.

196   What goes wrong is that her father-in-law, Judah, is afraid of marrying her to his youngest son, and many years pass by with Tamar in her parents' home and Shelah unmarried. It is a case of the woman getting the blame again: while Genesis clearly states that the death of the two men was due to their wickedness, Judah fears that it is Tamar's influence that has killed them. He withholds his youngest son out of fear that he, too may die.

The story continues: Judah is widowed, and takes some time to get over his grief. When he is feeling better, he goes to visit a friend and, on the way home, feels the need to use a prostitute. What he doesn't realise is that his daughter-in-law, Tamar, despairing of his ever giving her her rightful husband, has dressed up as a prostitute and deliberately put herself in front of him. He sleeps with her, and gives her his seal and his staff as pledge of payment that is to be sent to her later. When the payment is sent, the prostitute is not to be found. In due course, Tamar is found to be pregnant. Judah is horrified, and judges that she should be burnt to death.[29] She brings out the seal and staff, and Judah recognises them and says

> She is more righteous than I, since I wouldn't give her my son Shelah (v: 26).

Tamar has, he understands, been under enormous pressure because of her lack of children. Once again we see the pattern of women needing to produce heirs — preferably male — to establish their worth and identity. He also recognises his own fault, in keeping her dependent and without a husband. Perhaps he even recognises the irony that he used a prostitute without compunction, but was willing to sentence his own daughter-in-law to death for a similar act. Once again, we have the stress on female chastity and a different standard for men.

We also have hope: the man recognises his guilt, and treats the woman with dignity. Genesis tells us that he did not sleep with her again (v: 27), but he did own the children that he had fathered. God gave Tamar a double blessing: she bore twins, and from one of them was descended King David and all the royal house of Israel. Tamar has the honour of being one of the few women included in the genealogies of the Jewish people (Ruth 4:12; 1 Chron. 2:4), and in the genealogy of the Lord Jesus Christ in Matthew 1:3.

Potiphar's wife (Genesis 39)

The story of Tamar is an interruption in the story of Joseph. It comes just after Joseph has been sold to Pharoah's official, Potiphar, in Egypt. It is immediately fol-lowed by Joseph's adventure with Potiphar's wife.[30]

He becomes a much-trusted servant, entrusted with all the household affairs, and God blesses all his en-deavours, but:

> After a while his master's wife took notice of Joseph and said, 'Come to bed with me!' (Genesis 39:7).

He refuses: she persists, day after day after day. Eventually, she approaches him when the house is empty and grabs hold of his cloak. He runs, and she retains the cloak. When her husband comes home, she accuses Joseph of trying to rape her, and he is put into prison. Nothing more is heard of her, or of Potiphar.

198

What do we learn from this unnamed woman? She is, I think, a deliberate contrast with Tamar. Where Tamar seduces Judah out of desperation and to continue her husband's line, Potiphar's wife attempts to seduce Joseph because of her own infatuation and in defiance of her husband. Where Judah has to recognise that Tamar is more righteous than he, Joseph is clearly more righteous than his mistress. Where Judah indulges himself with a prostitute, Joseph resists protracted sexual temptation. Perhaps most importantly, where Tamar is a powerless woman dependent on men, Potiphar's wife is in a position of influence and has power over Joseph.

It is not only women who can be dependent and exploited; and women are just as capable as men of misusing power, if only they can attain it.

What do we learn?

Many Muslim writers mention these biblical stories with horror. They demean the prophets, they say. It is not fitting for a sacred text to describe such wickedness in detail, they suppose. And, since the stories are often told without any explicit discussion of how we are to judge the events, some even suggest that Genesis implies that God approves of them, and therefore demeans God himself!

Christian readers understand their Book quite differently. We believe that it describes the world as it is — in all its mess. Women can be glad that the Bible recognises their problems. It understands that they are often dependent and exploited. It records the agony of barrenness in a culture that judges a woman's worth by her fertility. It sees the jealousies of a polygamous marriage. It acknowledges the way that family honour can be invested in the chastity of women, while the unchastity of men is condoned. It also refuses to present women only as innocent victims: they are described as active, scheming, and, where they have power, sometimes using it to oppress dependents — both male and female.

If the Bible acknowledges all this, it implies that God sees it too. And the hints we have in Genesis show us that he does not like it. Again and again, he intervenes on behalf of the exploited. He speaks to Pharoah and to Abimelech on Sarah's behalf. He sends his angel to Hagar and provides for her and her son. He sees the unloved Leah and gives her children. He gives children to Tamar, and Judah admits his unrighteousness. There is hope!

4.4 How does it work out?

From this Genesis picture, the common predicament of women described at the beginning of this chapter is but to be expected. Human beings have gone wrong, and, as part of that going wrong, relationships between men and women have gone wrong. Where God made us together 'in his image', we tend to move apart. Where he gave us joint responsibility for caring for the earth and having children, we tend to divide our roles so that men do not help with the upbringing of children and women do not help with the care of the earth. Where he made us mutually dependent, the balance has shifted so that women tend to be dependent on men. Where he gave us joint domination over the earth, men tend to exert wrong domination over women. And, where we are all sinful and culpable, we all tend to blame other people, and, in particular, women tend to get blamed for everything. The 'mess' is universal.

The reader may have noticed the strong parallels between the women of Genesis and the predicaments described by the Muslim feminists in Ch. 2 above. There is the ownership and exploitation of sexuality, the problems resulting from concubinage and polygamy, the dependence of women on men to arrange their marriages, the family honour being bound up in female chastity, and the necessity for women to be married and bear children. The culture of Genesis is much closer to most Muslim cultures than it is to the West; but the patterns of blame, domination, dependency and role division can be found in the West, although they might take different forms.

There are laws in Britain which seek to curb some of these patterns: men and women are equally protected by law and have equal rights as witnesses; women are entitled to earn money and to receive state benefits; discrimination on the grounds of gender is illegal; and personal violence against women, even by the husband, is a criminal offence. However, access to these freedoms is by choice and can be limited by family power structures, so that the patterns still emerge. Amongst the white community, they are often most obvious in poorer areas, or in places where few people are active Christians. Elswick, where I live, has both characteristics.

It is one of the most deprived areas in the UK.[31] Everywhere we look, we see evidence that the world has gone wrong — in rubbish, vandalism, boarded-up and burnt-out houses, and young children playing unsupervised in the streets. We suffer high rates of crime, and there are increasing problems of drug and alcohol abuse.

Although there are large churches nearby, very few people in our parish[32] attend them, and the local parish church has an electoral roll of only 24. It is the only place of Christian worship within the parish boundaries.

Elswick is very mixed, with Muslims from rural Bangladesh and Pakistan living alongside overseas student families, elderly white residents and younger white families. Some get on well together, but there is plenty of racial harassment, and occasional outbursts of violence.

Over the years, I have met many women who are struggling valiantly to bring up their children in this area. They share the common 'mess', but the different aspects of it affect them in different ways.

> *Ruby's household was miserable again. Three of her five children had overslept and not gone to school, so they were watching the television and annoying each other. The oldest boy had gone an hour late, but the school had rung to say he had not turned up — he was truanting again. The husband was lying on the settee, fast asleep. And Ruby? In the midst of it all, she was quietly and determinedly doing the housework: vacuuming the floor, chopping the vegetables, washing the interminable piles of clothes.*

She stopped, and showed me her bruises from last night. Once again, her husband had come in, drunk and angry, at 2 a.m. Once again, he had woken the household, demanding his dinner and his marital rights. When she had objected, he had turned first on her, and then on the eldest boy who had stood up to him. He had then shouted at his teenage daughter, accusing her of everything he could think of from prostitution to drug abuse, and finally fallen asleep to leave his family to whatever night's rest they could manage.

Ruby is *dominated* by her husband. He is stronger than her and louder than her, and her whole life is dominated by her fear of him and her attempts to protect her children from the worst results of living in such a household.

Ruby is *dependent* on her husband. He earns the money, and she can do little without his permission. The whole family's happiness is dependent on his mood of the moment and how much he drank last might.

Ruby and her husband have very clear *roles* in the family. It is for him to manage the finances and exert his authority over the family, and it is for her to keep the house, care for the children and be available to provide him with food, comfort and sex whenever he requires them.

Ruby's husband *blames* her for his problems and the problems that are emerging in the childrens' lives. She does not look after them properly, he says, or they would not be late for school or truant. She is to blame for any violence he exhibits, because she angers him: she complains about feeding him on demand at two o'clock in the morning, she sometimes refuses to sleep with him, and anyway she is lazy and does not keep the house as clean as he likes it. Besides which, he says, she is stupid, and so were her parents before her.

So, Ruby's husband feels that he can treat her as he likes. After all, she is 'his': *she belongs to him.*

If Ruby were white, she would probably have left her husband by now. She would have set up her own home with her children, with the help of social services, and her husband would have only occasional, supervised access to the children. Or perhaps she would have 'given as good as she got': she would have opposed him from the early stages of the marriage. She would not have been meekly doing the housework, but sleeping herself, having woken the whole neighbourhood by shouting back at him when he arrived at 2 a.m., and perhaps had the police in to sort it all out. She might, of course, have stayed with him, whether out of fear or out of loyalty to him or to the children, but in that case she would probably have other women in similar situations to talk to. In one way or another, she would probably be fighting back.

There are many white 'Rubys', but this particular one happens to be a Muslim, from a traditional rural community, living in Britain. Her background limits her choices.

Should she leave her husband? She often toys with the idea. She can't imagine divorcing him, although she knows it is possible according to British law — she wants to be faithful to Islam, and knows only that the right to divorce lies with her husband. But perhaps she could go away, and take the children with her. 'If not, I might kill him one day', she says.

Then she considers:

'What about my children? People would say I was a bad woman to leave him. They would say my children were bad. Who would marry my daughter?'

'Who would help me? I have no brother or uncle or father in this country. My sister is here, but her husband would not let her help me.'

'How could I manage? My husband has always looked after the money and paid the bills and done the shopping. I can't even speak English properly. He never wanted me to learn, and now I have too many worries to be able to think.'

'He might come after me. Then things would be even worse.'

'I know another woman who left her husband. All the men think they can visit her now. All the women say bad things about her. I don't want to be like that.'

Should she stay? Perhaps there are ways of making life more bearable? What about her husband's parents and brothers: don't they know what is happening? Can't they help?

'They know a bit, but I'm ashamed to tell them more. They know what their brother is like, but he's their brother: they won't do anything that lets outsiders know too — they have to keep the family honour. Anyway, they think it's all my fault. If I were a better wife, he would not be like this.'

What about calling social services? What he's doing is against the law in this country. Or what about asking my friend's husband to talk to him? He's not from your community, and he has helped many families with problems like these.

'That would bring shame on him, and he'd be angry. He'd know I had told someone. Life would be even worse.'

Is there a religious leader who might challenge him?

'It would be the same. Anyway, they would probably just say I'm not a good wife.'

Eventually, I talk to her husband. His response:

'You don't understand. I'm a man. I'm a Muslim. She's my wife. She doesn't give me what I want.'

4.5 The Pattern in Elswick

Marriage

Maryam had been married for ten years and still had no children. Her husband refused to divorce her, despite the advice of some of his Muslim friends, and they decided to adopt. He encouraged her to earn money by taking in sewing, and helped her to care for the child. When she had to go into hospital for a hysterectomy, he took leave so that he could cook and clean and take the child to school. When she came home, he continued to care for her. Now, they share the running of a newly-aquired shop, and are proud of their intelligent and charming son.

Mary too was unable to have children. They were Christians, and neither even considered divorce. They too decided to adopt, and took into their family a baby with some brain damage. Mary then developed multiple schlerosis. Through it all, her husband supported her, cared for her, helped her and could always be relied upon to clean, cook, shop and take care of the child. Now, Mary is no longer able to do the housework, but they continue cheerfully and their son, though handicapped, is a great joy to them and their friends.

Good marriage relationships do exist in all communities in Elswick, but they are few. In the white community, decreasing numbers of people make the commitment of marriage, many choosing instead to live together in serial 'common law' monogamy. An indication of the unpopularity of marriage is that there were only six weddings at the local church in the period 1990–6, three being those of the vicar's daughters. In 1984, there were 10 weddings.

Often, the father is absent from the home: for a child to be living in the same house as both his or her parents is becoming the exception rather than the rule. One survey estimated that 22.8% of the children live in homes with only one adult[33] and approximately 20% of babies baptised at the local church have no father's name in the register. The church school catchment area has 637 households with dependent children and 216 lone parents, all but nine of the latter being women.[34]

In the Asian community, almost everyone gets married, and divorce and separation are relatively rare. However, as Elswick caters for the poorer members of the community, it is a place to which several women who have had to leave their husbands have come. Although there are some happy marriage relationships, there are others where there appears to be little communication between the partners, and the wife is subject to her husband's demands. Further, despite religious prohibition, alcohol and gambling can be as problematic for Muslims as for others; and in all cases I have observed locally, it is the husband who is caught up in them but the wife and children who have to bear most of the consequences.

However, one reason for lack of mutuality in Asian marriages seems to be the understanding of marriage on which they are built. Whereas the Genesis order is that the man should leave his family and give precedence to his wife, Islamic custom is generally that the wife should leave her family and join her husband's.[35] There is also traditional teaching about the mother-son bond discussed by Mernissi (see Ch. 2). While there are positive results of this, especially in the care of the elderly, it can lead to a young wife's being isolated within her own home: much can depend on the attitude of her mother-in-law.

Further, the husband-wife relationship is seldom perceived as friendship. Marriage is a contract between two families rather than a covenant between two people. While the Qur'an lays out the rights and responsibilities of both partners (e.g. Surah 4: 19, 34, 128–9), they do not necessarily involve the unity of mind and spirit as well as body envisaged in Genesis 2:23–4.[36]

Of course, expectations of marriage are determined by culture and personality as well as by religion,[37] and many of the younger Muslims have absorbed some western and romantic views. These can produce tensions, especially if not reciprocated by their spouses. In Elswick, it is still common for parents to seek spouses in their countries of origin. This can produce not only clashes in understanding, but also extended separation while the immigration department turns its slow wheels.[38]

Blame

The blaming of women is also characteristic of both white and Asian communities. Although most of the white community organisations are run by women, and they are usually the ones who stay with their children and bring them up, it is not uncommon to find the blame for a child's behaviour laid on the mother. This is particularly so if the mother is single, despite the fact that it is usually the father who is absent. A frequently heard comment on delinquent behaviour is, 'I blame the mothers.' It is less frequent that one hears, 'I blame the parents,' and I can recall only one person who said, 'I blame the fathers.'

In the Asian communities, any straying of husband or children is likely to be blamed on the wife. The idea seems to be that, if she were a good wife, her husband would not go astray. If her husband divorces her, the assumption is likely to be that it was her fault. If she leaves him, for whatever reason, she is in danger of being labelled 'bad', with unpleasant results for both herself and her children if they remain with her.

Childbearing

In the Muslim communities, and especially amongst the Bangladeshis, women are expected to have many children, and husbands are often opposed to contraception. They may perceive this opposition as Islamic, although this is by no means agreed by the religious authorities.[39] Whatever the basis, the result is that women may be pushed into deceiving their husbands. Others are worn out with bearing and caring for children from an early age,[40] and the 1991 census figures show very large proportions of children in the Muslim communities — 46% of Pakistanis and 48% of Bangladeshis but only 19% of whites were under 16.

Role divisions

Both white and Asian communities have strong ideas about male and female roles, but there are important differences.

Amongst the whites, women look after the children and the home, while men go out to work and earn money. There is also division over the sorts of jobs that are done in the home: women do sewing, washing, shopping, cleaning, cooking, and craft work. Men do repairs, plumbing, anything electrical, most decorating and heavy gardening. However, these roles are slowly changing. While the 'hard'[41] men will not readily do what they regard as 'women's work', circumstances are forcing many to re-think.

The general ethos of society is moving more towards the idea of partnership, and women are seeing that they can do things that have traditionally been the province of men. Men are therefore sharing more of the household chores, and most women are able to decorate, change plugs and do basic DIY. Increasing numbers of men are present at the births of their children, and are even willing to change nappies.

In Elswick, such changes are encouraged by the employment situation. The woman may be earning while the man is unemployed, so that there is no choice but for him to care for the children and the home. Where men are employed, wages are often so low that women also need to seek at least part-time work. The household duties must therefore, again, be shared.

In the Bangladeshi and Pakistani communities, the role division is not so much between caring for children and home and earning money as between public and domestic duties. There is some overlap here with divisions in the white community, since, for example, much child-care is done in the home, and much wage-earning is done outside it. However, there are important differences.

210   While shopping is usually the job of white women, it is usually the job of the Muslim men. They might also be expected to negotiate with schools, to take children to clinics, and to buy the family's clothes: all this is tradition-ally 'women's work' for the whites. On the other hand, the women are likely to be the ones to do the gardening and the decorating, which are traditonally men's jobs in the white community.

While this pattern can increase the dependency of the Muslim women by confining them to their homes so that they are unable to negotiate with the outside world, it can ease the situation in case of unemployment. A white man without a job can rapidly feel redundant as a person, since his major role of earning money has been lost. A Muslim man will still have control of whatever income his family may have, and will continue his roles outside the house.

Dependence and domination

Amongst Asians, the dependency-domination pattern is seen vividly in the lives of Bangladeshi women, and rather less so in Pakistani homes. While some women in both communities are the dominant powers in their house-holds, this does not generally happen until they become mothers-in-law. Where it does happen earlier, it may be because the husband is absent or inadequate, and the wife or daughter is forced to take on much of his traditional role.

Dependency of women is inscribed into the local Bangladeshi culture. Traditionally, women are not expected to be active outside their homes, and are entirely dependent on their men for finances and negotiations with representatives of outside organisations. The men even do the shopping. Typically, a new wife will leave her parental home and live with her husband's family, where she will be expected to prove herself in cooking and other household chores. She will have little opportunity to go out except for occasional visits to her own mother until she becomes a mother herself. All her activities must be approved by her husband, and usually also by her mother-in-law. Pakistani families follow a similar pattern, but women are usually more assertive and active outside the home.[42] This is partly because the community is more mixed, partly because it is longer established, and partly because of cultural differences.

The patterns described are generalisations, and there are many exceptions and variations. However, women are often left very dependent on their male relatives. The sudden absence of a husband due to death or an extended visit to the country of origin can leave them helpless or dependent on neighbours or children if there are no other responsible male relatives. More seriously, the alternative of separation from a violent or abusive husband becomes unthinkable, not only because of the resultant stigma but also because of the fear of being unable to cope.

Domination is the corollary of dependence. While some husbands are sensitive and respectful towards their wives, others enjoy their power over them. Inadequate husbands in particular may compensate by exerting their authority at home. Some claim that Islam gives them the right to demand obedience of their wives and punish them if they do not comply. Their physical strength combined with their position as 'husband' makes it difficult for the wife to do anything but submit.

The domination–dependency pattern can also be seen in the white community.[43] Men dominate 'their' women to varying degrees and by various methods — from persuasion, through emotional blackmail to mental or even physical violence. A typical way of getting one's own way is the 'tit for tat' method. The man gives 'permission' for his woman to do something provided that he can do something else that he wants.

Some men seem to feel at ease only when they see themselves as in control, and want to ensure that their women act only with their 'permission'. This results in women feeling unable to act without their man's approval. They suffer belittling of their characters and importance, undermining of their self-worth and breaking of their confidence. In cases of violence, many stay with an abusive partner out of fear. They have heard of cases where a man has gone after a woman who has deserted him, and she has suffered worse than before.

All this can be linked with a dependency on men, but this varies greatly. Some women see the man's role as providing for them practically, financially and emotionally, and, where the man agrees, a good partnership can be worked out.

In white families like Ruby's, where men seek un-balanced domination, various responses can be seen. Some women are cowed into dependency and submission. Some simply leave. Others are able to 'give as good as they get'. They stand up against all odds, and seem as 'hard'as their men. It is such partnerships that result in continual fight-ing, problems between neighbours and the need to call the police to settle domestic disputes. In general, however, most women are able to discuss their problems, and to give each other a great deal of the emotional support that they lack from their spouses. Few men have such suppor-tive networks, and admitting emotional needs would destroy their 'hard' image.

Financial dependency is not so much of a problem for white women as for Asian women, and is not so much of a problem as it was even a few years ago. This is partly because of changing employment patterns, and partly because of changes in state benefits. It is often easier for women than for men to find work, and some state benefits are now payable to the female rather than the male partner. This ensures that women have direct access to at least some of the family income. The same things are true for Asian families, but because women are often less familiar with the system than are men, their husbands may be able to cash benefits and to keep total financial control.

The importance of women

Non-Muslim as well as Muslim women in Elswick are subjected to blame, dependence and domination: this chapter has argued that the problems are not due to religion as such, but to sin. Religious and social systems are merely instruments of our sinfulness. However, Muslim women in Elswick often have heightened difficulties because of culture; and their cultures are at least perceived as Islamic. In addition, many have been dis-located into a cultural context which they experience as alien and often hostile, and in which coping mechanisms from their original culture are inadequate.

Women may find life particularly difficult because of the sharp differences between expectations of them at home and in the wider British community, as well as the basic problems of adjusting to different ways of washing, dressing, cooking, cleaning and looking after children. The cultural and environmental differences between home and school, village and town, Pakistan or Bangladesh and England add to the plight of local Muslim women. The great challenge to the communities is to re-build identity in their new context.[44]

Despite all the difficulties described above, it is largely the women who are the main carriers of culture and faith, and on whom this responsibility will rest. Campbell's analysis[45] suggests that it is women who hold the white community together, and who hold their men back from criminality. Shaw's study[46] shows that it was only when wives started arriving in Oxford that the Pakistani community there began to take its religion and cultural origins seriously.

Women may be dominated and dependent, but Genesis also teaches that men cannot manage without them (2:18). That women in Elswick should be able to fulfil their purposes in family and community is of the first importance to everyone. All the communities share the 'mess': the welfare of men and women alike depends on clearing it up.

Notes

1. A. Al-Hibri, 'A study of Islamic herstory: or, how did we get into this mess?', in A. Al-Hibri (ed.), *Women and Islam*, pp. 207–20.
2. N. Atiya, *Khul-Khaal*.
3. *Creation and Fall and the Women of Bangladesh*, pp. 9–13.
4. See for example part two of El Saadawi's *The Hidden Face of Eve*, which traces oppression through the Judaeo-Christian system as well as traditional Egyptian religion. Christian feminist treatments of the subject include E. Fiorenza, *In Memory of Her: A Feminist Theological Reconstruction of Christian Origins*, 1983, and R. Ruether, *Religion and Sexism*, 1974. A historical account that explores positives as well as negatives can be found in B.J. MacHaffie, *Her Story: Women in Christian Tradition*, 1986.
5. I would want to distinguish here between 'western' and 'Christian', since the two are by no means synonymous. The West has been deeply influenced by the Christian tradition, but there have been many other influences (e.g. those of classical Greece and Rome), and many consciously anti-Christian trends can be seen in it. Similarly, Christianity has been deeply influenced by the fact of its power in the West since Constantine, but it has not been confined to the West, and is Middle Eastern in its origins. There are churches in India, the Middle East and North Africa which pre-date the western churches, and in the twentieth century there are more Christians in the South and the East than in the North and the West.
6. This is in contrast with classical Muslim beliefs about the Qur'an. While the Bible is believed to have been written by human beings through the Holy Spirit of God, the Qur'an is believed to have been written in heaven from eternity and thence to have been dictated to a human being. The Bible is therefore read as

coming out of a culture, while the Qur'an is read as coming into a culture.

7. I have chosen to explore this rather than the role of women in public worship and church leadership because the latter questions seldom seem to arise for Muslims. There are a few discussions about the possibility of women taking political leadership (see, for example, Mernissi's work reviewed in Ch. 3.2), but, because of the separation of the sexes, women and men have usually worshipped separately, and women usually worship at home rather than in the mosque. Napoleon will discuss the passages on public worship in Pt. 4.2.

8. She is quoting here (p. 74) from M. Barth, *Ephesians*, Anchor Bible, New York: Doubleday, 1974, pp. 614, 618.

9. From J. and P. Alsdurf, *Battered into Submission*, p. 13. The book gives a disturbing analysis of wife abuse in professing Christian homes in the USA.

10. These are other passages which have often been used to keep women in subjection, but in the church rather than in the home. They are discussed at length by both Hurley and Evans, who, not surprisingly, come to different conclusions about them. An interesting treatment of them can be found in M. Hayter, *The New Eve in Christ: The Use and Abuse of the Bible in the Debate about Women in the Church*, 1987.

11. M. Barton, *Creation and Fall and the Women of Bangladesh*, p. 13.

12. And elsewhere in the Bible!

13. The most frequent use of the word in the Old Testament is to describe God as the helper of human beings, e.g. Psalms 30:10; 54:4.

14. The whole text of this chapter can be found in the Appendix, pp. 319f.

15. See pp. 12–13, Ch. 2 above.

16. It is important here that the blame should have fallen on both, and that the woman was no better than the man at admitting her responsibility — she blamed the serpent. Just because male interpreters have propagated the blaming of women, female interpreters need not 'turn the tables' by blaming men. The story warns that no human being likes to take responsibility for

disobedience to God, while God's pronouncements in vv.14–19 make it clear that each protagonist must bear the consequences of his or her action. As male and female share equal dignity, they share equal liability.

17. See, for example, Westermann, *Genesis 1–11*, pp. 262, 300 and Wenham, *Genesis 1–15*, pp. 81–2.

18. J. Calvin, *Genesis*, London: Banner of Truth, 1965 reprint, p. 172.

19. For example, Wenham, op. cit., pp. 70, 81.

20. See, for example, Genesis 5; 1 Chronicles 1–9.

21. Westermann (op. cit.) notes it but says that there is no good reason why the mother is the namer in v. 25 while the father is the namer in v. 26. On the other hand, neither does he make anything of its being Adam who names Eve.

22. See Numbers 13:33, where they are also called the sons of Anak, who are referred to in Deuteronomy 2:10 and 9:2, and Joshua 11:21–2 and 14:12. These were giants, and enemies of Israel.

23. She is not yet called Sarah (princess), but Sarai (perhaps meaning 'contentious'), and Abraham (father of many) is still called Abram (exalted father). Their names will be changed in Genesis 17, when God forms the covenant with Abraham and promises to give him many descendants through Sarah. For convenience, I shall refer to them as Abraham and Sarah throughout.

24. According to the Genesis version, the angel asks why Sarah laughs, and she denies it. The implication seems to be that she, and Abraham before her, doubted the promise. The Qur'an (11:71 and 51:29) has neither Sarah's denial nor Abraham's laughter; and most commentators insist that Sarah's laugh was not a sign of unbelief but of amusement or joy.

25. 1 Peter 3:5–6.

26. It is believed that she ran between the two hills Safa and Marwah looking for water for her son, and that the well of Zamzam, from which pilgrims bring water after the Hajj, was the one that God opened for her. These happenings are commemorated in the Hajj.

27. That is, only one daughter is mentioned, and that because there is a story about her. There may have been other daughters.

28. See Deuteronomy 25:5–6, but notice that this is followed by a discussion of what should happen if the brother is not willing to comply. It seems to be assumed that this practice is for the good of the wife as well as the deceased brother. The custom is still followed in some places e.g. amongst some of the Christians in Pakistan.

218 29. No such punishment is suggested elsewhere in the Bible.

30. The wife of Joseph's master is given more space in the Qur'an than any woman other than Mary, the mother of Jesus. The story of Joseph is the most detailed and coherent in the Qur'an, taking the whole of Surah 12. Its plot is very similar to that of the Genesis version, but with a much greater focus on the relationship between Joseph and his mistress. She is not named, and appears in a much better light than in Genesis. When she snatches Joseph's cloak, the other servants notice that it is torn from the back, and conclude that he was running away from her, so his master accepts his innocence. The gossip about the incident goes around, and she invites other women to meet Joseph so that they can see how amazingly handsome he is. When they see him, they cut themselves with their fruit knives in consternation, and start to pester him themselves. He chooses to go to prison rather than putting up with their advances. After he is released, she repents and turns to God.

In popular and Sufi thinking, the story has given rise to one of the greatest allegorical love stories in Islamic literature, with versions in many Muslim languages. The woman is called Zulaikha, and is an eastern princess. She dreams of Joseph, who says he is the *wazir* of Egypt. She gets her father to arrange her marriage with the *wazir*, the marriage occurs, and then she finds out that he is a eunuch. Eventually, Joseph appears on the scene, and the above story ensues. By the time Joseph emerges from prison, the *wazir* has died and Zulaikha has lost her youth and her beauty; but her impure love has been purified. Joseph prays for her, her beauty is restored, and 'they are married in pure and true love. Even so, their love was not perfect until they united their hearts in pure worship to God.' (Yusuf Ali, p. 599)

31. At the last census (1991), our parish was, on the Church of England's statistical deprivation indicator, the second poorest in the diocese, which is one of the poorest in the country. We scored 17.5, where 0 is the national average and 8 indicates deprivation. The next-door parish scored 17.6.

32. St Paul's, High Elswick.

33. This is for an area larger than Elswick. See City Challenge Report.

34. See St Paul's School Development Project *Survey Report*.

35. As actually happened to most of the Genesis women!

36. Doi's description of marriage (*Shari'ah: the Islamic Law*, p. 117) includes procreation, sexual and emotional gratification, piety, social placement and family alliance, but does not specifically mention companionship.

37. For a comparison of marriage expectation between two different Muslim communities in the same area of London, see H. Summerfield in Buijs, *Migrant Women*.

38. Noreen Hussain's piece in Ahmad and Raychaudhuri, *Daughters of the East* (pp. 51–3) offers thoughts on the selection of marriage partners from a Muslim woman in West Newcastle.

39. There are various opinions on the legitimacy of contraception within Islam. Musallam (*Sex and Society in Islam*) compares positive Islamic and negative Christian attitudes to birth control through the Middle Ages. Abdalati (*Family Structure in Islam*) (pp. 211–4) asserts that Islam permits birth control, but Maududi is of the opposite opinion.

40. Bangladeshi girls are usually married within a year of leaving school at 16, although some are allowed to continue in eduation. Many of the women who were brought up in Bangladesh married earlier. The present generation of Pakistani girls marry somewhat later, and several in the locality have gone on to further or higher education.

41. 'Hardness' is a characteristic much admired by many in Elswick. It means an ability to cope with all sorts of difficulties and pains without flinching, and usually implies a denial of the 'softer' emotions.

42. In the 1991 census, 25.4% of Pakistani women over 16 were economically active, compared to 17.8% of Bangladeshi women and 43.8% of white women. But the Tyneside Womens Employment Project (*Against the Odds*, 1991) found that 90% of Bangladeshi women interviewed want paid work.

43. I am indebted to Elaine Frame and Pat Moreland for this analysis, and for some of the ideas on role divisions in the white community above.

44. See, for example, J. Nielsen, 'Muslims in Britain: searching for identity' in *New Community*, Vol. 13 No.3 1987, pp. 384–94.

45. *Goliath: Britain's Dangerous Places*.

46. *A Pakistani Community in Britain* shows that religious practice for Pakistanis in Oxford was quiescent until the arrival of women.

5

The Jesus pattern

'All communities share the "mess": the welfare of men and women alike depends on clearing it up.' (p. 215 above). But clearing up the mess is not easy. The feminist activity of the past decades has challenged many of the worst practices, but it has often brought its own difficulties. The Genesis analysis suggests that the problem is a radical one, rooted in the very nature of human beings. The solution must therefore also be radical.

The Qur'an and *Hadith* offer patterns of action that can serve to regulate the 'mess'. In this chapter, we turn to the very heart of the Christian faith, to Jesus Christ himself, and only then consider New Testament patterns of action.

5.1 Jesus breaks the cycle

Ida Glaser

> There is neither Jew nor Greek, slave nor free, male nor female, for you are all one in Christ Jesus (Galatians 3:28).

> Husbands, love your wives, just as Christ loved the church
> and gave himself up for her (Galatians 5:27).

The New Testament teaching is that the person who puts
faith in the Lord Jesus Christ is 'in him'. That is, he or she
has a new identity, which is based on a new relationship.
The change is so radical that Jesus described it as being
born a second time:

> I tell you the truth, no-one can see the kingdom of God
> unless he is born again (John 3:3).

Such a change is not, according to Jesus, optional. It is the
radical beginning without which the human 'mess' —
whether with respect to women or otherwise — cannot
be challenged. With it, not only will relationship with
God change: human relationships will also change. In
particular, old distinctions of status will be removed, and
we will treat people in the same way that Jesus treated
them.

That is not to say that we will copy Jesus' ways in
eating, dressing, speaking, washing or even, unless God so
calls us, in celibacy. Rather, we will have the attitudes that
he had, and seek to apply them in our different situations
for the benefit of other people. This is summed up in the
idea that we should love others as he loves us. This, Jesus
said, is a general commandment which applies to relationships with all human beings:[1] the above quotation from St
Paul is an application of the commandment in the particular context of marriage.

This is the centre of all New Testament teaching
about behaviour. To understand its teaching about

women, then, we need to start by looking at Jesus'
relationships with them.

The Gospels are about the life and teaching of Jesus,
and contain hardly any direct teaching about women. Yet,
as I read them, I again and again see Jesus tacitly challenging the prejudices of his day concerning women, as well
as those concerning many other injustices amongst his
people.

Here, I want to explore how Jesus quietly reversed
the position of women. The Old Testament acknowledges
that they are blamed, dependent and dominated, and that
they are exploited because of sharp role divisions between
the genders. It shows that God sees this and cares, and
sometimes it offers rules that limit the damage. The
Gospels show us Jesus challenging fundamental assumptions, and breaking the cycle of male domination.

Role division

First century Palestine tended to divide male and female
roles as clearly as any traditional Muslim society.[2] The
religious leaders respected women in their own sphere —
that is, as wives and mothers, but did not expect them to
study, to take active parts in synagogue services, or to be
involved in public life. They were only admitted into the
outer courts of the temple, and their value as witnesses in
courts of law was that of a slave.

In contrast, in Luke's Gospel alone we see women
receiving messages from angels (2:26–38), composing
songs of worship (2:46–55), prophesying (2:36–38),
healed (4:39, 8:40–56, 13:10–17), used as examples of

faith (4:25–6, 7:36–50, 21:1–4), listening to Jesus' teaching (10:38–42), accompanying Jesus on his journeys (8:1–3), used as characters in parables (15:8–10, 18:1–8), following Jesus to the cross (23:27), and being the first witnesses to the resurrection (24:1–11).

224   That Jesus welcomed the many women who came to him and listened to him is itself indicative of his breaking of the mould. One incident serves as a paradigm:

> As Jesus and his disciples were on their way, he came to a village where a woman named Martha opened her home to him. She had a sister called Mary, who sat at the Lord's feet listening to what he said. But Martha was distracted by all the preparations that had to be made. She came to him and asked, 'Lord, don't you care that my sister has left me to do all the work by myself? Tell her to help me.'
>
> 'Martha, Martha,' the Lord answered, 'you are worried and upset about many things, but only one thing is needed. Mary has chosen what is better, and it will not be taken away from her' (Luke 10:38–42).

This has often been read as a story that teaches the general importance of being with Jesus and listening to his teaching. However, it takes on a new dimension when it is realised that this is a story about two *women*, and that it comes immediately after the parable of the Good Samaritan, with its challenge about racial prejudice. It becomes obvious that Mary is a woman who has neglected her female domestic role, and has slipped in with the men to listen to the religious teacher.

      Understandably, Martha expects Jesus to send her back to her job, and perhaps Mary expects it too. Jesus affirms Mary's choice: it is not necessary that the woman returns to the kitchen. The one thing that is needed — listening to Jesus — should be the priority for her as well as for the men.

Is Jesus saying that the traditional woman's role is an inferior one, and that the way forward for women is to take on traditional male roles instead? I think not, for Jesus himself sometimes did jobs that would traditionally have been done by women, and even by slaves.

He cooked the breakfast (John 21:8–12), he welcomed children (Luke 18:15–17): he even washed his disciples' feet (John 13:1–17), and he taught:

> Now that I, your Lord and Teacher, have washed your feet, you also should wash one another's feet. I have set you an example that you should do as I have done for you (John 13:14–15).

By his life as well as his teaching, Jesus affirmed the work of self-giving and serving others, and challenged those who wanted status and authority.

> You know that the rulers of the Gentiles lord it over them, and their high officials exercise authority over them. Not so with you. Instead, whoever wants to become great among you must be your servant, and whoever wants to be first must be your slave — just as the Son of Man did not come to be served, but to serve, and to give his life as a ransom for many (Matthew 20:25–28).

Jesus encouraged women to take part in traditionally male activities, but he did not encourage them to grab power for themselves. Rather, he called everyone — including his male disciples — to serve. Women should not be trapped in domesticity, but this is not because household management is demeaning. Rather, men too should see themselves as servants, for this is what it means to follow Jesus.

Dependency

226

> After this, Jesus travelled about from one town and village to another. proclaiming the good news of the kingdom of God. The Twelve were with him, and also some women who had been cured of evil spirits and diseases: Mary (called Magdalene) from whom seven demons had come out; Joanna the wife of Chuza, the manager of Herod's household; Susanna; and many others. These women were helping to support them out of their own means (Luke 8:1–3).

Mary, of low social status, and Joanna, of high social status, and many other women travelled with Jesus and his disciples. For women to travel with men probably challenged social norms in itself; but we see here another significant challenge. The role of these women was not to be dependent on the men: rather, Jesus and his disciples were dependent on their financial support.

Even in his birth, Jesus, the One whom Christians believe to be God himself come to us, was dependent on a woman. The Almighty could have come in any way that he chose, but the choice he made was to be carried in a woman's body and to be fed by her milk.

Yet the actions of Jesus also recognised the dependency of women in his society, and provided for them. Perhaps the most touching story is that of the widow of Nain, whose only son had died. Jesus saw the funeral procession:

> When the Lord saw her (the widow), his heart went out to her and he said, 'Don't cry.' Then he went up and touched the coffin, and those carrying it stood still. He said, 'Young man, I say to you, get up!' The dead man sat up and began to talk, and Jesus gave him back to his mother (Luke 7:13–15).

227

He understood the need of the woman for a male relative, and, without being asked, supplied her need. This is the more poignant in the light of Jesus' own death. As his widowed mother watched him die, he entrusted her to the care of one his disciples with the famous words from the cross:

> He said to his mother, 'Dear woman, here is your son,' and to the disciple, 'Here is your mother.' From that time on, this disciple took her into his house (John 19:26–27).

What he had done for the widow of Nain he was unable to do for his own mother. Yet he was able to provide for her, and he did so.

Blame

It seems that men in the time of Jesus were liable to blame women rather than men for sexual misconduct. One story (John 8:1–11) illustrates this, and Jesus' reaction to it. He is teaching publically in the temple, and the religious leaders bring a woman who has been caught in the act of adultery. They quote the Mosaic law, that adulterers should be stoned, and ask him whether they should carry it out. John tells us that they were not really wanting his ruling: they were looking for an excuse to accuse him of blasphemy. Jesus did not answer their question, but made them look at their own wrongdoing:

> Jesus bent down and started to write on the ground with his finger. When they kept on questioning him, he straightened up and said to them, 'If any one of you is without sin, let him be the first to throw a stone at her.' Again he stooped down and wrote on the ground.
>
> At this, those who heard began to go away one at a time, the older ones first, until only Jesus was left, with the woman still standing there. Jesus straightened up and asked her, 'Woman, where are they? Has no-one condemned you?' 'No-one, sir', she said. 'Then neither do I condemn you', Jesus declared. 'Go now and leave your life of sin' (John 8:6–11).

Jesus was well known for associating with people whom society labelled as 'sinners', and even had someone who had been a notorious prostitute among his followers. He often did things which were against the law as the religious leaders understood it. He was constantly seeking to show that the law was good, but limited in its purpose. More important was the spirit behind the law — the fundamental call to love God above all things and, as part of that love, to love all other human beings.

In this case, he is teaching and showing that God's greatest concern is not that people be punished for their sins, but that they should turn around, be forgiven, and live new lives. But there is something else here, because the victim of the religious leaders' zeal is a woman.

No-one knows what Jesus was writing on the ground, or why he stooped down. Some suggest that he was writing the great commandments — to love God and neighbour: others think he was merely 'doodling', as he turned away from the distasteful scene. Perhaps he was angry and embarrassed at the way the woman was being publically exposed. Perhaps, in the second instance, he was making the point that the men could recognise their own sin without his pointing at any one of them.

229

What is clear is that, if the woman was caught in the act of adultery, there must have been a man with her. He may even have been in the crowd. Yet, while the Torah makes it clear that both partners to adultery should be punished (Leviticus 20:10, Deuteronomy 22:22), it was only the woman who was blamed and brought for punishment. The religious leaders who accused her were male. Jesus was not only showing that no human being is blameless, but that these men who were blaming a woman were also sinful, and they knew it.

He did not exonerate the woman. Just as the men's sin was wrong, so her sin was wrong. What he did was to act with compassion: to abdicate his right to condemn and judge her, and instead to forgive her. She was to put adultery behind her, and to live a life pleasing to God.

Uncleanness

As in Islam, the Old Testament teaches that a woman is ritually unclean during menstruation and after birth (Leviticus 12; 15:19–24).[3] It even extends this to non-menstrual bleeding:

> When a woman has a discharge of blood for many days at a time other than her monthly period or has a discharge that extends beyond her period, she will be unclean as long as she has the discharge, just as in the days of her period. Any bed she lies on will be unclean, as is her bed

> during her monthly period, and anything she sits on will
> be unclean, as during her monthly period. Whoever
> touches them will be unclean; he must wash his clothes
> and bathe with water, and he will be unclean till evening
> (Leviticus 15:25–27).

230 The book of Leviticus contains many regulations about
ritual cleanliness. Other things that make people unclean
include certain kinds of food (11), skin diseases, especially
leprosy (13:1–45), and mildew (13:47–59). Some of this
makes good hygienic sense, but ritual cleanliness was
primarily an outward symbol of purity for a special group
of people whom God had called for a particular purpose:
that of bringing blessing to the whole world (Genesis
12:1–3). With the coming of Jesus, the special people had
fulfilled its purpose, and these symbols were no longer
necessary.[4]

Jesus saw that many of the religious people of his
time were so concentrating on the outward symbols that
they were forgetting the purity of heart and mind for
which God was primarily looking. He challenged them in
no uncertain terms:

> Woe to you, teachers of the law and Pharisees, you
> hypocrites! You clean the outside of the cup and dish, but
> inside you are full of greed and self-indulgence. Blind
> Pharisee! First cleanse the inside of the cup and dish, and
> then the outside will be clean (Matthew 23:25–26).

On the question of food, he is just as clear:

> Jesus called the crowd to him and said, 'Listen to me,
> everyone, and understand this. Nothing outside a man can
> make him 'unclean' by going into him. Rather, it is what
> comes out of a man that makes him 'unclean'.

After he had left the house, his disciples asked him about this parable. 'Are you so dull?', he asked. 'Don't you see that nothing that enters a man from the outside can make him "unclean"? For it doesn't go into his heart but into his stomach, and then out of his body.' (In saying this, Jesus declared all foods 'clean'.)

He went on: 'What comes out of a man is what makes him "unclean". For from within, out of men's hearts, come evil thoughts, sexual immorality, theft, murder, adultery, greed, malice, deceit, lewdness, envy, slander, arrogance and folly. All these evils come from inside and make a man "unclean" (Mark 7:14–23 (see also Matthew 15:10–20)).

With people suffering from leprosy, Jesus put his teaching into practice: where the religious leaders of his time avoided such people in case they came into touch with them and became polluted, Jesus touched them and healed them (e.g. Mark 1:40–42). He did the same with an 'unclean' woman: one who had been bleeding for no less than twelve years.

As Jesus was on his way, the crowds almost crushed him. And a woman was there who had been subject to bleeding for twelve years, but no one could heal her. She came up behind him and touched the edge of his cloak, and immediately the bleeding stopped.

'Who touched me?' Jesus asked. When they all denied it, Peter said, 'Master, the people are crowding and pressing against you.' But Jesus said, 'Someone has touched me; I know that power has gone out from me.'

Then the woman, seeing that she could not go unnoticed, came trembling and fell at his feet. In the presence of all

> the people, she told why she had touched him and how she had been instantly healed. Then he said to her, 'Daughter, your faith has healed you. Go in peace' (Luke 8:40–49).

232 Why was she trembling? Because, we suppose, she knew that she was 'unclean', and feared a rebuke for touching a 'clean' religious teacher. That was, perhaps, why she touched Jesus in the crowd, and had not come openly to him. He accepts her and reassures her, and she is unclean no more. Jesus will not accept that anything other than sin can make a person unclean and separate them from God and from other people.

And even the uncleanness of open moral sin cannot, in Jesus' eyes, remove a person's humanity and value. The sinner should not be shunned but sought, and offered forgiveness.

> Now one of the Pharisees[5] invited Jesus to have dinner with him, so he went to the Pharisee's house and reclined at the table. When a woman who had lived a sinful life in that town learned that Jesus was eating at the Pharisee's house, she brought an alabaster jar of perfume, and as she stood behind him at his feet weeping, she began to wet his feet with her tears. Then she wiped them with her hair and poured perfume on them (Luke 7:36–38).

Jesus' host was scandalised. Here was a notorious sinner — almost certainly a prostitute — actually touching a religious teacher, and the teacher was allowing her to do so! The Pharisee's conclusion was that Jesus did not realise that the woman was a sinner, and he could therefore not be a prophet. Jesus, however, did know who the woman was, and he also saw what the Pharisee was thinking. So he told a story:

> Two men owed money to a certain money-lender. One owed him five hundred denarii, and the other fifty. Neither of them had the money to pay him back, so he cancelled the debts of both. Now, which of them will love him more? (Luke 7:41–2).

233

The Pharisee gets the right answer: the one who owed more will love more, and Jesus then applies it to the present situation. The Pharisee has not even offered Jesus the standard hospitality of water for footwashing, or greeted him with the customary kiss. The woman has given not only water but her most precious possession, and has stooped to kiss his feet. It is she, and not the Pharisee, who sees the value of what Jesus can give her: like the men who brought to Jesus the woman taken in adultery, he does not even seem to recognise that he has sins which need forgiveness.

The story ends with Jesus' reassuring this woman as he did the one accused of adultery:

> Your sins are forgiven. . . . Your faith has saved you; go in peace (Luke 7:48, 50).

Domination

Domination of Jesus over women is simply absent from the Gospels. They never portray him as telling women what to do, or suggesting that men are in any way superior to them. On the contrary, Jesus takes women with the utmost seriousness. On many occasions, they are drawn into his life and work in ways which make them collaborators with him.

Jesus used women in his teaching

Luke 15 has Jesus' story of a male shepherd searching for his lost sheep: it also has his story of a female householder searching for her lost coin.

Luke 18:1–8 is the parable of the persistent woman and the unjust judge. The judge 'neither feared God nor cared about men', and would not give the woman the justice for which she was asking. But she persisted until he said:

> Even though I don't fear God or care about men, yet because this widow keeps bothering me, I will see that she gets justice, so that she won't eventually wear me out with her coming (Luke 18:4–5).

The story is told to encourage people to persist in prayer to God, the Just Judge; but it is not without significance that Jesus chose a woman to represent patient persistence in the face of injustice.

Luke 21 has Jesus commending a poor woman's devotion:

> As he looked up, Jesus saw the rich putting their gifts into the treasury. He also saw a poor widow put in two very small copper coins. 'I tell you the truth,' he said, 'this poor widow has put in more than all the others. All these people gave their gifts out of their wealth; but she out of her poverty put in all that she had to live on' (Luke 21:1–4).

Once again, the person who appears to be at the bottom of the social heap is affirmed by Jesus, at the cost of those who appear to have power.

Jesus revealed central truths to and through women

It was to a woman that, in John's gospel, Jesus first revealed himself as the Messiah.

In John 4, we read that Jesus was going through Samaria, a region between his home in Galilee and the main Jewish area around Jerusalem. He was alone, and sat down beside a well in the heat of noonday. Surprisingly, a woman came to the well — most people would have drawn their water in the coolness of the early morning. Jesus asked her for a drink. She was shocked:

> You are a Jew, and I am a Samaritan woman. How can you ask me for a drink? (v. 9).

Characteristically, Jesus was stepping over conventional barriers. It was not only that he was a man and was talking to a strange woman: there was a long history of antagonism between Jews and Samaritans, so he was stepping over ethnic barriers as well.

However, he did not discuss this. He went on to engage her in a theological discussion. In the course of this, he challenged her about her marital life: he discerned that she had had five husbands and that she was presently living with a man to whom she was not married. She was a woman who, whether by her own fault or through exploitation, had had a painful history and was now despised by her community — we presume that this was why she came to the well at such an unpopular hour.

Yet Jesus did not avoid her: he gave her hope. He offered her a whole new life. He answered her theological questions. And it was to her that he declared his messiahship (v: 26). She then went back to her village, and became a missionary to her people. 'Many of the Samaritans from that town believed in him because of the woman's testimony' (v: 39). Jesus respected this despised woman.

236 *It was through a woman that Jesus made it clear that he came not only as the Jewish Messiah, but also for the rest of the world.*

One of the things that the Jews of Jesus' time did not understand was that God had not called Israel for their own sake, but for the sake of the whole world. Even Jesus' disciples had not really understood this by the end of Jesus' life, and much of the New Testament tells us of the struggles they had to accept and adjust to non-Jews. A rather strange story in the gospels shows Jesus beginning to break into their misunderstanding. In both Mark and Matthew, it comes just after the passage quoted on pp. 230–1, in which Jesus challenges ideas of ritual uncleanliness. Here is Matthew's version:

> Leaving that place, Jesus withdrew to the region of Tyre and Sidon. A Canaanite woman from that vicinity came to him, crying out, 'Lord, Son of David, have mercy on me! My daughter is suffering terribly from demon possession.'
>
> Jesus did not answer a word. So his disciples came to him and urged him, 'Send her away, for she keeps crying out after us.' He answered, 'I was sent only to the lost sheep of the house of Israel.' The woman came and knelt before him. 'Lord, help me!' she said. He replied, 'It is not right to take the children's bread and throw it to the dogs.' 'Yes, Lord,' she said, 'but even the dogs eat the crumbs that fall from their masters' table.' Then Jesus answered, 'Woman, you have great faith! Your request is granted.' And her

daughter was healed from that very hour (Matthew 15:21–28).

What is going on here? Is Jesus reluctant to help the woman just because she is a foreigner? It seems to me that such an explanation is unlikely. He has just rebuked the religious leaders for their ideas about food and plates being unclean: it is unlikely that he is now acting as if a person is unclean. We have seen that he deliberately touched lepers and spoke to the Samaritan woman: it is unlikely that he is now being prejudiced and racist. The mere fact of the shock we feel at Jesus' being apparently uncaring towards this women indicates that something special is going on.

237

Jesus is delighted with the woman's faith, and he and she together are teaching the Jews, the disciples and us a lesson. She comes to him as the 'Son of David', which implies that she recognises him as the Messiah long expected by the Jews. In this, she is already ahead of Jesus' closest followers, who do not explicitly recognise this until the next chapter (16:16). She comes to him as a Gentile — a non-Jew — one of the people the Jews did not think their Messiah would be for. She comes with great persistence: so sure is she that Jesus will help her that she is not daunted by his silence or the disciples' discouragement. She has understood that God will not restrict his blessings to one particular people group.

Jesus tells her that his main calling is to reach the Jewish people, but she insists that she needs help. He quotes her what was probably a common saying of the time, and she replies in kind. The Jews thought of Gentiles as unclean, like dogs, but she insists that dogs have needs too.

238 It seems to me that Jesus, sure of her faith, is drawing her into a conversation that, with a touch of humour, overturns the current Jewish understanding of 'uncleanness'. The previous passage taught that it is illogical to think that foods, in themselves, can make someone 'unclean'. This passage teaches that it is even more illogical to think of a human being as 'unclean' because of their ethnic origin.

- Jesus' main ministry while he was on earth was to be to the Jewish people, but this did not prevent him from helping others. It was human need to which he responded, not a particular ethnic label.
- The Jews may have thought of the Gentiles as 'dogs', but all creatures need sustenance.[6] We can, perhaps, imagine a smile on Jesus' face as he agrees that a human being must be treated at least as well as a dog.

Onlookers would, no doubt, have felt rebuked for their prejudices. There are Christians around the world who remember the woman's words as they come to communion week by week. They confess:

> We are not worthy so much as to gather up they crumbs under Thy table. But thou art the same Lord whose property is always to have mercy.[7]

It was to women that Jesus first appeared after the resurrection; and it was they who were given the task of telling the men the good news.

All four gospels record that women followed Jesus to the cross while his male disciples forsook him.[8] They also agree that it was women who went to the tomb early on the third day to anoint the body, and that they were the first to witness the empty tomb and to meet with the risen Christ.

Every gospel, in its different way, goes on to show that the women were given the job of taking the good news of the resurrection to the other disciples.

- Matthew (28:7–10) has an angel saying:

  Go quickly and tell his disciples, 'He has risen from the dead and is going ahead of you to Galilee. There you will see him.'

- Jesus himself then meets them and says:

  Go and tell my brothers to go to Galilee; there you will see me.

- Mark (16:6–7) has the angel saying:

  He has risen! See the place where they laid him. But go, tell his disciples and Peter, 'He is going ahead of you into Galilee. There you will see him, just as he told you.'

- Luke (24:1–12) does not have the command to tell the disciples, but tells of the angelic message and of the women going back to tell the others what had happened. It also notes that they were not believed: the men had to go and see for themselves.
- John (20:1–18) has one particular woman, Mary Magdelene, finding the tomb empty and going to tell the disciples. After two male disciples had seen the empty tomb, Jesus came to Mary, and said to her:

  Go . . . to my brothers and tell them, 'I am returning to my Father and your Father, to my God and your God.'

The women's testimony matters. So striking is this that some have suggested it indicates the truth of the narratives. Given the position of women in society at the time, no-one would have chosen women as their major witnesses if they were making up a tale that they wanted to be believed.

240

Jesus, as we see him in the gospels, did not treat women as inferior in any way. They are not unclean. They are not relegated to secondary roles. They are not blamed, dominated or kept within the private realm. They are an essential part of humanity and therefore of his kingdom: they are co-workers with him, as Eve was originally made as a co-worker with Adam.

5.2 How it works out: marriage and authority

Napoleon John

> *Afri was brought up as a Brahmin, with the idea that women were basically possessions, useful for looking after the house and bringing up the children, but definitely inferior to men. He lived with a white woman for ten years and never once did the washing up — that was 'women's work'. Now, he is married and respects and works with his wife. He cares for the children, vacuums the carpets, and does the washing up after nearly every meal.*
>
> *What made the difference? 'It was seeing Jesus' attitude to women and children. He was so kind to them! He even washed his disciples' feet. And Paul taught that husbands should love their wives as they love their own bodies. That just never crossed my mind before I came to Christ.'*

The Lord Jesus Christ shows that women are to be treated as human beings fully equal to men, and challenges many of the things that have gone wrong for women. These are basic principles, but they leave open many questions.

Once, some people asked him whose wife a woman would be in the next life if she was given in marriage to more than one husband in this life. He replied:

> The people of this age marry and are given in marriage. But those who are considered worthy of taking part in that age and in the resurrection from the dead will neither marry nor be given in marriage, and they can no longer die; for they are like the angels (Luke 20:34–36).

Not all questions are relevant, and many are trivial in the light of eternity, but the New Testament does recognise and grapple with the problems of this life. It does this to some extent in the gospels, but more so in the epistles. The latter are letters written to various groups of Christians who were seeking to follow Jesus in their particular situations. They therefore often include advice about daily life, including male–female relationships. Because such advice is given in the context of first century Middle Eastern culture, it can be difficult for western readers to understand it and to see how to apply it in their own lives. This is not such a problem for Indian Sub-continental Christians: we live in a very similar culture to that of New Testament times.

Last year, I went to Israel with a party of white Christians. At one place, our guide drew our attention to some very ancient hand mills and oil presses such as were used in the time of Christ. While the others of my party excitedly took photographs, I stood aside in the shadow of a tree. One asked me why I was not excited about those very interesting things. My answer? I have seen all of them being used in my country.

It is not only on the level of instruments that we still live as in Jesus' days: many other aspects of our culture are even today similar to his. These cultural similarities are not exclusive to Asian Christians: they operate across religious boundaries. Yet, because of our background in the teachings of the Lord Jesus Christ, there are also profound differences between us and our Muslims compatriots. These differences can be seen in every walk of life, including the treatment of women.[9]

In what follows, I shall, from the perspective of an Asian who accepts the authority of the Bible, explore several aspects of male–female relationships that have caused controversy between Christians and Muslims.

The goodness of marriage

Maududi in his *Purdah and the Status of Woman in Islam*, pp. 8–9, writes:

> To cure the West of its moral ailments came Christianity. In the beginning it served the purpose well . . . But the concepts held by the Christian patriarchs of woman and conjugal relationships were not only opposed to human nature but unnatural to the extreme. Their basic doctrine was that woman was the mother of sin and root cause of all evil.

He quotes Tertullian's famous misogynist passage about women as temptresses (see p. 12 above), and adds one from the fourth century Greek theologian, St John Chrysostom: 'She is an inevitable evil, an eternal mischief, an attractive calamity, a domestic risk, a charming and decorated misfortune.'

As well as seeing women as evil, says Maududi, these early Christians believed that, 'the sexual relation between man and woman was in itself an objectionable, dirty affair, even if it was established within legal marriage.'

His conclusion is that, in Christianity, 'celibacy and spinsterhood became the criterion of the nobility of character, and married life came to be regarded as a necessary evil.'

It is certainly true that some early Christians had very negative ideas about women, and that there were movements that considered celibacy not only a better estate than marriage but the way to real freedom.[10] However, it is important to realise that their writings have no status in Christianity similar to those of Muhammad's companions or the early legal and religious authorities in Islam. Although some groups of Christians look to them for guidance and early ideas are very influential, what they said is considered their personal opinion and has no binding authority for future generations. A careful reading of the teachings of Jesus Christ would lead one to understand that their opinions did not always reflect what the Bible teaches: they were sometimes tragically wrong.

The Christian faith allows people to hold different opinions. But, as in Islam, it is the Scripture which is the measuring rod for Christian ethics and not the ideas of any theologian. Nowhere in the Bible is woman considered an evil being, although it does teach that everyone, male and female, falls short of God's standards. As for women, it teaches the very opposite of what some critics have suggested. For example, it is clear that marriage is good and that a wife is a precious gift to a man from his Creator:

244

> He who finds a wife finds what is good and receives favour from the Lord (Proverbs 18:22).

Some early Christians did advocate celibacy, and some continue to do so in the present. But this is not something that the Bible sees as being for all, or as better than marriage, although it was the way that the Lord Jesus chose to live. It does not push people into either marriage or celibacy: both are permissible, and both are good gifts from God. Marriage is good, but it is not the only option: women as well as men can find their value and identity in different ways, and not only as housekeepers and parents.

Those who have the gift of living a married life should, then, marry, and those who are gifted to remain single, should (of course, without living an immoral life) remain single (Matthew 19:10–12; 1 Corinthians 7). Those who enforce celibacy go against the will of their Creator:

> Such teachings come through hypocritical liars, whose consciences have been seared as with a hot iron. They forbid people to marry and order them to abstain from certain foods, which God created to be received with thanksgiving by those who believe and who know the truth (1 Timothy 4:2–3).

In Christianity, a husband and wife's sexual relationship is not 'a dirty affair' as Maududi has suggested. Sex is a gift of

God, although, like any other gift, it can be abused and polluted. Paul wrote to Christians who were showing the same doubts about sex that Maududi attacks:

> The husband should fulfil his marital duty to his wife, and likewise the wife to her husband. The wife's body does not belong to her alone, but also to her husband. In the same way, the husband's body does not belong to him alone but also to his wife. Do not deprive each other except by mutual consent and for a time, so that you may devote yourselves to prayer. Then come together again so that Satan will not tempt you because of your lack of self-control (1 Corinthians 7:3–5).

245

Sexuality is good, and wives and husbands have equal responsibilities to cater for their partners' needs.

The Old Testament also celebrates sexuality. It even includes the Song of Solomon — a whole book of poetry telling of the love between a bride and groom. Here is a sample:

> How beautiful you are and how pleasing, O love, with your delights!
> Your stature is like that of a date palm, and your breasts like clusters of fruit.
> I said, 'I will climb the palm tree; I will take hold of its fruit.'
> May your breasts be like the clusters of the vine, the fragrance of your breath like apples, your mouth like the best wine.
>
> May the wine go straight to my lover, flowing gently over lips and teeth.
> I belong to my lover, and his desire is for me.[11]

The permanency of marriage

> Another thing you do: You flood the LORD's altar with
> tears. You weep and wail because he no longer pays
> attention to your offerings or accepts them with pleasure
> from your hands. You ask, Why? It is because you have
> broken faith with her, though she is your partner, the wife
> of your marriage covenant. Has not the LORD made
> them one? In flesh and spirit they are his. And why one?
> Because he was seeking godly offspring. So guard yourself
> in your spirit, and do not break faith with the wife of your
> youth. I hate divorce, says the LORD God of Israel
> (Malachi 2: 13–16).

The attitudes of Islam and Christianity towards marriage
and divorce are very different. In previous chapters we
have already examined how easy it is, in practice, for a
Muslim man to divorce his wife. Most agree that the wife
has no option but acceptance:

> Ordinarily the marriage tie between a Muslim and his
> wife is dissolved by 'Talaq' which means a divorce given
> by a husband to his wife. It becomes complete when he
> pronounces it against her thrice and hands over to her her
> maintenance charges for the period of waiting (if he has
> not already maintained her till then) and the dower which
> he has settled on her at the time of the marriage. The wife
> in this case has no option.[12]

On the other hand, a husband retains the right of refusal if
the divorce is instigated by the wife:

> But when a wife, from an aversion to her husband, desires
> redemption from him, by resigning all her settlements and
> the presents made to her by him at the time of the
> marriage, it is called, 'Khula'. In this case the husband has
> the option of rejecting her offer . . . In 'Talaq' the wife

246

has no option. In 'Khula' the option lies with the husband.[13]

According to the commands of Jesus Christ, a Christian marriage is permanent. It is not a contract which can be terminated, but a covenant made in the presence of God: that husband and wife should live together in plenty and in need, in sickness and in health. Both husband and wife promise to one another in the presence of God that, forsaking all others, they will be faithful to one another as long as they both shall live.[14] Marriage is to be for ever, and is not dependent upon the wife remaining young and healthy, or even bearing children. Jesus did not teach things which were practical for the needs of men: he spoke of God's perfect intentions for both man and woman.

In Jesus' days it was a common practice among the men to divorce their wives. It was customary even among the Jews, regardless of God's hatred towards divorce taught in such passages as the one quoted above. Once some religious Jewish men came to ask Jesus whether it was right for a man to divorce his wife for any reason:

> Some Pharisees came to him to test him. They asked, 'Is it lawful for a man to divorce his wife for any and every reason?' 'Haven't you read', he replied, 'that at the beginning the Creator made them male and female, and said, "For this reason a man will leave his father and mother and be united to his wife, and the two will become one flesh"? So they are no longer two, but one. Therefore what God has joined together, let man not separate.' 'Why then', they asked, 'did Moses command that a man give his wife a certificate of divorce and send her away?' Jesus replied, 'Moses permitted you to divorce your wives

because your hearts were hard. But it was not this way from the beginning. I tell you that anyone who divorces his wife, except for marital unfaithfulness, and marries another woman commits adultery' (Matthew 19: 3–9).

248   The marriage relationship in Jesus' teaching is indeed exclusive and permanent. It is not a temporary agreement of convenience and should not be undertaken lightly. Jesus' words, 'What God has joined together, let not man separate' are solemnly pronounced during many Christian marriage ceremonies.

This is not to say that there is no possibility of divorce. The New Testament envisages two circumstances under which a believer can divorce his or her partner. These apply to wives as well as to husbands.[15]

- One of the partners is involved in grave sexual misconduct. This is indicated in Jesus' teaching above.
- One partner forsakes the Christian faith[16] and is not willing to live with the believer. This is taught by the Apostle Paul:

> But if the unbeliever leaves, let him do so. A believing man or woman is not bound in such circumstances (1 Corinthians 7:15).

Even then, divorce is a concession and not a command. This again contrasts with the Islamic position, in which, if one partner becomes a Muslim and the other does not, or if one apostasises,[17] a marriage is automatically dissolved:

> Ibn Abbas said: If a Christian woman embraces Islam before her husband by a short while, she will by no means remain as his wife legally . . . Al-Hasan and Qatada said regarding a Magian couple who embraced Islam: Their

marriage remains valid, but if one of them becomes a Muslim, the wife is regarded as divorced, and the husband has no right to keep her as a wife (*Sahih Al-Bukhari*, Vol. 7, pp. 157–158).

Marriage in Christianity is so important that even if one of the partners is an unbeliever the Bible encourages spouses to remain faithful to each other:

> If any brother has a wife who is not a believer and she is willing to live with him, he must not divorce her. And if a woman has a husband who is not a believer and he is willing to live with her, she must not divorce him (1 Corinthians 7:12–13).

Thus we conclude that Christianity takes marriage very seriously. It does not encourage partners to leave one another, although it does recognise that there are some circumstances in which separation is permissible. A Christian couple should not be preoccupied with possible grounds for divorce, but with thinking how to remain faithful to each other. As Jesus said, God has joined them together and no human being should separate them.

Divorce East and West

Christianity is often blamed for the frequency of divorces in the West. Divorce rates are certainly alarming, and it is sad to see so many marriages breaking down. But these divorces are not due to any fault in the Christian faith. The fact of the matter is that people in the West are so preoccupied with their own selfish interests that few have any time for God and the Bible. We have already seen that the Bible strongly condemns divorce and encourages people to love one another. I believe that, if the Lord Jesus

Christ were made the third partner in every marriage and the head of every household; if his teaching were taken seriously; families would not break up.

What I have found in my Christian ministry is that not many people even of those who marry in church are believers in Jesus Christ: they only want a church wedding because this is the tradition. In any case, westerners have made themselves so busy that few have time to sit down and learn what Christian marriage is all about. We clergy need to take marriage more seriously, and to ensure that couples understand their commitment to each other.

Some writers point out that Muslim marriages appear to be more successful than those in the West. For example, a Christian writes:

> In spite of appearances, the divorce rate in the Muslim world is estimated to be somewhat less than 10%, compared to our western world's figure of some 3 to 4 times higher than that. The current situation among those who would claim to be within the evangelical Christian community should also make many of us consider carefully before we are too ready to condemn others (Ed Challen: *To Love a Muslim*, p. 125–6).

This is, it seems to me, overstating the case. Challen's intentions are wholly admirable: he wants to encourage Christians to love Muslims. However, my own observation and that of many others suggests that, in similar circumstances, marriages amongst Christians are much less likely to break down than are those amongst Muslims.

Comparisons between Muslims and westerners can be misleading, since not only their cultures but also their respective understandings of marital relations are very different. Even comparisons between Muslims and Christians living side by side in the West are not likely to be helpful, since each group still tends to inhabit a different cultural world. A more meaningful comparison can be made between the Muslims and the Christians in countries where they have been neighbours for centuries, or between people from those countries who are now living in the West.

I come from one of the largest Christian communities in Pakistan. To my knowledge, divorces among the Christians from my home area can be counted on the fingers of one hand — they are far fewer than those among Muslims in the same area. As a student in Lahore, Pakistan, I lived among Muslims but had many contacts with Christians, and observed a similar contrast: there were far more divorces among Muslims than among Christians.

In the West, the pattern continues. In East London, where I live at the present, there is a very large Muslim community in the three boroughs of Waltham Forest, Newham and Redbridge. There are also many Asian Christian families. As in Pakistan, I find the divorce rate much higher among Muslims than among Asian Christians. During my time in Finland, where there were fewer people from my country, almost all the Pakistanis — Muslim or Christian — knew each other. Most of the Pakistani men were married to Finnish women. There were sadly many failed marriages between Muslim Pakistanis and Finnish women, but we knew not a single Pakistani Christian who, after having settled in the land, had divorced his wife.

I am not saying that all Asian Christian marriages are successful. My own parents' marriage was a difficult one. In my mother's old age, my father left her for a time and lived with a Muslim woman. But divorce did not take place. After a while my father came to his senses and asked my mother's forgiveness. She forgave him, and six years ago he died as a Christian man and a committed husband. The point I make is that divorce is rare among us as compared to our Muslim neighbours.

There are, I think, various reasons for this. Here are some:

First, this biblical understanding, 'one man one woman for life', is known to Christians even if they are brought up in a secular environment. In extreme cases there are Christian men who (like my father) walk out on their wives, but their conscience troubles them. They know they have wronged their wives and it is my experience that, like my father, they usually come back to their wives. An additional wife is not possible.

A second common reason for divorce or second marriage amongst Muslims in Pakistan is that the first wife is barren. Muslim scholars have justified second marriage in this case.[18] For Christians, leaving a wife because of barrenness is not considered an option. I think of two childless couples in one of the Asian Christian fellowships in East London. Their non-Christian Asian friends gave them all sorts of advice about how to get children, including the suggestion of divorce or conversion to Islam; but these men always kept to the view that 'what God has joined together let man not separate' (Matthew 19:6). They held that, if children are God's gift, so is a wife. If he did not bless them with both gifts, they can still be thankful to him for the gift that they have.

Thirdly, the dowry system creates problems. The Urdu newspapers often carry stories of young wives dying in home accidents.[19] We call them, 'kerosene oil stove victims'. To an outsider such deaths may appear to be accidents due to faulty stoves: those of us who come from Pakistan understand that women are likely to be the victims of their husbands or even of their mothers-in-law. In Pakistan, despite the Islamic ruling that the groom should give a dowry to his bride, the bride is expected to bring a large dowry to her husband's family. It is those who do not bring enough dowry who are liable to home 'accidents', or else to divorce. This may not end at the marriage ceremony: women may be continuously asked to get more money from their parents. If they fail, the result can again be divorce or 'accident'.

The *Sunday Times Magazine* published an investigation of the problem.[20] It claims that one city — Islamabad — had 84 reported 'stove burnings' in a six-month period, and that 81 of the women involved died. Across Pakistan, it is estimated that one such 'accident' occurs every day. Victims are usually in their twenties, and have almost invariably been judged to have brought too small a dowry. The magazine reports two stories of survivors:

After six years of marriage and bearing three children, Bushra Hasan was instructed by her husband to borrow 50,000 rupees (about £900) from her parents. On 7 December 1996, when she came back empty-handed, he beat her over a period of two days. On the second day, while she was sitting in the courtyard with her children,

253

her husband arrived with some members of his family. She described what happened:

> My sister-in-law took the baby from me and my mother-in-law held both my arms behind my back and pulled my head back by my hair. My husband began to rub my face with this wet cloth on a stick. After a few seconds, the pain began. It was excruciating and I was screaming. My husband stopped and his uncle took the stick from him saying, 'Come on, you are feeling sympathy, I'll do it.' The uncle painted the other half of my face and then pushed the whole cloth into my mouth saying it would stop my noise.

As a result of this acid burning, Hasan's face was so badly burnt that her husband eventually took her to hospital where he told the doctors that she had tried to commit suicide by hanging herself from a ceiling fan. The fan broke and burst into flames, he told them, burning his wife's face.

Zaenab Noor's husband punished her by tying her to a bed, then connecting electric wires to an iron rod which he inserted into her vagina and then switched on the electric current. He told the hospital that her burns were due to an upset cooking stove.

Christians in Pakistan also follow the dowry custom, but I do not know of any Christian woman who was either divorced or burnt to death because she failed to bring enough money to her marriage.

It is not only in the Indian sub-continent that one can observe different divorce rates amongst Christians and Muslims who share similar cultures. A Middle Eastern writer[21] observes:

If we take a quick glimpse at the Christian East, we will realize the rarity of divorce cases. I have lived dozens of years in Arab countries, especially in Egypt which has a population of thirteen million Christians, and yet I have heard about only one divorce in the Christian community. Westerners must recognize this fact in order to learn from the Eastern Christians this Christian biblical principle. Of course, premarital sexual relationships (which are in vogue in the West) are not practiced among Christian Easterners. It is possible to say that in the Christian East there is one divorce for every one hundred thousand marriages! (p. 115).

This does not necessarily mean that Eastern Christians have happier marriages than those in the West: some may not be at all successful by western standards. However, many marriages which would break down in the West survive in the East. This is because of our social structures as well as because of our Christian convictions. Marriage among us is not so much the union of two individuals as a relationship between two families. Some of our wedding customs may help the reader to understand how the newly-wedded couple are supported.

In a Pakistani Christian wedding, the groom is led by friends and close relatives as he comes to claim his bride. The party is welcomed at the door of the bride's parents' home, and there is a short time of prayer and praising God before entering the house. A popular hymn on this occasion is based on Psalm 133: 'How good and pleasant it is when brothers live together in unity . . .'

The *Milini* ceremony is then held: close relatives from both sides greet and hug each other. The girl's father will welcome and hug the boy's father, the girl's elder brother the boy's elder brother and so on. Other ceremonies similarly affirm the link between the two families. After the wedding, the bride goes with her new husband to his home, and there are more ceremonies. For example, the groom's younger brother will sit for a few seconds on the lap of the new bride, and she will give him some money. This is to show that the younger brother of her husband is like a son to her.

256

The purpose of all this is to involve both families in welcoming each other and the newly married couple. The bride and groom are thus assured of acceptance, help and support. If there is ever a crisis in the marriage, there are many people available to listen and to help.

There are similar ceremonies involved in Muslim weddings and not all of their marriages end up in such tragic situations as mentioned above. Very many marriages survive among the Muslims also, but again success may have more to do with social and family structures than with the wisdom and love of the husband. Such support systems generally do not exist in the individualistic societies of the West.

Another reason why some marriages which do not stand a chance in the West can survive in the East has to do with our approach to life's problems. In my opinion, most of our problems begin in childhood or early youth, regardless of cultural and ethnic backgrounds. There is no problem-free childhood or adolescence, either in the West or in the East. The difference is in how different cultures treat these problems.

Most people go into marriage with their personalities already marked by the dark shadows from the past. But, while in the West a couple is mostly left to solve their problems on their own, any young couple in the East is surrounded by many people who can help them to cope with their situation. Not all sisters-in-law or mothers-in-law are enemies. In many cases they provide advice, support and companionship which help the couple not to overburden each other with their past problems and present expectations.

Authority and headship

Authority

Muslims, Christians and atheists, East and West, have raised questions about the Bible's teaching about authority. Many have accused it of being totally patriarchal, and the root of all the misuses of male authority in societies influenced by the Judaeo-Christian tradition.[22] Here, we are going to limit ourselves to Muslim critics. It is my contention that they have misunderstood biblical teaching.

A New Testament verse frequently quoted in this connection[23] is:

> Women should remain silent in the churches. They are not allowed to speak, but must be in submission, as the Law says (1 Corinthians 14:34).

Such verses have raised all sorts of passions in recent years. The acceptance of women as priests in the Church of England has brought the issues into the open. Much has been written: my purpose here is not to join the controversy, but to reflect from my particular perspective on Christian ideas criticised by Muslims.

258

The verse quoted above certainly appears to suggest that men should have the upper hand in their relationships with women. This is the more striking in western cultures, where the equality of all human beings is held dearly. But if we read the verses in their contexts and in the framework of wider biblical interpretation, a different understanding emerges. We will use four principles:

- First, we need to look at the Bible as a whole. As the beauty of a painting cannot be appreciated from only a tiny part of it, so the Bible cannot be interpreted accurately by isolating one or two verses from the rest of the book.
- Second, all teaching, including that on authority and submission, depends on the Christian understanding of God.
- Third, in Christianity the Lord Jesus Christ and his teachings are *Sunnah*: the model for Christians. No human authority can be put above him, and above the Bible.
- Fourth, although I believe that the Bible is the Word of God, this does not mean that it was written in heaven and then sent down piece by piece to this earth through an angel. Rather, God spoke through different men and women. They were ordinary people of this world and the message was to the people of this world. The Bible does not speak only of timeless matters, but also about issues which mattered to the particular

people who wrote it. We therefore cannot apply the message of the Bible in today's situation correctly without looking at the situation in which the said passage or verses were written.

The verses we are looking at are about the place of women in the leadership of the church. To see them in the context of the whole Bible, we need to start in the Old Testament. This has very little to say directly about what women can and cannot do, and, as has been seen in Ch. 4, it was written in a culture which was clearly patriarchal. However, it does tell of several women in leadership positions. There were wise women, and female judges (Judges 4), prophets (e.g. Exodus 15:20; 2 Kings 22:14) and even rulers (2 Chronicles 22:12). Some did their jobs well, and some turned away from God, but even then there is no suggestion that this was because they were women. Many male leaders, too, chose their own interests rather than God's.

259

For the future, it was promised that, when the Messiah came, prophecy would not be the privilege of a few selected people. God would bestow this gift on all believers, male and female:

> And afterwards, I will pour out my Spirit on all people. Your sons and daughters will prophesy, your old men will dream dreams, your young men will see visions. Even on my servants, both men and women, I will pour out my Spirit in those days (Joel 2:28–29).

This promise was fulfilled after Jesus Christ returned to heaven. In Acts 2, we read that the Spirit came upon the followers of Christ, and that they all — male and female

— started to speak words from God. The Apostle Peter said that this was what the prophet Joel had meant. Women prophets are also mentioned later on in Acts:

> Leaving the next day, we reached Caesarea and stayed at the house of Philip the evangelist, one of the Seven. He had four unmarried daughters who prophesied (Acts 21:8–9).

This is not just a private matter: the New Testament encourages all believers to take part in public life and ministry. All, male and female, are eagerly to desire spiritual gifts, especially that of prophecy (1 Corinthians 14:1). These gifts were and are to be used in public, for the benefit of all.

Further, the first letter of Peter teaches that all believers in Jesus Christ are his priests,[24] and priesthood is certainly a public ministry.

> But you are a chosen people, a royal priesthood, a holy nation, a people belonging to God, that you may declare the praises of him who called you out of darkness into his wonderful light (1 Peter 2:9).

The Bible teaches that there is no slave or master, male or female in Christ, but all are one in Christ (Galatians 3:28). Although most of the leaders and prophets in both Old and New Testament times were men, there were also some women who took these roles with God's approval. This is the context in which we will try to understand statements like, 'women should remain silent in the church' and 'women should learn in full submission'.

Women are told that they should not speak in public worship. But the question is, what sort of public speaking is referred to here? Does it mean that women should never say a word in the church or in a public place to teach or even correct a male? I think not.

Traditionally, many commentators have made assumptions about what Paul meant, and have taken no account of the possibility that he might have been referring to particular problems. Here are two comments on 1 Corinthians 14:34:

> Whether [women] have the gift of tongues or of prophecy makes no difference, in fact, Paul's prohibition is intended for just such. And this prohibition is general and complete.[25]

> And we may add that if Paul's injunction had been respected and obeyed there would have been no opportunity for charlatans like Aimee Semple McPherson, Ellen G. White, and Mary Baker Eddy to have imposed their noxious wares upon a gullible public![26]

I believe that our verses have, like the rest of the Bible, authority for all times, but they are to be found in letters which were written to certain people about certain issues, and can only be rightly understood as such. For instance, it seems clear that the Apostle Paul wrote to the Corinthians because they had asked him some specific questions — about Holy Communion, about food regulations, about Christian morality, and about public worship. Some questions seem to have been general, and some to have concerned particular people.[27]

1 Corinthians 14:34–35 is part of an extended discussion of propriety in public worship in Chs. 11–14. Within this general question, the Apostle Paul's attention is drawn towards the behaviour of some particular people. This time, they happen to be women. In order to decide

what he is prohibiting, it is necessary to consider what the Corinthian problem might have been.

It seems to me unlikely that the public use of spiritual gifts by women was considered a problem in itself. Just a few chapters earlier (11:5), the Apostle Paul has acknowledged the right of women to pray and prophesy, so it is unlikely that he is forbidding prayer and prophecy here. In verses 27–30 of Ch. 14, which give general rules about the public use of the gifts of speaking in tongues and prophecy, men are also told to remain silent on certain occasions, and no one supposes that this is a general prohibition. Perhaps our verses, which follow almost immediately, are also dealing with particular occasions.

The concern of the whole of 1 Corinthians 14 is order in worship. It seems that the Corinthian worship services could be unruly, with many people speaking at once and causing confusion. The Apostle Paul exhorts them to speak one at a time, to wait for each other, and to reflect on what is being said. Each should be silent while another is speaking, 'for God is not a God of confusion but of peace' (v. 33). This is the context of our verses: they are to counter a particular problem to do with women speaking and disturbing the order and peace of the worship.

Women, like men, can abuse power, freedom and their position in society. Equality in Christ brought new power and freedom for women, and I would suggest that there were some women in Corinth who misused this and tried to impose themselves upon the whole congregation. Maybe some tried to enforce their own will by saying that the words which they received from the Lord were superior to certain men's words. This would explain Paul's rebuke:

> Did the word of God originate with you? Or are you the only people it has reached? (v. 36).

Perhaps some women behaved in public in such a way as to provoke their men to argue among themselves thus bringing shame to the whole company of Christ. We Eastern men protect our women jealously, so I can easily imagine such a situation arising; and I find it difficult otherwise to make sense of the Apostle's solution:

263

> If they want to enquire about something, they should ask their own husbands at home (v. 35).

The principle here, as elsewhere in 1 Corinthians, is that nothing was to bring Christian worship into ill repute. Christians are told to behave in public in such a way that people may see them and glorify God.[28] This will work out differently in different situations. In Corinth, while women were to pray and to prophesy, they were not to cause disruption by claiming priority or raising unhelpful questions. The final verses of the chapter (39–40) sum it up:

> Therefore my brothers, be eager to prophesy, and do not forbid speaking in tongues. But everything should be done in a fitting and orderly way.

Headship

> Now I want you to realise that the head of every man is Christ, and the head of the woman is man, and the head of Christ is God (1 Corinthians 11:3).

Ida has already discussed the way that different Christians interpret the passages about male headship and female submission within marriage. I want to add my perspective as an Asian husband. We start with the doctrine of God and the example of Jesus Christ. The above verse indicates that, although he was not married, his relationships with people are a pattern for a husband's relationship to his wife.

264

In fact, he offers a pattern for all human relationships. Elsewhere, Paul urges all Christian people to put the interests of others before their own interests, reminding them of the example of Christ:

> Your attitude should be the same as that of Christ Jesus: who, being in very nature God, did not consider equality with God something to be grasped but made himself nothing, taking the very nature of a servant, being made in human likeness . . . he humbled himself and became obedient to death — even death on a cross (Philippians 2:5–8).

Jesus Christ submitted to the will of his heavenly Father and became obedient even to death. Yet we believe that Jesus Christ is the second person of the Trinity, equal with his Father. The Christian creed says about Jesus Christ, 'We believe in one Lord Jesus Christ, the only Son of God, eternally begotten of the Father, God from God, Light from Light, true God from true God . . .' (the Nicene Creed). He submitted himself to the Father yet is equal with him: submission does not imply inferiority.

Submission in Christian faith is not that of a slave to his master. In the marriage relationship it means a wife accepting her husband's care with a grateful heart. Both man's headship and woman's submission are to be seen through the example of the Lord Jesus Christ. He is the true example of headship and submission. Thus we can say that the Christian wife's submission to her husband's authority is in response to his true and loving headship of the family, and is not an unthinking obedience to man's rule. The husband is to be a loving and caring head of his wife and not her taskmaster. He too is to follow the example of Christ.

265

At the last meal before he was crucified, Jesus Christ sat with his disciples to have a farewell meal. Before the meal started, he got up and washed their feet. He then taught something which is unique to him and is at the heart of the Christian faith:

> Jesus knew that the Father had put all things under his power, and that he had come from God and was returning to God; so he got up from the meal, took off his outer clothing, and wrapped a towel round his waist. After that, he poured water into a basin and began to wash his disciples' feet, drying them with the towel that was wrapped round him . . . When he had finished washing their feet, he put on his clothes and returned to his place. 'Do you understand what I have done for you?' he asked them. 'You call me Teacher and Lord and rightly so, for that is what I am. Now that I, your Lord and Teacher, have washed your feet, you also should wash one another's feet. I have set you an example that you should do as I have done for you' (John 13:10–15).

The biblical understanding of authority is very different from that of other systems. A person who has authority must first be a servant, as Jesus himself was:

> Whoever wants to become great among you must be your servant, and whoever wants to be first must be your slave — just as the Son of Man did not come to be served, but to serve, and to give his life as a ransom for many (Matthew 20:26).

266 So then, a person who has authority is the one who has, either metaphorically or literally, to wash the feet of others. He is to do the dirty jobs, and to take responsibility when all seems gloomy. Headship means care and not control.

On the social level, a man is to be the defender and protector of his wife and family and their interests. To protect women, men are, I believe, given authority to be the family's public spokesmen. Why this role of defender is given to man is very clear from the following passage in the Bible:

> Husbands, in the same way be considerate as you live with your wives, and treat them with respect as the weaker partner and as heirs with you of the gracious gift of life, so that nothing will hinder your prayers (1 Peter 3: 7).

This sort of protection may not be appreciated by people in today's western world where independence and freedom are all-important. But, in most of the world, the woman still is very much in a need of man's protection and does appreciate it. I believe that by nature woman needs protection and even if some deny it, western women, deep down, share the same need. This is my experience with my western wife. More than anything else, what she wants from me is the assurance that I love her. This simple sentence, 'I love you', gives her security: that is, a sense of protection. Thus in biblical faith woman is to be respected and protected both at home and in public. To protect her in public, the man should be the spokesperson for family and community affairs.

This model can be seen in operation in South Asian Christian homes and public functions. At home, it is often the woman who serves husband, family and guests. In public gatherings, it is often the man who cooks, serves, makes salads, clears tables and washes dishes. Some people might think that this sort of a system operates among South Asian Christians because of the Muslim culture and its understanding of *izzat*, or honour invested in women.[29] *Izzat* operates amongst both Muslims and Christians, but it means different thing to the two groups. For Muslims, *izzat* often involves segregation of sexes: keeping women away from men to protect their chastity. Anees Jung has written:

> The hold of religion is more on Muslim women than men. All the rules and regulations imposed by mullahs start and end with women. Women, they say, should stay at home, wear a burqa when they go out, should not go out alone, not talk to a man in public or study in a class alongside men . . . fifty per cent of Muslim families still do not allow women to take jobs. They are afraid that they will then lose their shame and not find the right husbands. Why do you need to work when we are here they say. That lends them honour and helps to keep their hold on women.[30]

Ghulam Sarwar, in *Islam: Beliefs and Teachings* adds that: 'Islam does not allow free mixing of grown-up boys and girls' (p. 166).

Generally there are no such restrictions upon South Asian Christian women.[31] They go out to work, and are

not separated from men in public functions. All sit together, but when the time comes to eat, the men get up
and serve the women. This is built into South Asian
Christian culture, and few realise why they do it — as,
perhaps, few English people realise why the top people in
government are called 'ministers'.

The Servant brings hope

As I look at the position of women in Pakistan today, I
want to say that the New Testament's teaching about
women is a beam of hope and light in a very dark world.
The Lord Jesus Christ, who saw himself as a servant and
not a dominator, brought to women a dignity and a
freedom that is second to none.

Evil men can, of course, be found in the Christian as
well as the Muslim communities in Pakistan. The question
is, what is to blame for the evil that people commit? Is it
their human nature, or do religious world views contribute? In particular, how are such views to blame, and how
do they contribute to the treatment of offenders and the
protection of their victims?

Let us consider, for example, the plight of women
involved in illicit sexual relationships. All sexual relationships outside marriage are considered wrong in Islamic
law, and are encompassed by the Arabic word *zina*, which
is usually translated, 'adultery'. It can be seen as the
greatest sin after *shirk* (associating anything or anyone with
God), and is severely punished.[32]

Some years ago, there was a television programme
broadcast in the UK under the title, 'Who will cast the

first stone?'[33] The allusion is to a story from John's Gospel, in which a woman is brought to Jesus by a crowd of (male) religious leaders, and accused of adultery (John 8:1–11). The men remind Jesus of an ancient law about stoning adulterers to death, and ask for his judgement. He responds by bending down and writing on the ground with his finger, and then says: 'If any one of you is without sin, let him be the first to throw a stone at her.'

Jesus bends down again, and the men slink away, one by one, until Jesus and the woman are left alone. Jesus asks her, 'Woman, where are they? Has no-one condemned you?' 'No-one', she replies. It is only now that Jesus declares his judgement: 'Then neither do I condemn you. Go now, and leave your life of sin.'

The programme was about the plight of Muslim women in Pakistan since the introduction of *shari'ah* laws under General Zia Ul Haq in the 1970s and 1980s. It focused on women who had been accused of *zina*, usually at the instigation of the husband, and were convicted by the Islamic courts. Particularly disturbing were the stories of women who were imprisoned for *zina* after being raped, while the men who raped them went free due to lack of evidence.[34]

Justice Zahoor Ul Haq, former Judge of the Federal Shariat Court (Islamic Court) of Pakistan, who had tried several of these cases, was interviewed. He explained that this was according to the Qur'anic requirement that there be four reliable witnesses to establish *zina*.[35] The verse, he said, has always been interpreted as referring to four male witnesses, as is specified in section 8b of the Pakistani

Offence of Zina Ordinance 1979.[36] This means that the testimony of a female rape victim is not accepted by an Islamic court. She must bring men who saw the rape take place.

Another Muslim scholar of Islamic law, Khalid Ishaque, disagreed with Justice Zahoor Ul Haq, saying that Islam teaches a different lesson about the treatment of their women. But the reference he gave from the Qur'an is itself problematic:[37]

> As to those women on whose part ye fear disloyalty and ill conduct admonish them (first), (next) refuse to share their beds, (And last) beat them, (lightly). But if they return to obedience, seek not against them means (of annoyance) (Surah 4: 34).

The programme gave examples. Blind Safia Bibi was raped by her landlord and his son. She got three years' imprisonment plus fifteen lashes in public as punishment for *zina*. Because she was blind and could not recognise the rapists, they walked free.[38]

Thirteen-year-old Zubeida was kidnapped and repeatedly raped. When at last she was found and the case was brought to court, Justice Zahoor Ul-Haq sentenced her to five years' imprisonment on the basis that she did not shout loud enough for help. When interviewed, he said that the medical reports suggested that the girl had experienced sexual intercourse more than once, so he concluded that she must have been 'sleeping around' for some time. Again, the men who raped her walked free.

The *Sunday Times* article referred to above (p. 253) also discusses women who are sentenced for *zina* when

270

they have been raped. It even reports that some have been raped by police when they have come to report sexual assaults.[39] Under Benazir Bhutto, special women's police stations were set up to help such women, but they are ineffective because the police women themselves have little power. The article reports that, in 1995, there were 140 complaints of which only six proceeded to a full investigation. Not one rapist was convicted.

The Human Rights Watch *Global Report on Women's Human Rights*, in its section on 'Police abuse of women in Pakistan', comments:

> Human Rights Watch does not object to laws founded on religion, provided that human rights are respected and the principle of equality before the law is upheld. However, the Hudood laws, as written and applied, clearly conflict with these rights and principles. Not only do they prescribe punishments that are cruel and inhuman under international law, but they clearly discriminate on the basis of gender (p. 149).

There are, of course, many people in Pakistan who seek to right such wrongs, and, as the Human Rights Watch report points out, 'the laws also conflict with the Pakistani Constitution which guarantees the right to equality and non-discimination on the basis of gender' (p. 149). But we have to face the fact that these laws are on the statute books, and that this is the way that Islam has treated and continues to treat women. It is professedly Islamic courts which pass these sentences, on the Qur'anic basis that a woman's testimony is not so valuable as a man's, and using the fact that there is physical evidence of a woman having been sexually used — whether by her consent or not — while it is not so easy to prove a man's involvement.

That is why I say that the New Testament brings light and hope. The woman brought to Jesus by the male religious leaders may have committed adultery, or she may have been raped: we do not know. What we do know is that there must have been a man involved, and that he was not brought for judgement. It seems that the men of Jesus' time were no more concerned to investigate the man's part than are the Islamic courts in Pakistan.

Jesus did not say that adultery was right — far from it. He told the woman to sin no more. But he did force the men to see the evil in themselves, and the injustice of their treatment of the woman; and he offered the woman a new life. The story is followed by one of Jesus' great sayings about himself:

> I am the light of the world. Whoever follows me will never walk in darkness, but will have the light of life (John 8:12).

How we all need that light — be we victims, rapists, adulterers, or 'respectable' people who stand in judgement over others.

Notes

1. John 13:34; John 15:12,17; Matthew 5:43–48; Luke 10:25–37.
2. See Mary Evans, *Women in the Bible*, pp. 33–7.
3. Also, as in Islam, bodily emissions can also make men ritually unclean. See Leviticus 15:1–18.
4. See Peter's lesson in Acts 10.

5. The Pharisees were members of a movement that was scrupulous about keeping even the smallest details of the religious law.

6. See also Luke 13:10–16, where Jesus points out that the religious leaders were likely to treat animals better than human beings in need.

7. *Book of Common Prayer*, Prayer of Humble Access.

8. John's Gospel has one male disciple at the cross (19:26).

9. On one visit to Pakistan, I met an Irish lady who was working among Afghan refugees. She had lived and worked there for some time, living amongst Pakistani Muslims. I took her to my home village, her first stay in a Christian majority area. She was surprised to see the difference between the condition of women in this Christian village and elsewhere in Pakistan.

10. E. Pagels, *Adam, Eve and the Serpent*, Ch. 4 has a fascinating analysis of such movements. She argues that they were particularly attractive to women and that they represented a movement for freedom understood as freedom from the demands of society and one's own body.

11. Song of Solomon 7:6–10.

12. Muhammad Valibhai Merchant, *A Book of Qur'anic Laws*, p. 156.

13. Ibid.

14. *Book of Common Prayer*, Marriage Service.

15. Mark 10:10–12 makes it clear that husbands and wives are subject to the same principles.

16. The passage is generally about one partner being an unbeliever. This can be due to one forsaking the faith, or to one partner in a previously non-Christian marriage turning to Christ. A believer should not marry an unbeliever (2 Corinthians 6:14).

17. See A.R. Doi, *Shari'ah: The Islamic Law*, p. 462. This is variously applied. For example, in India, the marriage is dissolved if the husband leaves Islam, but not if the wife does so.

18. See H. Abdalati, *Islam in Focus*, pp. 170–1.

19. I am not aware of any incidents involving Christian families, but this is not an entirely Islamic phenomenon. It is also a problem amongst Hindus, and can be seen as being linked to the idea of *sati* — the burning of a widow on the husband's funeral pile. See

R.S. Rajan, *Real and Imagined Women: Gender, Culture and Post-colonialism*, Ch. 4. The Pakistani dowry customs are also arguably of Hindu origin.

20. 7 December, 1996

21. *Behind the Veil*. The book bears the name of neither publisher nor author, perhaps because of its sensitive nature.

22. See relevant articles, S. Ferguson *New Dictionary of Theology*.

23. See, for example, J.A.Badawi, *The Status of Women in Islam*. The other passage which might be discussed in this context is 1 Timothy 2:1–12.

24. This has nothing to do with the ordained priesthood as understood by the protestant churches. The word 'priest' there is a contraction of the word 'presbyter', which comes from the Greek word for 'elder'.

25. R. C. H. Lenski, *Interpretation of 1 & 2 Corinthians*, p. 615.

26. G. B. Wilson, *1 Corinthians*, p. 209.

27. For example, 1 Corinthians 5:1–5 concerns a particular instance of sexual immorality.

28. See Matthew 5:14–16.

29. Literally, the word *izzat* means honour or greatness, but it has come to be used in different ways. It is either used for one's honour or for one's shame.

30. *Night of the New Moon*, p. 61

31. One occasionally meets Asian Christians whose attitudes are very much coloured by their contact with Islamic culture.

32. See A.R. Doi, *Shari'ah: The Islamic Law*, p. 236.

33. Channel Four, *Eleventh Hour* series, 12 December 1988, produced by Ahmad A. Jamal.

34. F. Haq, *Women, Islam and the State in Pakistan*, states that, since 1991, more than 2,000 women have been imprisoned for *zina*.

35. Surah 4:15.

36. M.W. ul-Haq, *Islamic Criminal Law*, p. 151.

37. The interpretation of this verse has been discussed in Ch. 3 above. Note that the words in brackets do not appear in the original Arabic.

38. This case was widely publicised by the Pakistan Womens' Action Forum, and is referred to in Mumtaz and Shaheed p. 103, F. Haq, 'Women, Islam and the state of Pakistan', in *The Muslim World*, Vol. 96. No. 2, 1996, p. 169, and the Human Rights Watch *Global Report on Women's Human Rights*. As a result of the campaign, the ruling was eventually overturned by the Federal Shari'ah Court, but this was not until Safia Bibi had spent some time in prison, since women are held in custody before trial for *zina*.

39. The Human Rights Watch *Global Report on Women's Human Rights* estimates that more than 70% of women in police custody in Pakistan experience physical abuse, including beating, rape and the insertion of chillies into the vagina (p. 148). 50–80% of those detained are accused of *zina*.

6
So what?

We started with a kaleidoscope of Islamic writings about
women:

- **The apologists**, who uphold traditional Islamic
  teachings about women's roles, and who argue that
  these are liberating to women. In fact, they say, they
  are more liberating than any other system, and in
  particular than anything that Christianity has to offer.
- **Some Muslim women**, who document gross injustices against women in Islamic societies. They argue
  that the systems they have witnessed in fact reduce
  female sexuality to male property, and disempower
  women.
- **Some of the** *Hadith*, which indicate the roots of
  misogyny and open possibilities of women being exploited within Islam.
- **The feminists**, who are seeking reinterpretations
  that reflect the positive attitudes of the Qur'an and
  Muhammad to women.

We then noted that there are parallels to all this within
Christianity. There are those who uphold traditional ideas

and say that these are positive towards women. There are those who point out how the same traditional ideas have been misused, and there are those who seek re-interpretations that will not allow for the misuses to be repeated.

However, we found that the Bible teaches us to expect misuses under any system: that the world has gone wrong for women. It also teaches us that God sees injustices, and is concerned for those who are oppressed — women included. In the life of Jesus, we have traced a reversal of the wrong pattern in male-female relationships, and in the New Testament we have seen some specific teaching that regulates the behaviour of men and women.

It would be far too simple to conclude that one system or other is better, and pointless to argue which has the better historical record. The fact is that both Christianity and Islam can point to many women who have been strong, independent leaders, and to many who have been weak, dependent and exploited. Both can point to great reforms for women: both can also admit that there have been gross misuses in their name.

Further, both systems have been subjected to considerable debate and re-interpretation in recent years. In neither has a definitive view about the position of women emerged. Both encompass a great variety of cultures, classes and ways of thinking, and almost any generalisation made about either will have many exceptions.

In this final chapter, however, we will focus on one tension that is evident in both Christian and Muslim discussions of women's issues; and we will dare the simplification of suggesting that the answer to it indicates the fundamental difference between Christian and Islamic ethics.

278   The tension is that between rules and principles: what is the balance between basic principles of relationships between men and women, and regulations about male and female roles and responsibilities? In Leila Ahmed's language (*Women and Gender in Islam*, pp. 65–6, see pp. 113–16 above), what is the relationship between the 'ethical voice' that tells us who we *are*, and the 'pragmatic voice' that tells us what to *do*?

Both Islam and Christianity have both voices. The question is, which comes first? Do we decide what to do on the basis of who we believe we are, or do we start from what we ought to do, and let that determine what we think of ourselves? For example, do we start by saying that males and females are equal and should therefore have equal shares in inheritance? Or do we start from the ruling that women should inherit a half share and thence argue that their equality with men is in the context of financial dependency on them?

The place of the law

A biblical view

In Ch. 5, Ida quoted the classic New Testament text about the equality of women: 'There is neither Jew nor Greek, slave nor free, male nor female, for you are all one in Christ Jesus' (Galatians 3:24).

This verse is embedded in a passage about the place of the law[1] in Christian thinking. Galatians teaches that even the God-given laws of the Old Testament cannot give human beings what they need: they cannot save us from the predicament of original sin. That sin has been dealt with by the life, death and resurrection of Jesus Christ, and the individual can appropriate what he has done through faith. The technical term is 'justification': God putting us in a right relationship with himself. The emphasis throughout the book is that justification is not something that we can do by keeping the law: it is something that God does in us as we put our faith in Jesus Christ:

> We . . . know that a man[2] is not justified by observing the law, but by faith in Jesus Christ . . . by observing the law no-one will be justified (2:15–17).

What, then, is the place of the law? Why did God give it, if it could not put us right? Paul explains:

> If a law had been given that could impart life, then righteousness would certainly have come by the law. But the Scripture declares that the whole world is a prisoner of sin, so that what was promised, being given through faith in Jesus Christ, might be given to those who believe.
>
> Before faith came, we were held prisoners by the law, locked up until faith should be revealed. So the law was put in charge of us to lead us to Christ that we might be justified by faith. Now that faith has come, we are no longer under the supervision of the law.
>
> You are all sons of God through faith in Christ Jesus, for all of you who were baptised into Christ have clothed yourselves with Christ. There is neither Jew nor Greek,

> slave nor free, male nor female, for you are all one in
> Christ Jesus. If you belong to Christ, then you are
> Abraham's seed, and heirs according to the promise.
>
> What I am saying is that as long as the heir is a child, he is
> no different from a slave, although he owns the whole
> estate. He is subject to guardians and trustees until the
> time set by his father. So also, when we were children, we
> were in slavery under the basic principles of the world
> (3:21–4:3).

280

It is not that we do not need directions: we do need to be
told what is right and what is wrong, and to learn what
pleases God. God's laws are good. However, they are
limited, and have a specific purpose. Only a few verses
earlier, Paul has quoted from the Torah:

> Cursed is everyone who does not continue to do every-
> thing written in the Book of the Law.[3]

Therefore, he says, 'all who rely on the law are under a
curse' (Galatians 3:10). The hard fact is that the law of
God teaches what is right, but human beings never keep it
in its entirety. Anyone who depends on keeping the law as
a way of pleasing God and earning heaven is going to be
disappointed.

The idea is that we start by being in 'slavery under
the basic principles of the world.' In the language of the
Apostle Paul, this refers to spiritual powers and to the anti-
God forces in the world. By nature, he teaches, we are
unable to resist these forces. Even if we try to obey God,
we will keep falling into their traps. In the sense that we
cannot help ourselves, we are slaves. This means that we
are not really free to follow the Right Way — we are
'prisoners of sin'.

In this situation, what is needed is 'supervision', or someone 'put in charge' of us. The same Greek word is used for both of these: *paidagôgos*. A *paidagôgos* was 'a person, usually a slave or freedman, to whom the care of the boys of a family was committed, whose duty it was to attend them at their play, lead them to and from the public school, and exercise a constant superintendence over their conduct and safety.'[4] This is the Apostle Paul's picture of God's laws. In a sense, they put us in another prison: that is, they tell us what to do rather than leaving us free to decide what is right. That is because, while we are slaves to the anti-God forces, we need telling what to do, and we need punishing if we do not do it.

The Apostle Paul uses another picture here: that of dependent children. Children need disciplining and training, because they have not yet learnt to make their own decisions and follow them. God's laws are given to discipline and train us.

But we are not supposed to remain as slaves or children. We are supposed to be set free, or to grow up. The law is given to prepare us for freedom, for adulthood, and not to keep us as we are. That is, the law is a temporary measure: the *paidagôgos* is to 'lead us to Christ' (v. 24) who puts us right with God, so that we are no longer slaves to the anti-God forces. The passage continues:

> But when the time had fully come, God sent his Son, born of a woman, born under the law, to redeem those under the law, that we might receive the full rights of sons. Because you are sons, God sent the Spirit of his Son into our hearts, the Spirit who calls out, '*Abba*, Father.' So

> you are no longer a slave, but a son; and since you are a son, God has made you an heir.'[5]

God's plan has always been to provide a way of release from the prison of law and sin. That is why the Apostle refers to Abraham and the promise. He has been explaining that God promised to bless Abraham and, through him, the whole world long before he gave the law through Moses. Abraham, he reminds us, 'believed God, and it was credited to him as righteousness.'[6] The promise to Abraham has been fulfilled in the Lord Jesus Christ, and when we put our faith in him, we are set free from our prison.

What, then, of the law? It keeps us in check until such time as we are set free to act righteously, says Paul, and our very inability to keep it helps us to see our need for Christ. We can therefore see God's law as having two functions in society:

- It limits human wickedness, by laying down what should be done and meting out punishment to those who disobey.
- It exposes human wickedness, by calling for a perfection that can be found in God alone.

The Old Testament law included many distinctions between Jews and non-Jews, which were symbolic of the special calling of the Jewish people. It also included rulings that distinguished between men and women and between slaves and free people: all were regarded as human beings to be respected, but the different groups had different positions in the cultures of the times, and the regulations accepted the situation.[7] Such laws were limited:

> There is neither Jew nor Greek, slave nor free, male nor
> female, for you are all one in Christ Jesus (Galatians
> 3:24).

This is the truth about human identity; and it is on this
basis that all laws should be interpreted.

Jesus exemplified this in his life and teaching. His   283
voice always brought people back to considering who
they were: what they should do was always secondary. As
Napoleon has noted (p. 247 above), he did not teach what
was practical, but God's perfect standards. Those standards
were not just stricter laws: they went behind the laws to
relationships. That is, Jesus did not see behaviour in terms
of following regulations, but in terms of human relationships with God and other human beings.

On the vexed question of inheritance, about which
the Qur'an has so much to say, for example, the gospels
record only this story:

> Someone in the crowd said to him, 'Teacher, tell my
> brother to divide the inheritance with me.' Jesus replied,
> 'Man, who appointed me a judge or arbiter between
> you?'
> Then he said, 'Watch out! Be on your guard against all
> kinds of greed; a man's life does not consist in the
> abundance of his possessions.'[8]

There follows the story known as 'the parable of the rich
fool'. A man has such a good harvest that he has no room
to store it all, so he decides to build bigger barns, so that
he can 'eat, drink and be merry' for many years. But God
says to him, 'You fool! This very night your life will be
demanded from you. Then who will get what you have
prepared for yourself?' (v.20) Jesus comments, 'This is how

it will be with anyone who stores up things for himself but is not rich towards God.'[9]

Jesus brushes aside the request for a legal ruling. That, he implies, is for the brothers to work out for themselves. He rejects the role of an arbiter, who makes decisions about the details of other peoples' lives. Instead, he teaches the principles by which the brothers should settle their dispute. The important thing is not how much inheritance they should have, but that they should not be greedy. This is because it is their fundamental relationship with God that matters, and not what they own.

Throughout his public career, the main area in which Jesus came into conflict with religious leaders was over the place of the law. It was not that he rejected the law — far from it. He declared that 'until heaven and earth pass away, not the smallest letter, not the least stroke of a pen, will by any means disappear from the Law until everything is accomplished' (Matthew 5:18). He had 'not come to abolish [the Law and the Prophets], but to fulfil them' (Matthew 5:17). That is, his approach to them fulfilled their deepest meaning; and, as in Paul's teaching above, Jesus had come to set people free to be able to fulfil that meaning in their own lives.

The correction of the religious leaders' view of the law was, then, at the centre of Jesus' life and teaching. The question of the place of the 'pragmatic voice' is a key concern of the gospels, and not only of our current debates on the place of women.

The view that Jesus frequently countered was the idea that keeping the regulations was of primary importance. Again and again, he flouted the rules, because he saw a deeper principle behind them. We saw in Ch. 5 (pages 229–233) how he dealt with 'uncleanness': he pointed out that the legal rulings about foods and bodily cleanliness were symbolic, and that true purity comes from the heart. He then flouted all the 'uncleanness' taboos: human beings mattered to him more than any rules, and no human beings could be considered 'unclean' because of any bodily problem. Even those who had become morally 'unclean' through their own sins were not to be shunned, but to be called back into relationship with God and therefore with his people.

Another sort of law, given much attention in the gospels, was the keeping of the Sabbath.[10] The seventh day of the week was a day set aside for rest and worship: no work was to be done on it. Religious leaders down the ages had focused on the meanings of work and rest in their interpretation of this injunction, and had spent much time considering what exactly was forbidden and what permitted. Jesus went against their rulings, and claimed his right to re-interpret:

> One Sabbath Jesus was going through the cornfields; and as his disciples walked along, they began to pick some ears of corn. The Pharisees said to him, 'Look, why are they doing what is unlawful on the Sabbath?' He answered, 'Have you never read what David did when he and his companions were hungry and in need? In the days of Abiathar the high priest, he entered the house of God and ate the consecrated bread, which is lawful only for the priests to eat. And he also gave some to his companions.'
>
> Then he said to them, 'The Sabbath is made for man, not man for the Sabbath. So the Son of Man is Lord even of the Sabbath.'[11]

'Son of Man' is one of Jesus' titles for himself. It is interesting that he chooses this title, with its stress on his humanity, as he puts himself above the traditional interpretations of the law and even above the law itself. It is because the law — in this case the law about the Sabbath — is for the benefit of human beings, and they can therefore interpret it as such. Jesus is the Great Human Being.

286

The Pharisees categorised plucking ears of corn as 'work'. Jesus does not discuss the categorisation: he is not interested in defining what can and cannot be done. Rather, he points out that even one of their greatest leaders had broken a much more important legal ruling when he had been in need. Human need must take priority over any details of law.

Jesus put this principle into practice on several occasions, and every time the religious leaders challenged him. Here is one example that concerns a woman:

> On a Sabbath Jesus was teaching in one of the synagogues, and a woman was there who had been crippled by a spirit for eighteen years. She was bent over and could not straighten up at all. When Jesus saw her, he called her forward and said to her, 'Woman, you are set free from your infirmity.' Then he put his hands on her, and immediately she straightened up and praised God.

> Indignant because Jesus had healed on the Sabbath, the synagogue ruler said to the people, 'There are six days for work. So come and be healed on those days, not on the Sabbath.' The Lord answered him, 'You hypocrites! Doesn't each of you on the Sabbath untie his ox or donkey from the stall and lead it out to give it water? Then should not this woman, a daughter of Abraham,

whom Satan has kept bound for eighteen long years, be set free on the Sabbath day from what bound her?'[12]

The famous Sermon on the Mount (Matthew 5–7) goes behind legal rulings in a slightly different way. Rather than looking at the effects of the law on the welfare of other human beings, it focuses on the heart attitudes of the person seeking to keep the law. Thus, for example, Jesus says:

> You have heard that it was said, 'Do not commit adultery.' But I tell you that anyone who looks at a woman lustfully has already committed adultery with her in his heart. If your right eye causes you to sin, gouge it out and throw it away. It is better for you to lose one part of your body than for your whole body to be thrown into hell.[13]

Throughout Matthew 5, Jesus insists on complete purity, and tells people to go to what look like ridiculous extremes in their quest for it. The religious leaders had, as we have seen, surrounded the laws with regulations to ensure their keeping, but Jesus says, 'unless your righteousness surpasses that of the Pharisees and teachers of the law, you will certainly not enter the kingdom of God' (Matthew 5:20). Is he, then, just giving an even stricter set of rules?

The above examples of his dealing with the Sabbath immediately contradict such a suggestion. He did not even keep the rules that there were; so how could he be giving another set of even heavier ones? What he is doing is calling people to the purity of life that is based on right relationships. The law on murder means not holding anything against anyone, the law on adultery means not lusting after anyone, the law on divorce means being faithful in marriage, the law on oaths means being honest in our dealings, and the law on retaliation means treating people well even when they do harm.

Matthew 6 moves on to religious acts — almsgiving, fasting and prayer. Again, Jesus refuses to give any regulations, but focuses attention on right relationships. If the laws discussed in Matthew 5 are about relationships with human beings, religious acts are about relationships with God. As each topic is raised, Jesus exhorts his hearers to do their acts of piety only for God, as an expression of the relationship that he wants to have with human beings — the relationship of father to child.

The law is, then, important to Jesus, as it is to Paul, but both of them see it as secondary. They both counter the view that religion is about keeping God's rules in order to please him and gain heaven: in fact, they both insist that the keeping of rules will neither please God nor earn heaven.

Jesus shows us that what pleases God is right relationships with him and with other people. God's concern is with our welfare, and any use of the law that puts regulations before people is wrong. Paul teaches that the law is there to restrain our wickedness, but also that it shows us our need of Christ. This is particularly clear from the way that Jesus teaches about the deeper implications of commandments about relating to people: he immediately shows us how far we fall short of his standard.

The teaching on divorce already quoted by Napoleon (pp. 247–8) sums it up:

> Some Pharisees came to him to test him. They asked, 'Is it lawful for a man to divorce his wife for any and every

reason?' 'Haven't you read,' he replied, 'that at the beginning the Creator "made them male and female", and said,
"For this reason a man will leave his father and his mother
and be joined to his wife, and the two will become one
flesh?" So they are no longer two, but one. Therefore
what God has joined together, let man not separate.'

'Why, then,' they asked, did Moses command that a man
give his wife a certificate of divorce and send her away?'
Jesus replied, 'Moses permitted you to divorce your wives
because your hearts were hard. But it was not this way
from the beginning. I tell you that anyone who divorces
his wife, except for marital unfaithfulness, and marries
another woman commits adultery.'[14]

Again, the religious leaders want to test him with a legal
ruling: again, Jesus refuses to take part in their debate.
Rather, he goes straight to fundamental relationships, in
this case between husband and wife. That fundamental
relationship, given by God at creation, is one of indissol-
uble unity: this is more important than any rule about
divorce.

What, then, the religious leaders want to know, is the
place of the law? Why did Moses give it? Jesus does not
reject the law, but tells them that it was given only because
of hard-heartedness. People were not able to live according to God's creation design, so they needed regulations.
There are passages in the Torah that ensure that women
cannot simply be dismissed from a marriage, or be charged
with sexual misconduct without redress.[15] These, according to Jesus, are only there because of human failure. In
Paul's terms, they function as supervisors until such time
as people are set free to be able to relate as God created
them to do.

A view of Islam

Mr Ahmad had requested a New Testament and had spent some weeks reading it. Now, he asked the local vicar to come and discuss it with him. The vicar was delighted. Here, he thought was an opportunity to discuss the central truths of the Gospel with his Muslim friend. They sat together over a cup of tea, and Mr Ahmad started the discussion: 'I have one main thing I want to ask. You know it says in Acts 15:20 that people should not eat blood? Why do Christians eat meat with the blood in it?'

The vicar was disappointed, but he learnt something: what seems important to Muslims might not be what seems important to Christians. Mr Ahmad was interested in the few legal prescriptions in the New Testament: to him, the wonderful story of the coming of Jesus Christ to save the world was not what really mattered.

Jesus refused to give legal rulings: Muhammad often gave them. *Hadith* after *hadith* relates how people came to him with questions about how to act in particular circumstances, and he gave his judgement or received a Qur'anic verse in response. It is on the basis of these judgements and verses, and on Muhammad's own actions, that the *shari'ah*, the Islamic law, has been built.

Shari'ah is an Arabic word meaning the Path to be followed. Literally it means 'the way to a watering place.' It is the path not only leading to Allah, the Most High, but the path believed by all Muslims to be the path shown by Allah, the Creator himself through his Messenger, Prophet Muhammad (P.B.U.H.). In Islam, Allah alone is the sovereign and it is he who has the right to ordain a path for the guidance of mankind. Thus it is only the Shari'ah that liberates man from servitude to other than Allah.[16]

Islam has two aspects: *iman* or faith and *'amal* or actions. The two are intimately related, for it is belief in God, his messengers and the Last Day that leads to acceptance of his guidance and to obedient actions. Obedience then strengthens faith. Christianity also includes both faith and actions, but the emphasis is different. Whereas any book on basic Christianity contains much more about faith than about deeds, books on basic Islam contain much more about deeds than about faith. Sarwar's *Islam: Beliefs and Teachings*, for example, gives 28 pages to 'basic beliefs', and 41 pages to 'basic duties'. Abdalati's *Islam in Focus* has 52 pages on 'ideology' and 'basic concepts', and then 85 pages on 'application'. The 'five pillars' of Islam include only one that concerns *iman*: the other four are all to do with actions.

291

The actions are specified in minute detail, even in areas of life which Christians would see as matters of personal or cultural choice. For example, where Jesus' specific instructions about prayer run only to a few verses,[17] Quasem's *Salvation of the Soul and Islamic Devotions* has 152 pages of detailed regulations about prayer. This excludes instructions about ritual ablutions, but includes, for example, 27 conditions for validity of prayers, 61 acts that corrupt prayers and 72 acts 'disliked' in prayers as well as details of times, postures and wording for different kinds of prayers.

As well as instructions for devotions, Islam has laws for every aspect of life. Doi's book *Shari'ah: The Islamic Law* quoted above has chapters on marriage and family law, and also on crime and punishment, inheritance and disposal of property, trade and commerce, the distribution of wealth, lawful and unlawful foods, international law and *jihad*.

Islam divides all human activities into five categories:

1. *Fard*: compulsory actions, which are rewarded, and the omission of which is punished.
2. *Mandub*: recommended actions, which are rewarded, but the omission of which is not punished.
3. *Mubah*: neutral actions, which are permitted but neither rewarded nor punished.
4. *Makruh*: disliked actions, which are disapproved but not punished.
5. *Haram*: forbidden actions, which are punished.[18]

It is the *shari'ah* that indicates which actions are in which category, which prescribes punishments to be administered in this life, and which enables people to know how to receive rewards and escape punishments in the next. Doi describes it as 'the path ... leading to Allah the Most High ... that liberates man from servitude to other than Allah' (p. 2).

One of the most frequent descriptions the Qur'an uses of itself is that it is *huda*, 'guidance'.

> This is the Book; in it is guidance, without doubt, to those who fear God.[19]
>
> These are verses of the Wise Book, a Guide and a Mercy to the doers of good, those who establish prayer and give regular charity, and have (in their hearts) the assurance of the hereafter. These are on (true) guidance from their Lord; and these are the ones who will prosper.[20]

God's mercy is, it is taught, seen in the giving of guidance; and response to that guidance is doing what is right, specifically here praying and giving as instructed and living in the light of life after death.

Islam is about believing that this guidance comes from God, and represents what he requires from human beings. It is then about doing what he wants.

293

> Submission to the good Will of God, together with obedience to his beneficial Law, is the best safeguard for peace and harmony. It enables man to make peace between himself and his fellow men on the one hand, and between the human community and God on the other. It creates harmony among the elements of Nature.[21]

Everything that exists is subject to God's laws, and, except for human beings, is bound to obey them. It is only we who have free will, and can therefore choose whether to obey or not. God tells us his will and calls us to submission through his prophets. This is the way to harmony.[22]

The first Surah of the Qur'an, which is recited in all the formal Islamic prayers, has as its only petition a request for guidance:

> Show us the straight way, the way of those on whom Thou hast bestowed Thy grace, those whose (portion) is not wrath, and who go not astray.[23]

Christianity, too has the concept of a way or a path. In fact, one of the earliest names for the faith of Jesus was 'The way' (Acts 18:26; 19:23; 22:4). But the concept is different: while Jesus Christ described himself as 'The way, the truth and the life' (John 14:6), Doi writes of God's laws as the path to follow. Where Jesus is primarily offering new relationships which will lead to right actions,

Islam is primarily offering a pattern of what should be done. Where the New Testament sees the law as restraining us until we are set free to choose what is right, Abdalati, like most other Muslim writers, sees obedience to the law as itself the way to right relationships.

294   This is reflected in the sorts of discussions about the place of women that have been explored in this book so far. Chapters 2 and 3, which considered Islamic teachings, were all about the status of women, and how men and women should therefore act and be treated. For example, the discussions on divorce included who can ask for it, how it should be carried out, and what responsibilities the divorcing partner should have towards the other.

In contrast, Ida noted that even the traditional interpreter of biblical teaching on women, J.B. Hurley, drew conclusions only about relationships and not about roles. Our Chs. 4 and 5 on Christian teachings, considered first how relationships have gone wrong and can be reversed, and only then looked at how the new relationships might work out in practice. Even then, Napoleon's account of New Testament teaching about marriage and authority was mostly about basic principles. On divorce, for example, he considered Jesus' teaching about the permanence of marriage, and circumstances under which divorce might be permissible. He then pointed out that forgiveness and reconciliation are preferable, because these are at the basis of the whole Christian faith. He gave no information about how a divorce should be carried out, or about divorce settlements or the custody of children. That is because the New Testament simply does not mention these things.

The fundamental difference

The situations of Jesus and Muhammad were different: Jesus was a wandering teacher, and Muhammad was establishing a state. Jesus was constantly challenging the establishment, while the new Muslim *umma* needed to develop an establishment of its own. As Christianity and Islam developed, their circumstances were again different. Where political power followed the dissemination of personal faith in Christianity, Islam spread first politically, and the conversion of individuals followed on.[24]

For nearly four centuries, Christianity was the religion of widespread but politically powerless minority groups. The early Christians had little hope of influencing state policy: they concentrated rather on how they could live according to the principles of the Gospel under rule that was often hostile. The first Islamic centuries were characterised by rapid conquest and the spread of the Islamic state. Non-Muslims had to adjust to living under Islam, and the Muslims had control of the political and legal systems.

The centrality of law and practice in Islam and the lack of such details in Christianity can therefore be explained on historical grounds. However, the difference also reflects a deeper difference in world views. It is not only that the early Muslim and Christian communities had different socio-political needs: it is also that Christianity and Islam offer different understandings of the human predicament, and therefore different solutions to it.

The underlying assumption in the New Testament teaching about the law is that human beings are 'hard-hearted', 'prisoners of sin', or 'slaves to the basic principles of the world', and that they need to be set free. In contrast, Islam rejects the concept of 'original sin.' It teaches that people are born innocent and are corrupted by their environment. The Bible agrees that environment can have a negative effect (e.g. 1 Cor. 15:33), but is clear that there is a tendency to sin in the very nature of human beings.

This is not to say that God made us wicked — far from it. As we have seen, Genesis teaches that human beings — male and female — were made in the image of God himself: that is, we are of infinite value, we are persons, and we have the capacity to choose and the responsibility to care for the whole world. What happened was that wickedness entered the world when our first ancestors sinned; and every human being since then has been born into a world-gone-wrong and as part of that world-gone-wrong. Christians describe this state as being 'fallen': as part of a fallen world, we all start life as fallen people, liable to worship our own interests rather than God. The predicament of women explored in Ch. 4 is only one aspect of a wider problem.

The New Testament puts it this way:

. . . in Adam all die . . . (1 Corinthians 15:22).

. . . sin entered the world through one man, and death through sin, and in this way death came to all men, because all sinned (Romans 5:12).

Some Islamic sources teach that God predestined some to sin and others not to sin:

Muslim b. Yasar said that when Umar b. al-Khattab was questioned about the verse, 'When your Lord took their offspring from the backs of the children of Adam . . .' he replied that he had heard God's messenger say when he was questioned about it, God created Adam, then passed his right hand over his back and brought forth from it his offspring, saying, I have created these for paradise and they will do the deeds of those who go to paradise. He then passed his hand over his back and brought forth from it his offspring, saying, I have created these for hell and they will do the deeds of those who go to hell (*Mishkat Al-Masabih*, Vol. 1: The Book of Faith p. 27).

This is quite different from the biblical idea of original sin. Rather, the idea is that all people — of every race, religion, gender and age — sin and fall short of God's glory (see Romans 1–3). This is not something that God has predestined them to do, but something that has become part of our nature since the first disobedience.

Muslim writers often criticise the idea of original sin. For example, Abdalati (1975, p. 31) writes:

It is commonly believed that sin started with Adam and Eve during their life in the Garden of Eden. That event led to the Fall and has ever since branded the human race with guilt, stigma, and bewilderment. Islam has taken a unique position on the whole issue, a position which is not shared by any other religion we know.

The 'common belief' is evidently that of Christians. Abdalati then recounts the Qur'anic version of the Adam and Eve story, in which they are not told that they will die if they eat the forbidden fruit, but that they will 'run into harm and injustice'. Their disobedience is largely the fault of Satan, who deceives them into thinking that eating the fruit is not a bad thing. When God calls them and reminds them that they have done wrong, they immediately pray for mercy and are forgiven. He explains:

> This symbolic event . . . tells that the human being is imperfect and ever wanting even if he were to remain in paradise. But committing a sin or making a mistake, as Adam and Eve did, does not necessarily deaden the human heart, prevent spiritual reform or stop moral growth. On the contrary, the human being has enough sensibility to recognise his sins and shortcomings. More importantly, he is capable of knowing where to turn and to whom he should turn for guidance (p. 31).

298

He is right in thinking that this is very different from the Christian position: there is a difference between 'committing a sin' and 'making a mistake' in Christian thinking, and Adam and Eve are believed to have done the former, by very deliberately disobeying God. The Bible describes people as spiritually blind, and even dead (e.g. Ephesians 2:1–5). We have not only gone wrong: we justify ourselves and even believe that we are right (see, for example, Romans 1:32). We certainly do not naturally know to whom we should turn to help us put things right.

This teaching Abdalati refers to with indignation:

> . . . discrimination on the basis of sex and hereditary guilt or sin are alien to the spirit of Islam. The idea of original sin or hereditary criminality has no room in the teachings of Islam (p. 32).

He is outraged at the idea that we all share a fallen nature. In contrast, he describes the Islamic position: 'Man, according to the Qur'an (30:30) and to the Prophet, is born in a natural state of purity or *fitrah*, that is, Islam, or submission to the will and law of God. Whatever becomes of man after birth is the result of external influences and intruding factors' (p. 32).

There are some misunderstandings of the Christian position here. As we have seen, there is no justification for the belief that the woman was to blame for sin and, since all people are sinners, original sin can be no reason for discrimination. More importantly, 'original sin' in Christian thinking is no more synonymous with 'hereditary criminality' than is Adam and Eve's sin with a 'mistake'. The biblical understanding of sin does not fit into the five Islamic categories of human action (see p. 292 above). The question is not one of which actions are punishable and which are not, but of whether our basic orientation is towards God or towards self. Sin, according to the Bible, is a fundamental rebellion against God, which can hide behind good citizenship and even religious devotion as well as behind robbery and murder. 'Crimes' are merely particular symptoms of sin.

From such a standpoint, Abdalati's indignation is but to be expected. If human beings are by nature not only sinful but blinded to the truth about themselves and about God, it is not surprising that they do not like the Bible's teaching about the fall. It is more comfortable to believe that people are born pure. However, there are passages in the Qur'an and the *Hadith* that seem closer to the Bible than to Abdalati's standard Islamic position.

For example, the devil is said to influence us at birth:

> Abu Huraira reported God's messenger as saying, except Mary and her son, no human being is born without the devil touching him, so that he raises his voice crying out

> because of the devil's touch (*Mishkat Al-Masabih*, Vol. 1, p. 20).
>
> Anas reported God's messenger as saying, the devil flows in a man like his blood (Idem).

This would appear to mean that we are attracted to sin as naturally as we have blood: this is not something that comes from the environment outside us, but from within. Even Muhammad had to have his heart made clean in his childhood:

> Anas told that Gabriel came to God's messenger when he was playing with some other boys, seized him, threw him down, split open his heart and took out of it a clot of blood, saying, this is the devil's portion in you. He then washed it with Zamzam water in a gold dish, repaired it, and put it back in its place (*Mishkat Al-Masabih*, Vol. 2, p. 1258).

The Qur'an usually speaks of sinners and believers as two different categories of people, but it also has hints that sin is universal:

> Nay, but man doth transgress all bounds, in that he looketh upon himself as self-sufficient (Surah 96:6–7).

Islam and Christianity are, then, agreed that something has gone wrong in this world, and that human beings are largely responsible for it. The question is, *What has gone wrong?* Is it that all of us are, by nature, rebellious against God and liable to live for our own comfort? Or is it that we are basically good and need to be given and then to choose to follow the right directions?

The Bible teaches the first. And, if we are basically rebellious, directions will not be sufficient. We are likely to convince ourselves that good is bad and bad is good, and, even if we recognise what is right, we are unlikely to choose to do it. If we do make the right choices, we will find ourselves too selfish to be able to carry them out consistently.

The question is then, not, 'What should we do?' but 'How can we change?' The biblical answer is, as explained in Galatians, 'Through faith in Jesus Christ.' His death and resurrection, as God incarnate, have opened the way to forgiveness and transformation: to a new life in which we can be set free to relate rightly and therefore to act rightly. Personal appropriation of this is the first and necessary step on the right path.

From an Islamic point of view, this is simply not necessary. If we are not 'fallen', we do not need a new life. All we need is a change in direction. If nothing has gone fundamentally wrong with human beings, and our sin has not disrupted the universe, nothing needs to be done to reverse the disruption. The death of Christ is not re-quired.

> *Peter and Doreen had to clean up the house of an elderly aunt who had been taken into hospital.*[25] *It was a mess, but it was no use trying to tidy it up. Everything was filthy and broken. There were cigarette burns all over the carpets, the upholstery and even the bedding, and the dog had fouled in every room. The stench was sickening.*
> *There was no option but to open all the windows, take everything to the rubbish tip, scour the house and re-furnish it. The aunt needed a whole new set of clothes.*

How do we perceive our 'mess'? Does it need just dusting and re-organising, or do we need a complete fumigation and re-furnishing?

Back to the women

We seem to have strayed far from our discussion of the position of women in Islam and in Christianity, but it was necessary. Christians and Muslims offer different rules for gender relationships, but it is only possible to judge between them on the basis of an understanding of the differing underlying assumptions.

We have already seen that it is dangerous to make judgements on the basis of practice: both systems have been subject to misuse over the centuries. It is also difficult to make judgements on the basis of the rules themselves. Something that seems obviously wrong to a Christian can seem obviously right to a Muslim: we all judge according to our own presuppositions.

Then, there is much overlap. Christians and Muslims would agree, for example, that fornication and adultery are wrong, that spouses should respect and care for each other, that women (and men) should dress modestly, and that motherhood is a high calling. Further, the writings of feminists within both religions can be remarkably similar. The anger at malpractice and focus on scriptural teaching about equality and mutuality is common. It is sometimes difficult to distinguish between what Muslim feminists think Islam teaches about women and what Christian feminists think Christianity teaches about women.

There is, however, a fundamental difference. The question is, What is the purpose of the rules? Are they to supervise slaves to sin, or are they themselves the path to freedom? If the former, they are temporary, and dependent on the way things have gone wrong in particular situations: getting free from the sin is more important. If the latter, they are permanent and universal; and they are what really matters.

This is, perhaps, why Christians have relatively easily accepted that, for example, the rule about women being silent in church discussed by Napoleon (pages 257–263 above) does not mean that women should never speak out in public worship.[26] It is the principle of orderly worship and bringing glory to God that matters: the details are situational. Similarly, it does not disturb Christian readers that details of, for example, marital rights and responsibilities are lacking in the Bible: it is the marriage relationship that matters, and such details are matters of custom and choice. As the Apostle Paul taught in Galatians, the law is secondary:

> By observing the law no-one will be justified (Galatians 2:17).

Islam has many more detailed regulations, and it can be difficult to challenge them on the basis of what is perceived as a prior principle. It is not so easy to argue that, for example, the permission for husbands to beat their wives was for the time of Muhammad only. While Muhammad may have disliked the ruling, the ruling was made, and Muhammad accepted it. As the Qur'an says in another context:[27]

> But it is possible that ye dislike a thing which is good for you, and that ye love a thing which is bad for you. But God knoweth and ye know not.

Those who believe that the rulings given to Muhammad are the right path for all peoples are likely to continue to see them as central and unchangeable. That is why the interpretations of such writers as Engineer and Mernissi (see Ch. 3.2 above) challenge much more than teaching about women. They question the heart of traditional Islamic understandings of the law by subordinating what have been regarded as divine rulings to their perceptions of the principles behind them. In doing so, they are using an ethical method which is closer to that of traditional Christianity than to that of traditional Islam.

The balance between the 'ethical' voice and the 'pragmatic' voice — between what we should be and what we should do — is clear in Christian ethics: what we do is to grow out of what we are, and the former therefore takes priority. There is no such priority in Islamic ethics: being Muslim is equated with doing what Islam requires. The very word *islam* implies submitting to God's will: doing what he commands.

This leads to authority being vested in the laws that are believed to have come from God, and in the people who are deemed to have the right to interpret them. In contrast, protestant Christianity sees every Christian as having received the Holy Spirit, through whom he or she can interpret the scriptures and make his or her own decisions about how to act.

This contrast too makes it easier for Christians to re-interpret the Bible. Traditional interpretation is considered important even by protestants, and new ideas have always to be carefully checked, but the principle that every believer — male as well as female — can comment on gender roles is clear, and the possibility that previous interpretations were wrong is always present. Mernissi's claim that every Muslim has the right and perhaps even the duty to scrutinise the *Hadith* and interpret the law is appropriating an individual autonomy that, common though it may have been in the early Islamic centuries, would appear to have more in common with protestant Christianity than with traditional Islam. The feminists are not the only Muslims moving in this direction:[28] the future development of Islamic law will depend on how influential such movement becomes.

There is another way of asking our question: How do the rules relate to gender relationships as we actually see them in the world? Are the basic patterns we see what God originally created, or do they represent relationships gone fundamentally wrong? If the former, we need to affirm them, but to recognise that they can be subject to misuse and therefore to **regulate** them. If the latter, we still need regulations to limit the damage, but we also need to **challenge** and to **change** them.

There are both Christians and Muslims who argue that the biological and psychological make-up of women makes them weaker than men and therefore that they should be dependent. They would proceed to male leadership and sharp distinctions of roles, and say that all these things reflect the way that God has constituted the two genders. Such gender differences should therefore be affirmed, and religious and cultural systems should regulate them to ensure that men and women take their appointed places without exploiting each other.

If we are fallen, this is a dangerous argument. The differences between men and women as we experience them today would reflect creation, but they would also reflect a creation gone wrong. It would therefore be of key importance to discern what is as created, and what have been the effects of the fall.

Muslims say that theirs is the 'natural' religion, in that human beings are born in a state of conformity to Islam.

306 There is some truth in this, in that the Islamic system accepts and regulates many of the 'natural' human instincts. From a Christian point of view, the problem is that some of these 'natural' instincts are wrong.

Fatima Heeren may be right when she says that there is a 'polygamous disposition undoubtedly inherent in some men'.[29] We would want to say that this disposition is due to original sin, and therefore wrong: it should be countered rather than encouraged. It may be that the Islamic system of divorce is, if properly applied, a good way of regulating marriages that have gone wrong. We would want to say that marriages only go wrong because of sinfulness: marriage should be a life-long commitment and not a terminable contract. It may be that Islamic laws on witness make sense in a patriarchal society, and even that male dominance is 'natural'. We would want to say that the apparently 'natural' is here due to original sin, and that women should never be thrust into situations in which their testimony is devalued.

Ida's analysis from Genesis suggests that the whole pattern of blame/domination/sharp role division is a distortion of God's purpose. At creation, he made male and female to work together and depend on each other. The distortion is a result of self-interest and power-seeking. The human beings who sought their own pleasure instead of obedience to God, and wanted to rival him in power, now seek their own pleasure rather than that of other people, and want power over one another. This is particularly seen in the relationships between the genders.

This means that regulations are desperately needed for every particular manifestation of the problem. We need the supervisor — the *paidagôgos* — to curb our tendency to use other people. But we need more than that: we need to challenge inbred patterns of rivalry so that, like the Lord Jesus Christ, we can reverse the wrong patterns and move towards accepting ourselves as God has made us and loving and serving one another. The criteria for judging rules for gender relationships are therefore, first, whether they are effective in preventing exploitation and, second, whether they challenge the pattern of blame/domination/ sharp role division and encourage mutual love and service. It is possible to do one without the other.

From a Christian point of view, however, it is not primarily the systems that need to be judged. Every system will have its strengths and its weaknesses. Even the God-given system of Old Testament laws was tailored to a particular community in a particular situation, so that it is not directly applicable in other contexts. For example, the ruling that a rapist should marry his victim if she is single (Deuteronomy 22:28) functioned as a protection for the girl and her family in a society in which women depended on marriage and the loss of virginity made marriage difficult: in twentieth-century Britain, it would have quite the opposite effect. It is the underlying principles about values and relationships that are changeless.

It is not, then, the system that is primary, but the way to right relationships. The question is not, 'Is this system correct?', but 'Does this way put relationships right?' This brings us at last to the answer to the question posed by Suzanna in our prologue (p. xiv above):

308 What has Christianity to offer women?

NOT western culture

Only one of the present authors is a westerner, and the westerner has a Jewish background that reminds her that the Bible was written in the Middle East and that the Lord Jesus Christ was not a westerner. His church can be found in every part of the world, and there are now many more non-western than western Christians.

Christianity has been strongly influenced by the West, and the West by Christianity, but the two are not synonymous. It was only during the anomalous interlude of western colonial power that Christian people thought that western culture was to be exported with Christian faith. Even then, the facts of Jesus' coming into a particular culture and the New Testament being written in Greek rather than Aramaic or Hebrew have encouraged Christians to translate the Bible and to encourage people to use their own languages rather than forcing them to learn English or Hebrew or Greek.[30] There are now growing movements of Christians who are deliberately reflecting on how their faith can best be incarnate in their own cultural situations.[31]

All of these would, like Napoleon, see much to criticise as well as much to respect in western culture. But they would strenuously deny that western culture is what

Christianity has to offer. The faith brings with it principles that challenge all cultures but can be worked out in any cultural context. In each situation, the culture will determine how the principles are applied and therefore the system that emerges.

Islam also adapts culturally to some extent, but it carries with it many detailed rules of behaviour that comprise a culture in themselves. This is, perhaps, why Muslims often suppose that, in criticising western laws, they are criticising Christianity. Dr Jamal Badawi quotes the *Encyclopedia Americana International* in his *The Status of Woman in Islam*:

> According to the English Common Law . . . all real property which a wife held at the time of a marriage became a possession of her husband. He was entitled to the rent from the land and to any profit which might be made from operating the estate during the joint life of the spouses. As time passed, the English courts devised means to forbid a husband's transferring real property without the consent of his wife, but he still retained the right to manage it and to receive the money which it produced. As to a wife's personal property, the husband's power was complete. He had the right to spend it as he saw fit (p. 9).

It would be right to ask why the Church was so slow to realise that such laws could result in gross injustice, but wrong to suppose that the laws are intrinsically Christian. They arose from the interaction of Christian principles — that husband and wife are so united that they are 'one flesh' (Genesis 2:24) and that the husband is the 'head' of the household (but see Ch. 3.2 on this) — and the particular system of ownership in England. Where other

309

Christian principles — such as the husband loving his wife enough to die for her — are not followed, or where — as over the past century — the system of ownership has changed, the laws do not work.

310 We have said that a system needs both to counter exploitation and to promote an ideal reversal of the 'fall'. While the traditional Islamic system does only the first, since it denies the 'fall', the problem with any Christian system is that it may so focus on the ideal of what ought to be that it does only the second. It may also confuse contextual laws with eternal principles, and thus cling onto laws which are no longer appropriate.

Past laws have assumed that people were Christians, and would therefore love one another and seek to live according to biblical principles of, for example, sexual purity and lifelong marriage. The present situation in Britain is that many people have rejected such biblical principles, and that only a minority aspire to self-giving love. There is an ideal of freedom, to be sure, but it is not the biblical freedom to obey God: it is the individual 'freedom' to do as we please that the Apostle Paul sees as slavery to anti-God forces. Such 'freedom' needs supervision: it is our prayer that the British legal system will soon adapt to provide it.

NOT a perfect system of regulations for the conduct of gender relations

From a biblical point of view, some of the Islamic teaching about women is entirely praiseworthy — that they should be faithful to their husbands, for example, and that motherhood is to be honoured. Some, like that on divorce, is open to misuse; some, like the Shi'ite teaching on temporary marriage, is wrong;[32] and some, like that on removing bodily hair, deals with practices which should be entirely a matter of cultural or personal choice.

But that is not the point: the key difference between Christianity and Islam is that Christians do not accept that regulations are what meet fundamental human need. They are useful, and some are necessary, but they are not sufficient. As Jesus flouted many of the regulations of his day and called people to right relationship with God and each other, so the focus of Christianity now should be, we have argued, not regulations but relationships. Even if we had a perfect legal system, it would not be enough, because we would not be able to follow it. The legal system is needed only to keep society in check, so that people can move towards the new relationships that are available through the Lord Jesus Christ.

In the end, what does it matter who does the housework and who earns the money? Both need to be done, and both have drawbacks as well as rewards. The need is not to decide who does what, but to recognise that neither can in themselves either increase or decrease human worth.

Men and women are different: all systems have to adapt to the fact that, for example, women carry children and men can on average carry heavier physical weights. In some things, we have no choice: Napoleon cannot give birth to a child, and Ida, much to her chagrin, cannot budge the nuts on a car wheel without help.[33] The problem is not how we organise ourselves to allow for these differences, but whether we think that one of us is therefore better than the other.

The 'mess' in gender relationships that Ida has described is not only about who should do what, and what should happen if they step out of line. It is also about the anger felt by women at how they feel they have been treated. It is about jealousy and rivalry and fighting for recognition and affirmation. It is, at base, about people who want to be valued and loved.

Without the value and love, no system will improve matters. And without people recognising where they have been wrong, and learning to forgive and be forgiven, they are not going to value and love each other. Without being forgiven, people will continue to hide their guilt and blame and exploit others. Without forgiving, people will continue to be angry and to fight for systems that give them more power.

It is here that Christianity has something to offer:

The Lord Jesus Christ himself

> If anyone is in Christ, he is a new creation; the old has gone, the new has come! All this is from God, who reconciled us to himself through Christ and gave us the ministry of reconciliation: that God was reconciling the world to himself in Christ, not counting men's[34] sins against them. And he has committed to us the message of reconciliation (2 Corinthians 5:17–19).

Reconciliation was a key word in Napoleon's consideration of divorce: Muslims and Christians alike recognise that reconciliation is better than separation. Here, the Apostle Paul calls people to an even more important reconciliation: the reconciliation with God that enables reconciliation with other people. This reconciliation is, he says, through the Lord Jesus Christ and specifically through his death on the cross (v. 15, 21).

The key to reconciliation is that God no longer 'counts people's' sins against them.' However bad they were, they are forgiven; and without forgiveness there can be no true reconciliation but only an uneasy truce. In Jesus Christ, we are offered God's forgiveness: it is the teaching of Jesus that, when we know we are forgiven, we should — and can — forgive others (Matthew 6:14–15; 18:21–35).

In Jesus Christ, says the Apostle Paul, we can also be a 'new' creation. That is, we are offered a return to being what God meant us to be: a path towards reversing the 'mess'. It is thus that we can move towards Jesus' reversal of the 'mess' in male-female relationships, and towards all people — male and female — learning the way of sacrificial love that he modelled for us.

> *Sewa comes from a high caste Sikh family, and used to see women's roles as producing children and being available to serve and please men. When he started to follow Jesus, he realised that men and women were equal. 'It was hard to accept,' he says. 'I wouldn't have done any housework before, but now, I will do anything. Now, I believe that women should be involved in public speaking, in planning, in everything.' He acts according to his beliefs: since his wife has been ill, he has not only done the cooking and housework but has attended to all her personal needs in hygiene and dressing. He has laid down much of his life for her, while encouraging her to continue her work as far as she is able.*

Susan came to Christ as a teenage atheist, and attended a church in which young men were told that, if they really wanted to follow Jesus, they should not have girl-friends. This was, doubtless, to encourage them towards single-hearted devotion, but Susan felt that women were dangerous and that, in order to please her new lord, she should become as sexless and as like the men as possible. It was only later that she slowly came to understand that God really loved her, just as she was — a woman. She now knows that God's love in Christ is for all people, just as they are, and feels her value as a sexual being. She puts her beliefs into practice by accepting and valuing other people, especially women, from all cultural backgrounds.

Jim and Alison were living together. They would have said that they were Christians, but that didn't mean much. Then they came to the Lord Jesus Christ, and everything changed. They made the commitment of marriage and discovered a love that is based on giving and not on getting. 'I had realised that the way I was treating Alison was not very helpful to her,' says Jim, 'But I had no intention of doing anything about it. I thought of women as people to possess — as ways of boosting my own ego — so I thought about leaving Alison, not about changing. When we came to Christ, it was not that I tried to make amends for the past, but that we had a whole new way of living. The Bible says, "We love because he first loved us" (1 John 4:19). It was Jesus' loving us that opened a whole new vista of how to relate to one another.'

Zubaidah came to Britain as a bride, but found that her in-laws disliked her. After three miserable years and a baby who died at three months, her husband divorced her under Islamic law and she was sent back to her family. Her father refused to take her in, because of the shame it would bring on him, so she was sent back to Britain — with no place to go and only temporary permission to enter the country. She found Christian friends who gave her a home, cared for her through a long period of depression, and helped her to get a work permit and a home of her own. One

> *day, she asked them: 'How can I follow your Jesus?' She is now following him, and finding that his acceptance of her heals all her previous rejections.*

That is what Christianity has to offer: not a system but a Person, the Lord Jesus Christ, God giving himself to this world-gone-wrong so that we can be forgiven, God sending his Holy Spirit to change us from the inside, so that we can live as pleases him. And what pleases him? That every human being — male and female — should act and be treated as what they are — infinitely precious beings made to reflect his image. That is the status and dignity of women.

In the Name of God,
the Father, the Son and the Holy Spirit.
Amen.

Notes

1. 'Law' can mean different things in the New Testament, and the Old Testament contains several different kinds of laws. Here, we refer to law as instructions from God about how to act.
2. The Greek has the word for a human being, not the word for a male man.
3. Deuteronomy 27:26, quoted in Galatians 3:10.
4. S. Bagster, *The Analytical Greek Lexicon*, p. 298.
5. Galatians 4:4–7.
6. Genesis 15:6, quoted in Galatians 3:6.
7. For example, the laws about extra-marital sexual relationships in Deuteronomy 22:13–30 are clearly in the context of a largely rural society in which women were members of their father's or husband's household.

8. Luke 12:13–15

9. v. 21

10. See, for example, Genesis 2:2–3; Exodus 20:8–11; Jeremiah 17:19–7.

11. Mark 2:23–28.

12. Luke 13:10–16.

13. Matthew 5:27–30

14. Matthew 19:3–9

15. See Deuteronomy 22:13–21; 24:1–4.

16. Doi, *Shari'ah: The Islamic Law*, p. 2

17. Matthew 6:5–15; 18:19–20; Luke 11:2–4. The rest of his teaching about prayer is encouragement to keep on praying, because God loves and sees us.

18. See Doi, *Shari'ah: The Islamic Law*, p. 950–51 and Sarwar, *Islam, Beliefs and Teachings*, p. 164.

19. Surah 2:2.

20. Surah 31:2–5.

21. Abdalati, *Islam in Focus*, p. 9.

22. Idem.

23. Surah 1:6–7.

24. This is a very broad picture: the interplay between faith and power is a complex one in both faiths. However, this broad picture draws, I think, a valid distinction that underlies the different emphases of the two systems.

25. It was not that the old lady had been neglected, but that she was stubborn. She had been regularly visited by family, and received as much help as she would accept from the social services, but she would not allow anyone to keep her home clean.

26. There are, of course, exceptions. There have always been debates about which laws are to be kept by all Christians at all times, and which were for particular situations.

27. Surah 2:215, on the subject of fighting.

28. Individual reading of the Qur'an is also being encouraged by some of the increasingly popular lay movements which are often labelled 'fundamentalist'. In Britain, Qur'anic study circles are growing up which include only people who have little or no

316

traditional Islamic education. Although the importance of traditional interpretation is acknowledged, young people are told that their own understandings may well be valid. See the arguments and instructions for Qur'anic study in K. Murad, *Way to the Qur'an*, Chs. 5 and 6.

29. Heeren and Lemu, *Women in Islam*, p. 41. See p. 40 above.

30. See L. Sanneh, *Encountering the West*, 1993.

31. See, for example, R. S Sugirtharajah, *Voices from the Margin*, 1991; C. Wright and C. Sugden (eds.), *One Gospel — Many Clothes*; B. R. Ro and M.C. Albrecht, *God in Asian Contexts*.

32. Most Christians would agree that polygamy is also wrong, and the New Testament certainly teaches that a man should have one wife (1 Timothy 3:2). However, others point out that some Old Testament characters had many wives, and that, although this always caused problems, their practice was not denounced. They therefore believe that, in some cases, polygamy may be the best option — that, for example, if a man has several wives on his conversion to Christ, he should not be required to divorce them since this would be unjust to them.

33. Mechanical or masculine.

34. There is no word for 'men' in the Greek, but a general 'their'.

Appendix: Genesis 3

[1]Now the serpent was more crafty than any of the wild animals the Lord God had made. He said to the woman, "Did God really say, 'You must not eat from any tree in the garden'?"

[2]The woman said to the serpent, "We may eat fruit from the trees in the garden, [3]but God did say, 'You must not eat fruit from the tree that is in the middle of the garden, and you must not touch it, or you will die.' "

[4]"You will not surely die," the serpent said to the woman. [5]"For God knows that when you eat of it your eyes will be opened, and you will be like God, knowing good and evil."

[6]When the woman saw that the fruit of the tree was good for food and pleasing to the eye, and also desirable for gaining wisdom, she took some of the fruit and ate it. She also gave some to her husband, who was with her, and he ate it. [7]Then the eyes of both of them were opened, and they realised that they were naked; so they sewed fig leaves together and made coverings for themselves.

⁸Then the man and his wife heard the sound of the Lord God as he was walking in the garden in the cool of the day, and they hid from the Lord God among the trees of the garden. ⁹But the Lord God called to the man, "Where are you?"

¹⁰He answered, "I heard you in the garden, and I was afraid because I was naked; so I hid."

¹¹And he said, "Who told you that you were naked? Have you eaten from the tree from which I commanded you not to eat?"

¹²The man said, "The woman you put here with me — she gave me some fruit from the tree, and I ate it."

¹³Then the Lord God said to the woman, "What is this that you have done?"
The woman said, "The serpent deceived me, and I ate."

¹⁴So the Lord God said to the serpent, "Because you have done this,

> Cursed are you above all the livestock and all the wild animals!
> You will crawl on your belly and you will eat dust all the days of your life.
> ¹⁵And I will put enmity between you and the woman,
> and between your offspring and hers;
> he will crush your head, and you will crush his heel."

¹⁶To the woman he said,

> "I will greatly increase your pains in childbearing;

with pain you will give birth to children.
Your desire will be for your husband, and he will rule over
you."

[17]To Adam he said, "Because you listened to your wife and
ate from the tree about which I commanded you, 'You
320   must not eat of it,'

Cursed is the ground because of you;
  through painful toil you will eat of it all the days of
    your life.
[18]It will produce thorns and thistles for you,
  and you will eat the plants of the field.
[19]By the sweat of your brow you will eat your food
  until you return to the ground, since from it you
    were taken;
for dust you are and to dust you will return."

[20]Adam named his wife Eve because she would be the
mother of all the living.

[21]The Lord God made garments of skin for Adam and his
wife and clothed them.

[22]And the Lord God said, "The man has now become like
one of us, knowing good and evil. He must not be
allowed to reach out his hand and take also from the tree
of life and eat, and live for ever." [23]So the Lord God
banished him from the Garden of Eden to work the
ground from which he had been taken. [24]After he drove
the man out, he placed on the east side of the Garden of
Eden cherubim and a flaming sword flashing back and
forth to guard the way to the tree of life.

Glossary

adam Hebrew for a human being. Can also be used of a male human.

adamah Hebrew for the ground.

'A'ishah Muhammad's favourite wife, married to him as a child.

aqiqa Shaving of hair and sacrifice following the birth of a child. Two sheep or goats are sacrificed for a boy, and one for a girl. Silver of the weight of the shaved hair is given to charity.

bazaar Market.

bid'ah Innovation. In Islamic law, used to refer to practices that have no precedent in classical *shari'ah*.

burqa Loose garment covering a woman from head to toe, sometimes including the face.

fitna Disorder, chaos. Also charm, temptation.

hadith Report, usually of what was said or done by Muhammad. Usually refers to items recorded in one of the classic *hadith* collections.

hajj The pilgrimage to Mecca. One of the five pillars of Islam.

halala Making something lawful. Used to refer to the requirement that a woman be remarried and the marriage consummated before a wife is lawful for a husband who has divorced her.

Hawwa Arabic for Eve.

hazrat Honorific title, used for prophets and other people perceived as holy.

hijab Veil or curtain (Arabic). Usually used to refer to a woman's head covering.

ijma' Consensus: the agreement of scholars in the development of Islamic law.

'ish Hebrew for man (i.e male).

'ishshah Hebrew for woman.

isnad Chain of transmission for a *hadith*.

ijtihad Use of personal judgement.

izzat Family honour.

jihad Striving in the way of God. This includes the personal struggle to please God as well as social and physical struggles for the defence and propagation of Islam.

kafa' Equality.

khalifah Vicegerent: someone who stands in another's place. Used in the Qur'an to refer to Adam.

khul Divorce at the instance of the wife, literally self-redemption.

iman Faith.

islam Submission. From the same root as *salaam*, peace.

isra'iliyyat Material that expands the Qur'anic references to biblical stories, and is derived from Jewish sources.

matn The content of a *hadith*.

mehr Dowry given by groom to bride, required by Islamic law.

mut'ah Temporary marriage contract, acceptable in Shi'a Islam but not to Sunnis.

Pharisee Member of a Jewish group devoted to keeping the laws of the Torah.

purdah Veil or curtain (Persian/Urdu). Also refers to the privacy of women and hence to their separation from unrelated males.

qiblah The direction for prayer: the Ka'aba at Mecca.

qiyas Method of analogical reasoning whereby established Islamic law is applied to new situations.

324 *salah* Ritual prayer. One of the five pillars of Islam.

sawm Fasting. One of the five pillars of Islam.

shahada The confession of faith, said in Arabic: 'I bear witness that there is no god but God, and Muhammad is the Messenger of God.' One of the five pillars of Islam.

shalwar Loose trousers worn with *kameez* (tunic).

shari'ah The Islamic law.

shirk Associating anything with God: the greatest sin in Islam.

Sufi Belonging to one of the 'mystic' orders of Islam. Sufis seek to follow the path to personal enlightenment and knowledge of God.

sunnah The practice of Muhammad.

surah Chapter of the Quar'an.

tafsir Commentary on the Qur'an.

talaq Divorce.

umma A people. Used to refer to the Islamic community.

zakah 2.5% of capital to be given towards Islamic causes as one of the five pillars of Islam.

zina Sexual sin, especially adultery.

Bibliography

Abdalati, H., 1975, *Islam in Focus*, Indianapolis: American Trust Publications.

— 1977, *Family Structure in Islam*, Indianapolis: American Trust Publications.

Afkhami, M., 1994, 'Women in post-revolutionary Iran: a feminist perspective', in Afkhami and Friedl 1994, pp. 5–18.

Afkhami, M. and Friedl, E. (eds.), 1994, *In the Eye of the Storm: Women in Post-Revolutionary Iran*, London: I.B. Tauris.

Ahmad, R. and Raychaudhuri, S. (eds.), 1990, *Daughters of the East*, The Common Trust in association with West Newcastle Women.

Ahmad, R.M., 1990, *Dreams into Words*, The Common Trust.

Ahmed, L., 1992, *Women and Gender in Islam*, Yale University Press.

Al-Galaleen, 1983, *The Commentary of Al-Galaleen*, Egypt: Al-Azhar, Egypt.

Al-Hibri, A. (ed.), 1982, *Women and Islam*, Pergamon Press.

Al-Hujwiri, A.U.A-J., 1953, *Kashful Mahjub*, translated by R.A. Nicholson, Lahore: Highway Publishers.

Ali, F., 1969, *Al Qur'an Al Hakim* (Urdu translation), Lahore: Chand Company.

Al-Kanadi, A.B.M., 1991, *The Islamic Ruling Regarding Women's Dress*, Jeddah: Abul Qasim Publishing House.

Al-Masih, A., undated, *Islam under the Magnifying Glass*, Austria: Light of Life.

Alsdurf, J. and Alsdurf, P., 1989, *Battered into Submission*, Sussex: Highland Books.

Al-Zamakhshari, undated, *The Commentary of Al-Zamakshari*, Dar Al Kasshaf.

Atiya, N., 1988, *Khul-Khaal: Five Egyptian Women Tell their Stories*, London: Virago.

Azad, A.K., 1968, *The Tarjuman al-Qur'an*, translated and edited by S. Abdul Latif, Lahore: Sind Sagar Academy.

Badawi, J.A., undated, *The Status of Woman in Islam*, UK: Islamic Propagation Centre International.

Bagster, S., 1967 reprint, *The Analytical Greek Lexicon*, London: Samuel Bagster & Sons Ltd.

Barton, M., 1992, *Creation and Fall and the Women of Bangladesh*, Dhaka: Netritto Proshikkhon Kendro.

Bhutto, B., 1988, *Benazir Bhutto:Daughter of the East*, London: Hamish Hamilton.

Breaking the Silence: Writing by Asian Women, 1984, London: Center-prise Trust.

Buijs, G. (ed.), 1993, *Migrant Women*, Oxford: Berg.

Campbell, B., 1993, *Goliath: Britain's Dangerous Places*, London: Methuen.

Challen, E., 1988, *To Love a Muslim*, London: Grace Publications.

Doi, A.R.I., 1984, *Shari'ah: The Islamic Law*, London: Ta Ha.

El-Saadawi, N., 1980, *The Hidden Face of Eve: Women in the Arab World*, London: Zed Press.

Engineer, A.A., 1992, *The Rights of Women in Islam*, London: C. Hurst and Co.

Evans, M.,1983, *Women in the Bible*, Exeter: Paternoster.

Ferguson, S. et.al. (eds.), 1988, *New Dictionary of Theology*, Leicester: IVP.

Fiorenza, E., 1980, *In Memory of Her: A Feminist Theological Reconstruction of Christian Origins*, London: SCM.

Gauhar, A. (ed.), 1978, *The Challenge of Islam*, London: Islamic Council of Europe.

Hamid, A.S. (trans.), 1986, *Sahih Muslim* (English), Vol. 1–4, New Delhi: Kitab Bhavan.

Haneef, S., 1979, *What Everyone should Know about Islam and Muslims*, Lahore: Kazi Publications.

Haq, F., 1996, 'Women, Islam and the state in Pakistan', in *The Muslim World*, vol. 86 no. 2, pp. 158–75.

ul-Haq, M.W., 1994, *Islamic Criminal Laws (Hudood Laws and Rules)*, Lahore: Nadeem Law Book House.

Hasan, A. (trans.), 1988, *Sunan Abu Dawud* (English), Vols. 1–3, Lahore: Sh. Muhammad Ashraf.

Hayter, M., 1987, *The New Eve in Christ: The Use and Abuse of the Bible in the Debate about Women in the Church*, London: SPCK.

Heeren, F. and Lemu, A., 1978, *Women in Islam*, Leicester: The Islamic Foundation.

Human Rights Watch, *Global Report on Women's Human Rights*, London and New York: Human Rights Watch, 1995.

Hurley, J.B., 1981, *Man and Woman in Biblical Perspective*, Leicester: IVP.

Ibn Kashir, undated, *Commentary* (Urdu), Karachi: Noor Muhammad.

Iqbal, S., 1992, *Women Talking*, West Newcastle Local Studies.

Jackie & Hodan, undated, *Hijab: An Islamic Obligation*, London: Al-Khilafah Publication.

Jeffery, P., 1979, *Frogs in a Well: Indian Women in Purdah*, London: Zed Press.

Jung, A., 1993, *Night of the New Moon*, London: Penguin.

Khan, M.M. (trans.), 1986, *Sahih Al Bukhari* (English and Arabic), Vol. 1–9, 6th Ed., Lahore: Kazi Publications.

Khan, M.U.H., 1972, *Purdah and Polygamy*, Peshawar: Nashiran-e-Ilm-o-Taraqiyet.

Khan, S., 1993, *Why Two Women Witnesses?*, London: Ta-Ha.

Knott, K. and Khokher, S., 1993, 'Religious and ethnic identity among young Muslim women in Bradford', in *New Community*, Vol. 19, pp. 593–610.

Lenski, R.C.H., 1963, *Interpretations of 1 and 2 Corinthians*, Minneapolis: Augsburg Publishing House.

MacHaffie, B.J., 1986, *Her Story: Women in Christian Tradition*, Philadelphia: Fortress Press.

Mallouhi, C., undated, *Mini-skirts, Mothers and Muslims*, anonymous.

328

Marsh, C.R., 1973, *Share Your Faith with a Muslim*, Chicago: Moody Press.

Maududi, S.A.A., 1948, *Birth Control*, Lahore: Islamic Publications Ltd., 7th ed., republished 1968.

— 1988, *Purdah and the Status of Woman in Islam*, Delhi: Markazi Maktaba Islam.

— 1988–93, *Tafhim al-Qur'an*, translated as *Towards Understanding the Qur'an* by Z.I. Ansari, Leicester: The Islamic Foundation, Vols. I–IV.

Merchant, M.V., 1980, *A Book of Qur'anic laws*, 3rd Ed., New Delhi: Kitab Bhavan.

Mernissi, F., 1985, *Beyond the Veil: Male-female Dynamics in Muslim Society*, London: Al Saqi Books, revised ed.

— 1991, *Women and Islam: An Historical and Theological Enquiry*, Oxford: Basil Blackwell.

— 1994, *The Harem Within*, London: Bantam Books.

Mirza, K., 1989, *The silent cry: second generation women in Bradford speak*, Research Paper No. 43, Centre for the Study of Islam and Christian–Muslim Relations.

Moghadam, F.E., 1994, 'Commoditization of sexuality and female labour participation in Islam: implications for Iran 1960–90', in Afkhami and Friedl 1994, pp. 80–97.

Moshay, G.J.O., 1994, *Who is this Allah?*, Bucks.: Dorchester House Publications.

Muhajir, A.M.R., 1965, *Lessons from the Stories of the Qur'an*, Lahore, Sh. Muhammed Ashraf.

Muhammad, A., undated, *Marnee Ke Bade Kay Ho Ga, (Life after Death)*, Delhi: Madina Book Dept., Jame Masjad.

Muhammad, S., 1995, *Women in Islam versus the Judaeo-Christian Tradition: Myth and the Reality*, Middlesex: Institute of Islamic Studies in the UK.

Mumtaz, K. and Shaheed, F. (eds.), *Women of Pakistan: Two Steps Forward, One Step Back?*, London: Zed Press, 1987.

Murad, K., 1985, *Way to the Qur'an*, Leicester: The Islamic Foundation.

Musallam, B.S., 1983, *Sex and Society in Islam:Birth Control before the Nineteenth Century*, Cambridge University Press.

Newcastle-upon-Tyne City Council, 1992, *The West End: a Partnership in Community Regeneration*, City Challenge Action Plan.

Nielsen, J., 1987, 'Muslims in Britain: searching for identity', in *New Community*, Vol. 13 No. 3, pp. 384–94.

Nomani, M.K., 1988, *Iranian Revolution and the Shi'ite Faith*, Lucknow: Furqan Publications.

Pagels, E., 1988, *Adam, Eve, and the Serpent*, New York: Random House.

Pickthall, M.M., 1953, *The Meaning of the Glorious Qur'an*, New York: The New America Library.

Quasem, M.A., 1983, *Salvation of the Soul and Islamic Devotions*, London, Boston, Melbourne and Henley: Kegan Paul International.

Qutb, A., 1990, *A Treatise on Competing Faith Oriented Family Norms*, New Delhi: Qazi Publishers.

Rajan, R.S., 1993, *Real and Imagined Women:Gender,Culture and Postcolonialism*, London: Routledge and Kegan Paul.

Ro, B.R., and Albrecht, M.C., 1988, *God in Asian Contexts*, Taiwan: Asia Theological Association.

Robson, J. (trans.), 1981, *Mishkat Al Masabih* (English). Vol. 1–2., Lahore: Sh. Muhammad Ashraf.

Sanneh, L., 1993, *Encountering the West*, London: Marshall Pickering.

Sarwar, G., 1984, *Islam: Beliefs and Teachings*, London: Muslim Educational Trust.

Sasson, Jean, 1995, *Princess*, London: Bantam Books.

Saint Paul's School Development Project, 1994, *Survey Report*.

Scherman, N. and Zlotowitz, M., 1980, *Bereishis, Genesis: A New Translation with Commentary Anthologized from Talmudic, Mirdrashic and Rabbinic Sources*, New York: Mesorah Publications.

Schleifer, A., 1986, *Motherhood in Islam*, Cambridge: The Islamic Academy.

Shaw, A., 1988, *A Pakistani Community in Britain*, Basil Blackwell: Oxford.

330

Smith, J.I. and Haddad, Y.Y., 1982, 'Eve: Islamic image of woman', in Al-Hibri 1982, pp. 135–144.

Sugirtharajah, R.S., 1991, *Voices from the Margin*, London: SPCK.

Suyuti, J.U.D., 1982, *Al Itqan* (Urdu) Vol. 1–2, Lahore: Idarah Islamiyat.

Thanvi, A.A., 1990, *Bahishti Zewar (Heavenly Ornaments)*, trans. F. Uddin, New Delhi: Taj Company.

The Life of Muslim Women, undated, Surrey: F.F.M. Publications.

Trible, P., 1978, *God and the Rhetoric of Sexuality*, Philadelphia: Fortress Press.

Tyneside Women's Employment Project, 1991, *Against the Odds: Inner-City Women and Fair Paid Employment*, Newcastle Council for Voluntary Services.

Usmani, S.A., 1991, *Tafsir-e-Usmani*, translated as *The Noble Qur'an* by M.A. Ahmad, Lahore: Aalameen Publications.

Watt, W.M., 1980, *Muhammad: Prophet and Statesman*, Oxford University Press.

Wilson, A., 1987, *Finding a Voice: Asian Women in Britain*, London: Virago.

Wilson, G.B., 1978, *1 Corinthians*, Carlisle: Banner of Truth Trust.

Wright, C. and Sugden, S. (eds.), 1990, *One Gospel, Many Clothes*, Oxford: EFAC/Regnum.

Yusuf Ali, A., 1946, *The Holy Qur'an* – Text, Translation and Commentary, Islamic Education Centre, Jeddah.

331

Videos

Badawi, J. and Shorrosh, A., 1988, *Bible or the Qur'an?* (Debate), USA.

Deedat, A. and Shorrosh, A., 1988, *Which is God's Word?* (Debate), Birmingham, UK.